TEENS LOOK AT MARRIAGE

Also by Jeanne Warren Lindsay:

Do I Have a Daddy?
A Story About a Single-Parent Child

Teens Parenting:
The Challenge of Babies and Toddlers

Pregnant Too Soon: Adoption Is an Option

Teenage Marriage: Coping with Reality

TEENS LOOK AT MARRIAGE:

Rainbows, Roles, and Realities

850068

By Jeanne Warren Lindsay

Morning Glory Press
Buena Park, California

First Edition

Copyright © 1985 by Jeanne Warren Lindsay

Printed in the United States of America

All Rights Reserved

No material in this book may be copied, reproduced,
or used in any way without written permission.

Lindsay, Jeanne Warren.
    Teens Look At Marriage.
    Bibliography: p. 170
    Includes index.
    1. Teen-age marriage—United States.
    2. Youth—United States—Attitudes. I Title.
HQ799.2.M3L565 1985   306.8'4   84-18954
ISBN 0-930934-16-4
ISBN 0-930934-15-6 (pbk.)

MORNING GLORY PRESS
6595 San Haroldo Way   Buena Park, CA 90620
Telephone (714) 828-1998

To Bob
Who Has Given Me
Trust, Respect, and Caring
Plus Lots of Love
For 33 Years

Contents

Nationwide survey developed; Married/living-together teenagers respond; Data analyses compare attitudes; Teen Mother Program alumnae provide data; Interviews offer additional insight

Few recommend teenage marriage; Is marriage forever? Living together more acceptable; Fewer "shotgun" weddings today; Summary and conclusions

Parents as role models; Ethnic/religious group preference; Early marriage not recommended; Summary and conclusions

Teen years often missed; Continue school after marriage? Partners change; Summary and conclusions

Communication important to intimacy; Counselor helps with communication; Handling the arguments; Who has the last word? Summary and conclusions

Sex is part of total relationship; Importance of sex within marriage; Viewpoints on premarital sex; Contraceptive information needed; Summary and conclusions

Traditional roles are reality; Variations in attitudes expressed; Housework often disliked; Traditional pattern is changing; Summary and conclusions

Contents 9

Foreword

Before the turn of the century, it was common for teens to be parents in the United States. The average age of first marriage during this time was sixteen, and children soon followed. The shift to industrialization and urbanization, and the resulting need for more extensive education changed this pattern of early matrimony. Today, the average age of first marriage is twenty-three, and yet, the phenomenon of teen parenthood persists. During 1984, a million teens are parenting more than a million children.

Jeanne Warren Lindsay has contributed much of her professional life to assisting teenage parents in adapting to their new roles and responsibilities of parenthood. As a teacher in a pregnant minor and school-age parent program, she has developed a unique understanding of the phenomenon of early parenthood and the young people involved. For me, it is a true privilege to write a foreword for Jeanne's latest book. She is a person I admire and respect, not only for her insight and knowledge, but also for the compassion and human sensitivity she has displayed in her work with youth.

My experiences as a therapist, educator, spouse and parent provided a context for me as I reviewed the draft of *Teens Look At Marriage*. Jeanne has provided us with an indepth picture of the attitudes that today's youth hold with regard to marriage, cohabitation, communication, sex, etc. She has clearly achieved her goal of providing insight that will assist in our understanding of adolescent marriage.

While this insight and understanding will be extremely valuable, I believe Jeanne has done us an even greater service. She has captured her data in such a manner as to allow us to create a springboard from what *is* (the attitudes of today's teens) to what *could be* (more positive, meaningful relationships within teen marriages). In my work as a therapist with young people, I believe this concept of using what is to see what could be is a tool of incredible value. If we will use the increased understanding of our youth provided by Jeanne's research as a foundation for helping them to continue to grow, to become all that they can be, to stretch for compassion, caring, respect for themselves, and for each other, then we will have used it well.

Gary L. Yates, M.A.
Counselor, Children's Hospital
Los Angeles, California

Preface

Fewer teenagers marry today as compared to thirty years ago. In fact, the percentage of young people who marry before reaching age 20 has been cut in half in one generation. (Planned Parenthood Federation of America, 1981).

Offsetting this change, however, are the many unmarried teenagers who are moving in with their partners. In the survey described in this book, 359 teenage respondents were living with partners, but only 37 percent of these young people were married. In the Teen Mother Program which I teach in Cerritos, California, I have seen the same trend. Ten years ago about half of our students married before their babies were born. Now about one-fourth are married, but an additional quarter have simply moved in with the baby's father.

These young couples, whether married or not, face many difficulties including financial hardship, communication problems, three-generational living, sexual adjustment, and, for many, adjusting to parenthood before they have time to strengthen their relationship with each other. While in the throes of developing their own identities, they must learn to adjust to couple living.

Early marriage is followed by early divorce for many. According to Weeks, author of *Teenage Marriages: A Demographic Analysis* (1976), the probability of divorce for women married at 17 or younger is twice as high as for women aged 18 or 19 when they marry — and four times as high as for women who wait until they are 25 or older to become brides.

Very little research is available on teenagers' attitudes toward marriage. Teenage pregnancy has received increasing attention from researchers and from the media in the past decade but the "problem" is generally identified as primarily a single mother event. Not long ago, most special schools for pregnant teenagers were intended only for unmarried students. If she married, the "problem" ceased to exist so she no longer had a need for special services.

But the problems of too-early entry into the job market, too little money, and the end of formal education continue for many young people who marry and/or move in together. In fact, nearly four in five of those who marry, whether or not they bear a child immediately, drop out of school. Of those who are pregnant but not married, about one in four drop out. More than 90 percent of teenage women who are neither pregnant nor married graduate from high school. (Moore et al, 1979)

About half of all teenage brides are pregnant at their weddings. (Elkin, 1977) Babies born to very young married couples experience the same medical risks as do babies born to single teenage mothers. Some teenage wives obtain good prenatal care and adequate nutritious food for themselves and their babies. In many young families, however, the lack of money and knowledge may cause the young married woman to go without these essential ingredients for a healthy pregnancy.

Too-early childbearing is accepted as a problem by many adults. Adults, too, tend to be negative toward teenage marriage - unless she's pregnant. But how do teenagers feel? *Teens Look at Marriage* attempts to provide insight into this topic.

Teens Look at Marriage is not a discussion of what should be. Rather, it is a study of the realities in the lives of teenage couples today. It is also a discussion of a research project which examined attitudes toward marriage of teenagers who are neither married nor living with partners.

The life of a teenage couple is seldom easy. The goal of this book is to assist professionals and other caregivers in understanding the world of teenagers who settle into a partnership, often before they have developed their own identities. For some of these couples, it is a world of poverty, jealousy, spousal abuse and other hardships. But for others, it offers the rainbow of hope for a satisfying and long-lasting partnership filled with trust, respect, caring, and love.

September, 1984   Jeanne Warren Lindsay, M.A.

Acknowledgments

About 3400 people helped with this book. Included were the 3118 teenagers who, at the cost of an hour of each one's time, participated in the nationwide survey of teenagers' attitudes toward marriage. At least 100 adults, most of them teachers, were involved in administering this questionnaire, and I am grateful for their help and for the help of their students and clients.

Students in our school's Teen Mother Program have been sharing their lives with me for 12 years, and through them I have learned about the pain and the joy of early partnerships. Eighty-two of these young women completed a questionnaire for this research. I appreciated their help and, especially, their letters.

High points of the research were the 76 interviews, almost all with former students and their partners. I was continually amazed at the openness and the honesty with which these young men and women shared their lives. Those who talked with me before *Teenage Marriage: Coping with Reality* was published are listed in the Acknowledgments for that book. Although their names are omitted on this page, I thank them again.

Those interviewed specifically for *Teens Look at Marriage* included Karen Lind, Maria Torres, Jo Ann and Chris Harris, Beth Ann Chapel, Dawn Coleman and Carl Manfrates, Shanita Marble Judon, Cathy Thuss and Steve, Tina and Isaias Lombera, Carol Pace, Suzette LeBlanc, Jackie and Keith Fuhriman, Rhonda Long, Teresa Zaragoza, Mary Zaragoza, Christina Hurtado, Maria Rios, Nancy McKinney, Teri Tait, and Carol Schecter. I am grateful to each one. Quotes from these young people are all "real" except that names and unimportant details have been changed to conceal their identities.

An entirely different - but important - kind of help was provided by Nick Konnoff, California State University, Long Beach, who handled the computer analyses of the nationwide survey data. Anthony Jurich, Ph.D., Kansas State University, offered helpful suggestions concerning presentation of the research data.

By far the most helpful individual among these 3400 people was my daughter, Erin, who provided hundreds of hours of research assistance during the past two years. She translated a six-foot high stack of computer readouts into useable charts, checked and rechecked her numbers and mine, proofread the tables with me, performed most of the library research, and managed to make me laugh at tense moments.

Claudia Miller designed the cover of *Teens Look at Marriage*. Joyce Young of Buckner and Young Photography provided the photographs. Judi Root and Bette Marcoe, First Impression Typesetting, did the typesetting and layout of the book. Delta Lithograph printed the book.

Friends who helped with the editing of the manuscript included Catherine Monserrat, Jean Brunelli, Gary Yates, Julie Vetica, Barbara Elmore, Sr. Maureen Joyce and Marilyn Lanphier.

Bob provided careful editing of the final manuscript as well as encouragement along the way. When deadlines became impossible, he handled the dinners, the laundry, and the crises. I appreciate and love him.

Introduction

During the past dozen years I have worked closely with pregnant adolescents and school-age parents. Some of these young women were married while others were no longer with their babies' fathers. Some had on-going relationships with the young men but did not live with them, and other couples lived together without being married.

Some people feel marriage is a solution to a problem. Young wives in our school program occasionally comment, "I don't have problems - I'm married." Yet it is these young wives who are more likely to drop out of school, have a second baby - and then are divorced two or three years later. Teenage marriage is seldom a cure for other teenage problems.

Coping with pregnancy and single motherhood without the support of the baby's father is a difficult task for a teenage woman. She needs an abundance of parental and community support, but if she has this help, she may be able to continue her education and master the job skills which will enable her to become a productive citizen and a good parent. Later she may develop a more satisfying relationship within marriage than she could ever have achieved while still in high school.

These were my observations, but I wanted to know more about teenagers' attitudes toward marriage and about the phenomenon of very early marriage. To obtain additional information, I designed a four-part research project.

Nationwide Survey Developed

First, I developed a cross-country survey of teenagers, most of whom were still attending high school. In 1983 this 12-page two-part questionnaire was mailed to teachers and other professionals who had agreed to participate in the survey. Generally these were people who were either familiar with my work with teenagers or had read one or more of my books on the subject. They administered the questionnaire to teenagers, most of them in high school, and returned the answer sheets to me. Respondents were not identified by name, but a record was kept of geographic origin of each response.

These teenage respondents represent all parts of the United States, various religions, ethnic groups, socio-economic levels, and urban/suburban/rural backgrounds. Of the 3,118 young people involved, 22.7 percent were male and 77.3 percent female. The following chart provides more information on this group:

AGE	14 or Yonger		15		16		17		18 +	
	F	M	F	M	F	M	F	M	F	M
PERCENTAGE	6.3	3.9	35.4	33.4	28.2	28.6	26.2	30.0	3.9	4.1
NUMBER	218	43	354	91	589	168	707	198	487	190

SCHOOL GRADE	8 or Lower		9-10		11		12		Not in School	
	F	M	F	M	F	M	F	M	F	M
PERCENTAGE	6.3	3.9	35.3	33.4	28.2	28.6	26.2	30.0	3.9	4.1
NUMBER	146	27	827	229	659	196	611	206	92	28

PLACE OF OF RESIDENCE	Inner City		Urban Area		Suburb		Town: 10,000 or less		Farm	
	F	M	F	M	F	M	F	M	F	M
PERCENTAGE:	29.8	20.8	22.9	17.6	20.2	34.4	17.4	14.6	9.8	12.5
NUMBER	694	143	532	121	469	236	405	100	227	86

GEOGRAPHIC AREA	N. Cal		N.W.		S. Calif.		NM/TX		M. West		NE		SE	
	F	M	F	M	F	M	F	M	F	M	F	M	F	M
NUMBER	167	29	312	50	581	287	319	79	525	173	241	76	250	57

ETHNIC GROUP	Black		Anglo		Asian		Native American		Hispanic	
	F	M	F	M	F	M	F	M	F	M
PERCENTAGE	17.9	8.7	58.2	60.6	1.3	2.2	5.0	7.2	17.5	21.3
NUMBER	417	59	1355	413	31	15	116	49	408	145

RELIGION	Catholic		Born-again		Protestant		Jewish		Other	
	F	M	F	M	F	M	F	M	F	M
PERCENTAGE	41.0	48.3	18.9	19.5	14.7	13.9	.8	.7	24.6	17.7
NUMBER	859	292	396	118	307	84	17	4	515	107

MARITAL STATUS	Single		Engaged		Married		Separated		Divorced/ Widowed	
	F	M	F	M	F	M	F	M	F	M
PERCENTAGE	80.7	90.2	12.1	6.0	6.3	2.3	.7	1.0	.2	.1
NUMBER	1898	618	284	41	147	16	17	7	5	3

PARENTS' INCOME	Under $5000		$5000- $10,000		$10,000- $20,000		$20,000- $50,000		Over $50,000	
	F	M	F	M	F	M	F	M	F	M
PERCENTAGE	14.5	9.4	19.6	14.4	29.8	27.4	28.5	36.5	7.6	12.4
NUMBER	285	57	386	87	586	166	560	221	183	88

Most of these teenagers were not yet married or living with a partner. They answered questions concerning a good marriage based on what they would like to have in their future unions. Compared to the realities around us, some of their answers appear overly optimistic. However, those who look for the rainbows of a good marriage are more likely to find them than are those already convinced they do not exist.

Married/Living-Together Teenagers Respond

The second part of the questionnaire was administered only to the 359 young people in the survey sample who were already married and/or living with a partner. These young people were asked about the realities of their relationships, and were encouraged to add additional comments to their answer sheets. Both parts of the questionnaire are included in the Appendix.

At the time they completed the questionnaire, approximately one-fourth of the respondents were attending special schools for pregnant adolescents and school-age parents. This emphasis on special schools was deliberate because I wanted a good sample of young couples, married and/or living together. I realized young people already married and/or living together would be more likely to attend these schools because of the special services they offer.

About two-fifths of the female respondents had been pregnant, and three percent had had abortions. About 20 percent of the young men either said they had caused a pregnancy or didn't know. Of the 379 mothers in the survey, less than half (180) had babies older than six months. Only 34 had children aged two years or older.

As mentioned above, the second part of the questionnaire was designed for those who were already married and/or living with a partner. These young people, too, represented a variety of ethnic, religious, and socio-economic backgrounds and came from all parts of the country. About two-fifths of this group were married.

Only 28 were males. Fewer men of high school age marry and of those who do, many drop out of school. In fact, almost half of these 28 respondents were no longer enrolled in school while in the total sample, all but 4 percent of the males were attending school.

Relying only on females' viewpoints when researching the lifestyles of teenage couples results in slanted data. Therefore, in spite of the disappointingly small sample, I have included these young men's responses in this book.

Of the living-together females, almost 90 percent were still in school, a far higher percentage than that of the general population of school-age wives and mothers. Conclusions drawn from statistics based on responses from this group should include consideration of this pro-school bias.

This group of married and/or living-together teenagers responded to additional questions concerning the *realities* of their relationships. While the main survey asked for "what should be" opinions, this section was designed to elicit information on "what is."

Data Analyses Compare Attitudes

All questionnaires were completed anonymously. Answer sheets together with any additional comments from respondents were returned to me by mail. The resulting data were coded by Nick Konnoff, a professional computer programmer at California State University, Long Beach. He ran frequencies and percentages according to the SPSS program (Nie et al, 1975).

These young people shared their feelings concerning best age to marry, qualities of a "good" spouse, traditional versus equal marriage, importance of sex in marriage, problems with jealousy, attitudes toward spousal abuse, and other relevant topics.

Attitudes and realities of teenagers from the various ethnic, religious, and socio-economic groups, of different ages and marital status, and from different geographic areas were compared. Of the living-together group, responses of those who said they were happy were compared with those who weren't, and of those who found living together harder than they expected with those who found it easier. Within this smaller group, those living with a partner of the same religious faith and/or from the same ethnic group were compared with those who weren't.

Obviously not all of the survey data could be included in *Teens Look at Marriage*. The various analyses were made in an effort to learn of possible differences in opinions and in realities. For many questions, for example, few differences appeared among young people living in different geographic areas. Therefore, few geographic analyses are included in the Appendix. When statistics are mentioned in the narrative, supporting tables of data will always be found in the Appendix. These tables are arranged by chapter topic and numbered accordingly.

In the narrative I have attempted to strike a balance between providing research data and making the book quickly readable for those who want only the basic information. Bar graphs are frequently used to illustrate specific points, and for these graphs, percentages are rounded off. Each graph in the narrative is backed by a supporting table of data in the Appendix, and percentages in these tables are all exact to one decimal point.

Teen Mother Program Alumnae Provide Data

After the major survey was completed, I felt I needed more statistical data, especially in the area of sex role realities. About half of the young women enrolled in our school's Teen Mother Program during the past dozen years have been married and/or lived with their partners. Many of the others, while still teenagers, married after either graduating or dropping out of school. I felt these young women could provide more information about the realities of early marriage.

Current addresses were available for about 300 alumnae of this program. I mailed a two-page questionnaire to these young people and asked them to complete and return it *if* they had married or moved in with a partner while still teenagers. The questionnaire is included in the Appendix.

Ninety-six responded, and 82 of this group had either married or moved in with a partner while still a teenager. Fifteen were no longer with their first partners, but the others were still together, a few for ten years or longer. They represented a variety of ethnic, religious, and socio-economic groups. Their input added more reality to the research, especially on the topics of roles, living with in-laws, and attitudes toward parents' marriages.

Tables illustrating the data obtained from this survey of Teen Mother Program alumnae are clearly marked "Teen Mother Program Survey." All other tables are from the computer-analyzed nationwide survey.

Interviews Offer Additional Insight

As an anthropologist, I don't believe that statistics are enough. Some hopes, dreams, and realities can be counted but many cannot. The people behind these statistics are real teenagers, each one different from all the others. Working with relatively small groups of teenage parents, I have learned well the wonderful uniqueness of each individual in our program. These young people have shared their rainbows and their realities with me throughout the years.

For this book and for its companion volume, *Teenage Marriage: Coping with Reality* (1984), I interviewed 76 young people, almost all of them married or living with a partner while still of high school age. Included were 60 women and 16 men. Forty-three were still teenagers at the time of the interview, and all the others were in their 20s.

Represented in the interviews were 37 married couples, seven living-together couples, nine divorced women, three women separated from spouses and planning to file for divorce, and four single mothers. All of the married and divorced couples were married while one or both were teenagers. Length of their marriages at the time of the interview ranged from one to ten years. White, Hispanic, and Black couples were included.

These interviews occurred over a period of two years. At least three of the seemingly stable married couples interviewed in 1982-1983 were divorced a year later.

Comments of the young people interviewed were used extensively in *Teenage Marriage* with the belief that other teenagers would learn more from these young people than from anything a professional could say. Additional comments are used in *Teens Look at Marriage*, but for a different reason. Adults who work with teenagers need to be acutely aware of the culture of school-age couples, a culture which includes many school-age parents. I believe these young people's comments give insight into this special culture, a culture quite different from that of young marrieds a few years older.

If a quote is so identified, it is from the nationwide survey. Otherwise, all quotes are from the interviews with the Teen Mother Program alumnae and their partners.

To summarize, *Teens Look at Marriage* is based on four research projects: a coast-to-coast survey of 3118 teenagers and their attitudes toward marriage; an additional survey of 359 of these young people who were already married and/or living with a partner; a survey of the realities of the relationships experienced by 82 alumnae of the Teen Mother Program in Cerritos, California; and on extensive interviews with 76 young people, nearly all married and/or living with partners while still teenagers.

Teenage Marriage: Coping with Reality was written for teenagers. Suggestions are offered for working toward a good marriage. For teenagers not yet married who have a romanticized idea of the happily-ever-after marriage, reading *Teenage Marriage* may put them in touch with some of the realities of too-young partnerships.

Teens Look At Marriage is a resource book. It contains a great deal of information about teenage relationships and teenagers' attitudes toward those relationships, but it offers little advice. It is not designed to be therapeutic. Rather, it is meant to provide insight into the culture of teenage couples, thereby helping teachers, other professionals, students and parents increase their understanding of teenagers' attitudes toward marriage and to learn of the realities of teenage partnerships.

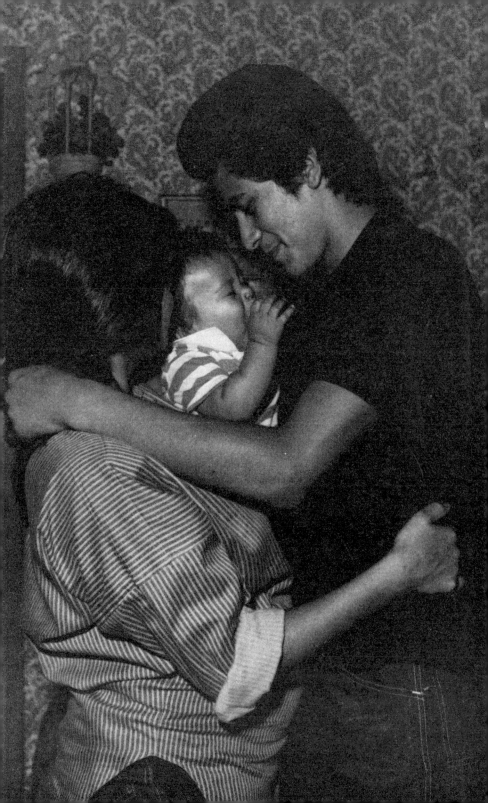

Chapter 1

Marriage —
If, When, Why

*I would tell high school kids to wait, definitely
wait — because there is so much you miss.
Trying to make ends meet and trying to satisfy
each other is a lot of responsibility. I can't even
go out with a girlfriend. If you get married,
you'll see that same person day after day and
come home to that same person. I wouldn't mind
getting married now that I'm 19, but not when I
was 16. (Jean, married at 16 to Dick, 17)*

*Marriage right after high school? Oh no, it's
too soon — although when the pressures build up
at home sometimes I think about going off and
getting married. But I wouldn't rush into it
because I know those feelings are because I'm
depressed, or there is too much pressure...there
has to be planning for a marriage to work. I'm
not rushing into it. (Glenna, 17)*

Are teenagers ready for the rainbows, roles and realities of
marriage? Or are adolescents likely to stop with the rainbow — the
hope that marriage, when it happens, will be a live-happily-ever-
after affair?

The reality is that many teenage marriages end within a few years. Some research results suggest a failure rate of 60 percent within five years. Teen marriages are two to four times more likely to break up than are marriages of people in their 20s. (Weeks, 1976)

Few Recommend Teenage Marriage

Most of the teenagers in the survey do not consider the teenage years good for marriage. Less than one in fifty of these young people think a man or woman should marry at 17 or younger. Some do not plan ever to marry.

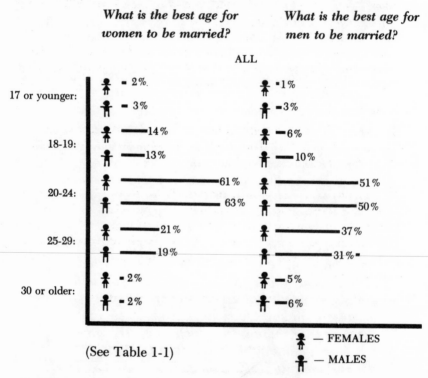

| | *What is the best age for women to be married?* | *What is the best age for men to be married?* |

ALL

	Women	Men
17 or younger:	♀ ▪ 2%	♂ ▪1%
	♂ ▪ 3%	♂ ▪3%
18-19:	♀ ——14%	♂ —6%
	♂ ——13%	♂ ——10%
20-24:	♀ —————————61%	♂ ————————51%
	♂ —————————— 63%	♂ ———————50%
25-29:	♀ ————21%	♂ —————37%
	♂ ———19%	♂ —————31% ▪
30 or older:	♀ ▪ 2%	♂ —5%
	♂ ▪ 2%	♂ —6%

(See Table 1-1)

♀ — FEMALES
♂ — MALES

Todd married Evangelina when he was 21 and she was 18. He now wishes he had waited:

> *Don't get married until you're at least 25 or until you've made a business for yourself. If I had stayed home until next*

year, I'd be in business and I'd be doing what I wanted. I'd be more free. I'm a machinist and I'll still go into my own business someday, but it's taking a lot longer this way.

Annalee married Curt three years ago when she was 17 and he was 20. They're still together but their relationship is deteriorating rapidly. She tries to help others avoid the pain of a too-early marriage:

My cousin was going to get married recently and I said, "Mary, don't get married. Move in with me." I even told her I'd lend her my car, and I don't lend nobody my car. I wanted her to see what it's like being married. My mom knew what I was trying to do and she said, "Annalee, you can't talk her out of it." But I kept telling her, "Don't do it."

I have a real good friend. She and her boyfriend started seeing each other about the same time we did. And now she's just going through hell with him. I see people going through it all the time, and I try to tell them.

Is Marriage Forever?

Teenagers don't want the trauma and heartbreak of divorce. When they marry, they want it to last forever. Kathleen, married at 17 to Henry, 21, says firmly:

Our marriage better last the rest of our lives. There was one time we almost split up. I was going to get a job and be on my own. We weren't getting a divorce, but I decided I was missing out on too much. Then I got pregnant again and I stayed and I'm glad I stayed. My God, I'm glad I stayed. I don't ever plan on leaving.

When you get married, do you expect it to last the rest of your life?

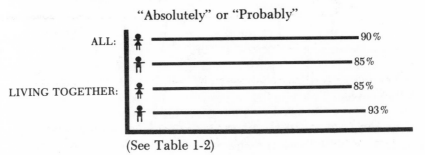

"Absolutely" or "Probably"

ALL: 90%
85%

LIVING TOGETHER: 85%
93%

(See Table 1-2)

Note the high percentage of young people who said they expect marriage to last the rest of their lives and who are already living with a partner. However, almost 200 of these same young people also responded to the open-ended question, "Do you think *your* partnership will last 'forever'? Please comment." Only 40 percent answered affirmatively.

Almost one-fifth of these young people were no longer living with their partners. Some had been married and were already separated or divorced, while others had lived with partners but were no longer with them.

About two-thirds of these teenagers had been living with their partners for less than a year. When they started living together, two-fifths of the women were pregnant and about one-eighth already had a child.

Only 298 young women and 24 young men responded to the final question, "Are you happy with your partnership?" Women were more positive than men — 89 percent said they were happy at least most of the time while 75 percent of the men agreed. (Table 1-3)

Finding only one-fourth of the males and one-tenth of the females stating they were unhappy is surprising considering the general instability of teenage relationships. This may be partly due to the fact that many of these young people had lived with their partners less than a year.

Alyssa and Brian, married at 16 and 17, are coping well:

> *Why don't teenage marriages last? I don't think they face reality before they get married. I don't think anybody thought we knew what we were facing, but we just sort of take it as it comes. We know that every day we'll have a new problem, not necessarily between us, but something we'll have to face. I think we're rare — usually the bigger the problem, the more we seem to bond together. We're always on the same side.*

Less than half of these living-together couples were married when they completed the questionnaire — a trend among school-age parents today. The Guttmacher Institute reports that 31 percent of first births to adolescents in 1970 were delivered to single mothers. That number increased to 46 percent by 1978. (Planned Parenthood Federation of America, 1981) Some young single mothers live with their babies' fathers and some non-parent couples live together without marriage.

Living Together More Acceptable

Back in the 1940s my great-aunt Belle rented two apartments in her home in a small Kansas town. I remember hearing a hushed conversation between her and my mother, a discussion not meant for my ears. Aunt Belle had discovered the young couple in the back apartment were not married. She was horrified, and, as I recall, she gave them three days to get out.

Aunt Belle's livelihood depended on those rentals. If one was empty, her income was cut in half. She was willing to risk that hardship rather than be associated with a couple "living in sin."

Even twenty years ago it was unthinkable in most families for teenagers — or older couples — to live together without being married. "Shotgun" weddings were a common answer to premarital pregnancy. The marriage rate for teenagers has fallen during the past two decades partly because of changes in attitudes toward forced marriages.

Today, television soap operas, movies, and sometimes the people next door imply that marriage is not that important. The value of a marriage license is questioned. "What good does that piece of paper do anyhow?" young people ask.

A dozen years ago in my class of pregnant teenagers and school-age mothers in Cerritos, California, half of our students were married before the baby was born. Today only about one-fourth marry, but another quarter live with their babies' fathers, generally at his or her parents' home.

Gloria and Derek lived together briefly before their wedding two years ago. When asked if she recommended this approach, Gloria responded:

> *No, not really. You need to know him but you know, they talk about things like the toothpaste and stuff and I think that's silly. If you love each other, you can handle those things. But you do need to know each other. I don't think I learned any more about him when we were living together than I did when we were just dating.*
>
> *My dad wanted us to get married when I got pregnant but I wasn't going to let anybody tell me when. We wanted to get married when we wanted to. We waited until July because I didn't want to be married in school. I guess that was just a good month.*

How do other teenagers feel about this? Do young people not yet
pregnant or parents have different attitudes than those who have
faced this situation? How do boys' and girls' attitudes differ?

Are there differences in opinions among teenagers from different
ethnic groups and religions? Do rural youth have similar attitudes
to those of inner-city teenagers? The survey was designed to
provide information on these topics.

Teenagers' responses to "How do you feel about a man and
woman living together if they aren't married?" varied. About one in
six of the females and one-eighth of the males said flatly, "It's
wrong." Others replied, "It's OK but I wouldn't do it." The others
approved of cohabitation, with some specifying marriage plans as a
prerequisite.

*How do you feel about a man and a woman living together if they
aren't married?*

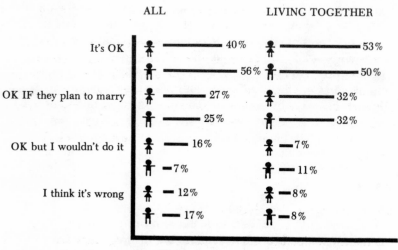

(See Table 1-4)

More Born-again Christians than young Catholics disapproved of
cohabitation. Views of Protestant teenagers fell between the other
two groups. (Table 1-5)

Comparing young people from different ethnic groups showed
variations in opinions. Responses from Anglos, perhaps because
they comprise slightly more than half the total sample, were
similar to those of the total group.

Native American youth were more likely to approve of cohabitation — half of the 116 women and almost three-fourths of the 49 men said it was OK. Less than 10 percent of the women and 5 percent of the men think it's wrong. (Table 1-6)

Fewer teenage women from small towns or farms than from urban or suburban areas favored cohabitation (Table 1-7). Few differences were apparent when responses were analyzed according to parents' income.

One-third of the young people from the southeastern part of the United States felt cohabitation is wrong as compared to only 10 percent of the women and 6 percent of the men from New Mexico and Texas. Other groups showing lower percentages of young people disapproving of living together before marriage included women from southern and northern California, men from southern California, the Middle West, and the Northeast. (Table 1-8)

Twice as many of the never-pregnant respondents thought cohabitation was wrong as did young women who had had an abortion, those who were pregnant, young mothers, or fathers. (Table 1-9)

Tables in the Appendix give detailed responses to this question. Certainly a number of young people still feel marriage precedes living together. Nevertheless, almost three-fourths of this entire group of teenagers think living together without marriage is all right with the proviso for some that wedding plans be made. . . a decided shift in opinion from my great-aunt Belle's era of strong disapproval and condemnation of couples living together before marriage.

Fewer "Shotgun" Weddings Today

As mentioned before, marriage because of pregnancy has decreased over the past decade. In years past, if a couple's unmarried daughter became pregnant, the father's first thought was to find the young man responsible and insist on marriage. If a shotgun was needed to enforce the request, he'd find one.

Few parents bring out the shotgun today, but some still are convinced a marriage will make things "right." Estimates are that one-third to one-half of all teenage brides are pregnant at their weddings.

Maralee did not marry Lyle. She explained:

*If you get married just because you're pregnant, it's always
going to be that idea in the back of your mind, "I married him
because I was pregnant." That's not good at all. If I had
married him he would have told me, "No school," and how I
would have resented that! My world can't stop because I had a
kid.*

More teenage men than women think a couple should marry if
she becomes pregnant. Among those already living with partners,
women are less likely to recommend marriage because of
pregnancy while men are more apt to do so. In fact, almost twice
as high a percentage of these young men as young women favor
marriage in this situation.

**When a high school-age girl gets pregnant, should she and her
boyfriend get married?**

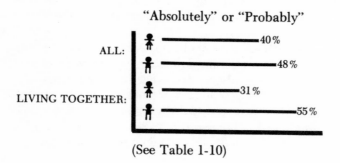

"Absolutely" or "Probably"

ALL:

40%

48%

LIVING TOGETHER:

31%

55%

(See Table 1-10)

Almost half of the never-pregnant women said the pregnant
couple should marry, more than twice as high a percentage as the
total group of mothers. (Table 1-11) Are these young mothers
accepting what may be their own situation? Or do they believe
they are coping well by themselves and don't need to marry? Or, if
married, do they regret the decision? Such information is not
available from this survey.

More than half of the teenagers living in small towns or on farms
believe that if pregnancy occurs, marriage should follow. Urban
and suburban youth are less convinced. (Table 1-12)

Slightly more Born-again Christian teenagers (44 percent)
"absolutely" or "probably" recommend marriage if pregnancy
occurs than do either the Catholic or Protestant youth. (Table 1-13)

Black males were about half as likely to favor marriage because of pregnancy as were the other men in the sample. Black females, too, were less positive about such a marriage than were women from other ethnic groups. In all but the Black group, the men were more positive toward marriage than were the women. (Table 1-13)

When Alyssa and Brian discovered she was pregnant, they talked about marriage but decided to wait until several months after their baby was born. A year later, they are convinced they made a good decision:

We didn't live together before we got married. My parents didn't want him to move in unless we got married, but we knew anyway that him moving in would be the same stress as if we had gotten married. So he didn't. In the long run, it was our decision to wait.

I don't mean to brag but I feel we made some good decisions after I was pregnant. We did think about it and we decided we didn't want to put two kinds of stress on our relationship. We knew we couldn't postpone the baby but we could postpone the wedding. So we waited and it worked out fine. By then my dad was over his upset, and he and Brian were back to being friends. We were used to the baby. I was further along in school. That's why we decided to wait. . .we figured it would be less stressful. And it has worked out fine.

As Alyssa and Brian understand so well, a good marriage decision is not a decision made under undue stress. A mature decision takes not only love, but time and careful thought. A shotgun approach to marriage may mean disaster to the couple involved — and to their child.

Summary and Conclusions

Very few teenagers recommend marriage before age 20. When they do marry, more than 85 percent expect their partnerships to last the rest of their lives.

Almost three-fourths of the teenagers in the survey think it is all right for couples to live together before they marry. Less than half of the survey respondents already living with partners are married. Getting married because of pregnancy is not advocated by the majority of the young people in the survey sample.

Many of these young people apparently understand that marriage seldom solves problems. It is not a cure for unplanned pregnancy, nor will it solve problems of low self-esteem or hassles with one's family.

Developing a good relationship takes hard work and commitment from each partner, a difficult task for teenagers who are still working on forming their own identities. A good sense of self-worth on the part of both is important if they are to develop the long-lasting partnership of trust and commitment on which the rainbows of a good marriage are based.

Chapter 2

Making That Big Decision

I want Janie to know enough about my situation so she'll wait. The majority of younger marriages don't last. My friends who got married young have split up or they're talking about divorce. I wish I could've been on my own first. It's not worth it.

At the time you think it's the right thing to do, that you can get out of the house, but there are better ways to get out than this. I wish I could have continued my schooling.

Where I work I see 16-year-olds coming in and getting their marriage licenses. Sometimes I talk with them. They look real scared and I ask them what they want to do, and tell them they don't have to get married. I tell them they still have choices. (Sally, married at 17 to Hugh, 19. Divorced two years later.)

Choosing a lifetime companion is a big decision. For an adolescent to understand and act upon this concept is difficult. Ninety percent of the teenagers in the survey expect their marriages to last the rest of their lives, yet four times as many marriages of teenagers fail as do marriages of older couples. (Weeks, 1976)

A successful marriage, irrespective of the partners' ages, depends on such things as commitment and agreement on expectations. Similar interests and family backgrounds may make life easier for the couple. Most (96 percent) of the survey respondents thought this was important for husband and wife. A majority of those already living with partners said they and their mates have similar interests. (Table 2-1) However, about half of these respondents also said lack of similar interests is a problem at least part of the time. (Table 2-2)

Parents As Role Models

Having a good marriage model in her/his own parents as s/he grows up is likely to help a young person understand the commitment and caring needed in a marriage relationship. However, many teenagers have watched their parents separate and divorce. In their homes they have not had this model of the long-lasting relationship they covet.

Only three-fifths of the total group said they had spent their growing-up years with their mothers and fathers. Even fewer of those still single but living with a partner had been reared by both parents. Having parents separate when a young person is in the throes of early adolescence can make life doubly hard for that young person.

For how long have you lived with both of your parents?

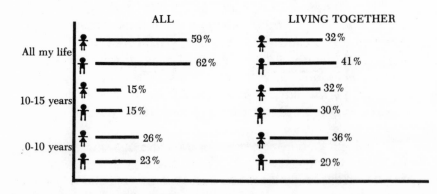

(See Table 2-3)

For how long have you lived with both of your parents?

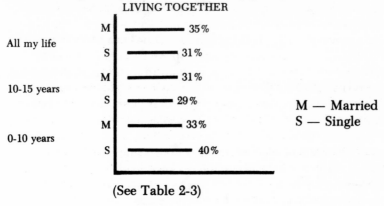

(See Table 2-3)

Time after time in our Teen Mother Program, the students talk about happy childhoods, good family relationships, and good experiences in elementary school. Then, when they reach junior high school age, their world changes. Mother and Dad, perhaps partly because of the stress often inherent in parenting 12- to 14-year-olds, decide to separate. The resulting situation is likely to be rough for everyone, but especially for this young adolescent.

Very few of the teenagers in the nationwide survey want their marriages to be like their parents' unions. In fact, the majority do not. Among the young people already living with a partner, almost three-fourths want something different.

Do you want your marriage to be much like your parents' marriage?

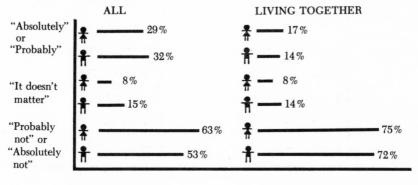

(See Table 2-4)

In the nationwide survey, Black youth were most opposed to having marriages like those of their parents, and Asian and Hispanic males least opposed. (Table 2-5)

Eighty-two young people, alumnae of the Teen Mother Program mentioned above, returned a survey in which they were asked about their partnerships. Less than one-third said they wanted their marriages to be like those of their parents. Only about half of the parents of these young people were still married at the time of the survey. Time after time these teenagers shared their negative feelings about their parents' divorcing as they responded to the question, "Do you want your marriage to be much like your parents'? Why or why not?" They wrote:

My parents just didn't love each other.

My dad is the boss in my house, but I think decisions should be made by both persons.

No, because they hated and fought with each other. I wouldn't want anyone's marriage to be like theirs.

They were a sorry sight — as young as I was, I remember. (They divorced when I was 6.)

My dad worked too much and didn't have any time for us, then found time for another woman.

My parents never got along. They didn't know how to manage money and were always in debt and we had very little to eat.

George, married at 21 to Maura, 18, explained how he feels:

No, I don't want a marriage like my parents. My mom is an alcoholic and my dad almost is, too. They just don't communicate at all. I've seen a lot of hard times, especially since I was 11 or 12 until I moved out at 20. I've seen a lot of fights, a lot of booze.

Some of these young people made positive comments about their parents' marriages:

They loved each other very much, communicated well, and had fun together.

My parents are still very happy together after more than 25 years of marriage and that's what I want to be able to say in 25 years.

Some young couples simply want a more equal marriage than their parents have had. Brian, 18, and Alyssa, 17, have lived with Alyssa's parents since their marriage more than a year ago. They get along well, but Alyssa is outspoken about not wanting a marriage like her parents have:

Marriage like my parents? No, because I don't let Brian get away with things like my dad does. My dad is a typical husband like he wants the house clean but he'd better not do any of it. I feel like my dad associates women with the housework and the babies, not with people who can also go to college, have a career. I don't think my dad likes women wanting to do things men do. Like I wanted to go back to school and learn some things. Instead of understanding, he said, "Oh, you can't have a career and get married and have a baby."

But Brian knows I need something else in addition to being a parent. I need to feel like I'm contributing to what we buy, to what we're doing. He understands that. He supports me when I work part-time because he knows I'm doing something I want to do. He has always told me he doesn't want me to have to work but he has never said I shouldn't work. He wants me to be happy in what I do. My dad never wanted my mother to work.

Ethnic/Religious Group Preference

In the late 1960s I taught a class of mostly Black women at a local community college. One night the discussion turned to interracial marriage. These women, most of whom had adolescent children, were outspoken in wanting their sons and daughters to marry within their race. A few years later when my daughter was dating a Black man, my Anglo parents and a few neighbors disapproved. Not too many years ago, interracial marriage was against the law in some parts of the United States. In some areas, prejudice against "mixed" marriage still exists.

Teenagers in the survey were queried about their attitudes on this subject and on marrying outside of one's religious faith. Less than 60 percent of these young people said they would prefer to marry a person from their own ethnic group or within their own religion. Most of the others said "It doesn't matter" although a few did not want to marry within their own groups. (Tables 2-6 and 2-7)

Even fewer of those already living together think it's important that one's partner should be from the same ethnic group and religion as oneself. (Tables 2-6 and 2-7) Very few of these young people think marrying a person from a different ethnic group or religion would cause problems within a marriage. (Tables 2-8 and 2-9)

When opinions of young people from the various ethnic groups are compared, quite different feelings on the subject of marrying outside of one's own ethnic group or race are revealed. Black men were least concerned. Only 29 percent said they want to marry within their own group while almost 60 percent say it doesn't matter. The other 12 percent don't want to marry someone from their own race. Among the Black women, 56 percent expect to marry another Black while most of the others say it doesn't matter.

About two-thirds of the Anglo youth want to marry other Anglos. Smaller percentages of Asian, Native American, and Hispanic youth think it's important to marry within their own ethnic groups. (Table 2-10)

Young people living in small towns and on farms were more likely than were urban and suburban youth to want to marry a person of their own race or ethnic group. Almost 70 percent of this group think it is important to do so. (Table 2-11)

Born-again Christian youth and Protestant males are more concerned than Catholic youth or Protestant women about marrying within their own ethnic group. They also want their partners to have the same religious faith. Of the three groups, the Born-again Christians were most likely to expect problems in either an interracial or interfaith marriage. (Tables 2-12, 2-13, 2-14, and 2-15)

Of the young people already living with partners, 277 shared the same religion with their mates, and 72 had different beliefs. Both partners were from the same ethnic group in 258 cases, but this was not true for 94 couples. Comparing these young people's responses about their relationships shows some differences.

Almost half of the couples with different religious backgrounds found this was a problem occasionally, a problem to their parents, or was a big problem for the couple. Fewer couples considered their different ethnicity a problem, perhaps because ethnicity is "fixed" while religion generally isn't. (Tables 2-16 and 2-17)

Allison and Orlando were married when she was 14. She was pregnant, but she continued school throughout her pregnancy and afterward until she graduated. Now, ten years and three children later, they're still together. While their different ethnicity apparently has not been a problem, Allison continues to be bothered by the difference in their religious beliefs:

> *Orlando won't let me have my freedom of choice when it comes to church. The kids are baptized Catholics but I don't go for that. He's concerned about what his family will think, yet he doesn't even go. He's a hypocrite because he'll quote the Bible but he won't go. We've only been to church once since the kids were baptised.*
>
> *My brother is going to be a preacher and he talked to me a lot about the Bible last Christmas. I'd like to get into a church but Orlando won't let me. I started going to Mass three or four weeks this spring, but they read out of a book they had typed up a year ago and I didn't think that was right.*
>
> *The kids' Godparents want me to get them involved, and I can't tell them it's because Orlando won't give me freedom of choice. If I'd had my way, I would've waited until they were old enough to decide for themselves, then get baptised.*

Couples with the same religion and of the same ethnic background were more likely to report more interests in common with their mates than did the young people in the "mixed" partnerships. (Table 2-18) They also found it easier to talk with their mates. (Table 2-19)

The mixed-religion or mixed-ethnic couples tended to find living together harder than they had expected, and they were a little more likely to say they were unhappy with their partnerships.

Simply being reared in two different families means young couples enter marriage with different world views. If their families represent different ethnic groups or religions, they may need to work a little harder to achieve a satisfying relationship.

Is Early Marriage Recommended?

Over and over the young people I interviewed advised against early marriage. Many feel they have missed out on being teenagers and want their children to have a different life:

I hope Derek waits until later. It's hard now for me and I'm
sure it's hard for Arnie. It's got to be hard for anybody. I hope
he waits because I don't want him to go through everything we
did. You're still a teenager and you want to go out and do
things like a teenager but you have bills to pay and you have to
buy groceries — so you can't. And if you move in with his
parents it's a mistake — it's a mistake to move in with either
set of parents. And Arnie keeps saying he wants to go back to
school but he has to work instead. It's hard. I wish we had
waited. (Lucia, married at 17 to Arnie, 18)

Although she was pregnant during her senior year, Glenna didn't
marry her baby's father. They continued seeing each other, and a
year later she was still pondering the pros and cons of their choices.
Should she and Jeffrey each continue to live with his/her own
parents? Should they move into an apartment together without
getting married? Or should they get married?

The problem is — if we get married as soon as we move out
with each other, what happens if we don't like it? If all of a
sudden I don't like the way he does things, the way he brushes
his teeth, or we don't agree on money, all those things.
The bad thing is if we do live with each other and don't get
married, what happens to Babs if she grows up and we still
aren't married? When she's old enough to ask if we're married,
how do we answer her? I guess it also goes back to religion —
if a child lives with her mother and father, they should be
married. But I would hate to get married, then go through a
divorce.

When asked if she would have liked to marry Jeffrey when she
was pregnant, Glenna replied thoughtfully:

No, it would have been too soon. I had to learn how to
handle the baby and adding the marriage would have been too
much. It would have been more of a strain to both of us.
Having the responsibility of bringing her up — I know if I
were married, there would have been a lot of new experiences
— and half my time would have been spent caring for the
baby. Men can't understand that — and I wouldn't have had
enough time for him.

I had goals and Jeffrey didn't believe in them at the time.
He would have wanted me to stay home with the baby. And
there were the families — my family especially who didn't like
him, thought I was too young to get married. They thought I
would get involved in something I wouldn't be able to handle.
They thought eventually Jeffrey would not have been able to
handle it, would leave, and I would be out in the street. I'm
glad we didn't get married. But the decision was really mine. I
was scared and if you're scared, you aren't going to jump into
something right away.

I hope we make it together eventually, but we're very
different, have very different backgrounds. It won't be easy.

Counselors can help teenagers understand they need to know as
much as possible about each other before they marry. Sometimes
young people don't understand how important this is. When Marge
told her parents she was pregnant, they talked about marriage.
When they realized her boyfriend was 21, they asked what he did
for a living. "I don't know," she replied. "I can't pry into that kind
of thing. That's too personal."

But marriage *is* a very personal affair and it is also a public affair.
Fitting in well with each other's family is tremendously helpful. As
an old saying puts it, "When you marry, you don't marry just your
spouse — you marry the whole family." If he doesn't like her family,
can he handle visiting them when she wants him to? If she can't
stand his mother, will she be able to live there until he or the two of
them make enough money to move out?

A young couple may find it helpful to complete the questionnaire
on which this book is based. (See Appendix.) When they compare
their answers, they may gain fresh insight into each other's
attitudes toward marriage, insight which may help them decide
whether or not to marry.

Summary And Conclusions

Although many teenage marriages fail, most young people want
their own marriages to last a lifetime. The majority of the young
people in the survey hope to have marriages quite different from
their parents' relationships, partly because so many of their parents
are divorced.

Almost half of these teenagers don't care whether or not they
marry someone of their own religious faith and/or ethnicity. Very

few feel an interfaith or interracial marriage would cause problems. Some of the respondents were already living with a partner from a different religious and/or ethnic background. They indicated slightly more problems within their partnerships than did those whose families were more similar.

Young people need to be reassured that lifetime marriages are possible, but that achieving this goal takes a great deal of hard work. Before marriage, each partner should be positive the other is indeed the person with whom s/he wants to live "forever." Agreement on expectations, what each wants out of life, is important. A thorough discussion of this topic is included in *Your First Year of Marriage.* (McGinnis, 1977)

Choosing the "right" marriage partner is perhaps the most important decision one can ever make. It deserves time and careful consideration of each person's goals, personality, life style, the widest possible view of each other.

Once the decision is made, a steady diet of trust, respect and caring built on a solid foundation of love and commitment may result in the forever marriage most teens want.

Chapter 3

Coping With Changes

What did I give up for marriage? My teenage years — going to high school — just leading a normal teenage life. Sometimes I miss that. (Annie, married at 15 to Jose, 17)

I gave up my freedom to go where I wanted and with whomever I wanted. I have none of the friends I had before I got married. I have a few that are married but we don't go out together. We call each other once in awhile. There's a loss of freedom unless you have a real liberal husband who doesn't care whether you go out or stay home. (Elise, married at 18 to Hector, 20)

The Lost Adolescence Syndrome, as described by Anthony P. and Julie A. Jurich (1975) is a pattern often found in couples having difficulty with their marriages. An individual who marries while still a teenager frequently has not had time to develop a firm individual identity. S/he has not experienced a "typical" adolescence, and after awhile may fantasize about the "single carefree life" s/he has missed, according to these authors.

Teen Years Often Missed

Teenagers who marry face many changes in their lives, changes which often include a loss of individual freedom and at least some of the friends they had before marriage.

A poignant letter from a former student who married while still in high school typifies this Lost Adolescence Syndrome:

> *Sometimes I wish I would have never married, had my baby and gotten older. I'm doing fine, I guess. I've never known any other way of life, but I'm really starting to miss the teenage years that passed me by so very fast. I went straight from having to be in the house when the lights went on to having to be in when the child cried or the husband called.*
>
> *I don't know what's going on with me. Dick treats me good and we never really fight. He's always there when I need him but he's never there when I don't. Please try to tell me what's wrong. I still love him very much...*

This young woman was one of 82 alumnae of the Teen Mother Program who responded to a questionnaire concerning their marriages. The majority (52) said marriage "tied them down." Often in interviews young men expressed the same feeling:

> *I thought it would be the same as before, but I feel a lot of responsibility now. Once in awhile it gets to me, but then I think of where Maura is coming from. She has to watch the baby and I think that's a pretty big job, taking care of the baby all day. I have to work, I have to bring money into the house. It's changed our lives a lot.*
>
> *I feel like I'm still young. I see all my other friends going out doing this and doing that. I get this feeling that I want to get away, that this is for the birds, but then I remember I love them both and just keep going. (George, married at 20 to Maura, 17)*

Time after time these young couples talked about losing friends:

We found out who our friends were. Our real friends would still come over and visit but other people kind of shined us off. When we became a family and didn't party any more, we weren't fun. I have only two friends now. (Kathleen, married at 17 to Henry, 21)

Some insisted the change in lifestyle didn't bother them:

I'm happy because he's a good father and he doesn't go out with his friends. We don't go out — we just stay home on the weekends and we're always together. It doesn't bother me — I feel if I have a responsibility I should stay home and take care of it. (Rowena, married at 17 to Tom, 17)

Our marriage didn't change our relationships with our friends, but being parents did. It's nobody's fault... we're just in different worlds now. We don't like to go out to parties, stay out late, see whose car will go the fastest. (Alyssa, married at 16 to Brian, 17)

Yet in the survey of the 3,000 teenagers and their attitudes toward marriage, only 22 percent of the girls and 20 percent of the boys would expect marriage to mean fewer friends. Almost this many, in fact, would expect to have more friends because of marriage. The others anticipate either no change or they think marriage would bring different friends. (Table 3-1)

One survey question concerned changes in recreation which may occur after marriage. A slight majority expect to be able to party less after marriage. One-fifth expect more, and the rest, no change. (Table 3-2) Comments from the interviewees expressed their realities:

I used to drink a lot and she used to drink a lot, before the kids, but no more. You can't be a good parent and be drinking. And you don't have time to be out drinking... you can't take a kid to a party. (Henry)

Nancy had her first baby when she was 16. The baby's father left when he learned Nancy was pregnant. Two years later she married Ronnie and feels she made a good decision:

*I honestly don't feel like I gave up anything important to me
when I got married two years ago. The only thing I don't do
now is go out with my friends all the time. But I feel that's a
change for the better because I used to neglect my baby and
leave her with my mom a lot. I realize now that was wrong. I'm
still feeling guilty about it and am trying to make it up to her
now.*

Continue School After Marriage?

According to the survey, marriage is not likely to change high
school attendance. Only 6 percent of the women and 13 percent of
the men say they would drop out if they got married. Of those
living together, a few more felt marriage would mean quitting
school. (Table 3-3)

Reality is often quite different. About four out of five of those in
the United States who marry before they finish high school drop out.
(Moore et al, 1978) Howell and Frese (1982) studied the antecedents
and short-term consequences of teenage marriage, parenting, and
school-leaving. They point out that being married or a parent is
more often than not associated with dropping out of school.

The survey results considered here are biased for two reasons.
First, those not yet married are reporting their expectations —
what they *think* they would do if they married. Second, since the
survey was mostly administered within schools, few of those who
had dropped out could be included.

Time after time in our school's Teen Mother Program, students
drop out after they marry. Often they assure me that marriage won't
make a difference in their attendance, and some do continue
attending regularly. Others, however, either come intermittently or
not at all. Often they say their husbands don't want them in school:

*Not finishing high school bothers both of us. I want that RN
so bad I can taste it. On that graduation day it will be so
wonderful. I'll get it some day, somehow. (Elaine, married at
16 to Lloyd, 17)*

When teenagers marry, they often find their priorities must
change. School may not seem important anymore. If he has

already dropped out, he may feel threatened if she continues. One young wife called to tell me she would not be back in class. "He says I know enough to keep house," she reported.

But sometimes that change in priorities goes the other way:

> *After I got married I had to set my priorities, had to understand I was married and I had a baby. I realized that if I dropped out of school, who would hire me? I didn't see much of my daughter because of school and work, but now I'm a priority person, and if it's going to be better in the long run . . . that was hard for me to learn because I was mostly an impulse person before that. (Rosemarie, married at 15 to Steve, 15. Divorced a year later.)*

About half the young men in the survey and 43 percent of the young women expected marriage to limit their freedom. Response was almost identical from young women already living with their partners. Only half of the young men living with partners, however, said marriage means less freedom for them. (Table 3-4) Young women who were interviewed often spoke of staying home while their partners went out with friends. This is a reality for many of these young people.

The same reality was described several years ago by Vladimir de Lissovoy (1974) who reported a study of 48 teenage couples in Pennsylvania. These young people were systematically followed for a period of 30-36 months after their marriages. Almost all of the young women expressed feelings of loneliness and loss of friends and social life. Most of the men, however, continued seeing their friends, tinkering with cars, and other social activities. They didn't seem to be aware of their partners' loneliness. "Somebody has to stay with the baby" was a frequent answer to a wife's complaint about staying home alone, according to de Lissovoy.

Partners Change

Almost half the people in the living-together survey had lived with their partners less than six months. Nevertheless, the majority reported changes in their partners and about one-fourth said these were negative changes.

**Has your partner changed much since you were married or started
living together?**

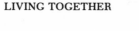

LIVING TOGETHER

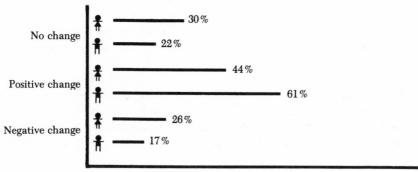

No change — 30%, 22%

Positive change — 44%, 61%

Negative change — 26%, 17%

(See Table 3-5)

More negative change was reported by young people whose
partners were of a different religious faith or from a different
ethnic group than their own. More than 40 percent of those with a
partner with a different faith and 38 percent of those in an
interracial relationship reported negative changes in their partners.
About the same percentages from each group reported positive
changes. (Table 3-6)

Some of the young women spoke of the "Ownership Syndrome."
Because their husbands seem to feel marriage means ownership of
one's wife, their freedom is drastically limited. "He thinks he has a
right to tell me what to do," they say.

> *Marriage changes your life a whole lot. He tells you what to
> do more. Like before when we weren't married, he would tell
> me what to do and I would say, "Why should I do this —
> there are no strings attached to me." Now when he tells me to
> iron his clothes and to cook, I do it. When he says, "Don't go
> there," you have to do what he says. You don't have to, I
> suppose, but if you do, it causes less fights and arguments.*
>
> *I could do things better if I was single. I could go to church, I
> could get a job, take my kids where I want, dress them like I
> want. But Joel won't let me. (Estella, married at 18 to Joel, 20.)*

Jean didn't feel Dick was afflicted with "Ownership Syndrome," but she reported a difficult first year:

> *The first year wasn't that great. I think it was the hardest, perhaps because I wasn't used to it. All of a sudden I had this other person to pick up after and it was hard. He worked graveyard and slept during the day. When he went to work I would go to bed by myself. I guess I figured you were supposed to see each other...*

Many young people already living with partners are finding life together is harder than they expected. Lack of friends, loss of freedom, and the often overwhelming responsibilities these young people must face are undoubtedly involved in these opinions.

Compared to what you expected before you started living together, is living together:

LIVING TOGETHER

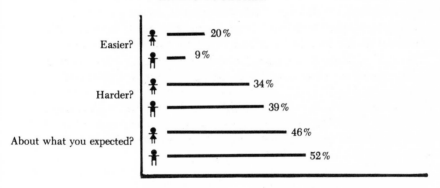

(See Table 3-7)

Marriage or moving in with a partner brings many changes into a teenager's life. His familiar world of friends and parties may vanish. Her relationship with her family may be altered. Trina and her husband were one of the couples that didn't make it. They were divorced six years after they married. She commented:

> *I think it's hard when you go from a close-knit family right to a husband and a little family unit, and I never really*

*became just one person. I think it's important to become an
individual first before you're ready to move into another kind
of unit.*

Summary and Conclusions

Teenagers in the survey sample generally did not expect marriage
to bring drastic changes into their lives. However, many young
people already married and/or living with partners find they have
given up a great deal — their friends, their freedom, sometimes
their education and career goals — because of their relationship.

The majority of survey respondents reported changes in their
partners, some positive and some negative. A higher percentage of
those in interfaith or interracial relationships reported negative
changes in their partners although many of these young people said
their mates had changed for the better.

The "Ownership Syndrome" is a problem for some young couples
— the situation in which one partner, usually the man, takes
charge and expects the other one to comply. Good communication
between the partners may help solve this problem.

Almost all couples face changes when they marry. Adolescents
themselves change rapidly. Place two adolescents together in
marriage and the changes are likely to be overwhelming.

If the young couple can work through these changes and through
the process of bonding to each other, they may be able to develop a
long-lasting partnership. Going into the partnership with a firm
realization that changes will occur coupled with a determination to
work through these changes are solid steps toward achieving a
satisfying relationship.

Not all teenage couples survive as a unit — but with lots of trust,
respect and caring in addition to unlimited love, some manage to
change and grow together.

Chapter 4

Learning to Communicate

We have a common problem. I feel like I don't communicate enough. I feel I should talk a lot more and I'm working on it. I think it would help our relationship. A lot of times we just sit there and watch TV and don't say a word to each other. I know Maura wants more.

My family didn't communicate much. They were TV freaks and my mother was an alcoholic. Maybe that's part of our problem — different families. It helps to communicate, and we're both working on it. We're trying to get over those bumps and keep the communication going for both of us. I'm trying to talk more, bring up anything. (George, married at 21 to Maura, 18)

George and Maura have been together almost two years and their relationship is deteriorating. George blames some of their problems on his inability to talk freely, to share with Maura. Lack of good communication is a problem in many young marriages. In this survey, more than half of the young people already living together found this to be true in their own partnerships. (Table 4-1)

They often mentioned communication as one of their biggest problems. They think their relationship would improve with more open sharing between them of thoughts, feelings, plans, and dreams.

More talking is not always the solution, however. In our busy lives, we speak of the need for "quality" time with children and with spouse. Research studies have shown it isn't the amount of time a parent spends with her/his children that matters as much as the way s/he spends that time. The same is true of communication between partners.

In some partnerships, one person talks a great deal while the other partner develops a good tuneout system for survival. In our culture the "talker" is more likely to be the woman. If this couple is having marital problems and they and/or their counselor decide better communication would help, more doesn't necessarily mean better. Instead, the partner who already communicates freely may help the other become more open and at the same time cut back a little on his/her verbiage.

With some partners, improvement of both quality and quantity of communication is important. There is no standard recipe for good communication between a couple.

Communication Important To Intimacy

Good communication between partners is an important part of intimacy, and most couples strive for intimacy. Trust, respect, and caring provide a good start toward intimate communication.

According to Erik Erickson (1963), an adolescent needs to develop a strong personal identity before s/he is ready for intimacy. Without this self-identity or autonomy, a person is likely to have trouble finding true intimacy with a partner.

Toews (1980) describes the paradox encountered by very young couples. On the one hand, they need to share intimately with each other, but at the same time, each may still be in the identity formation stage. Young people need to separate from their parents as they form their independent identities.

Toews maintains that young couples sometimes turn to each other for the security still needed from the families of origin. Then, as each matures, the rebellion normally directed toward parents may cause a crisis in their relationship with each other.

Learning to share intimately with one's spouse may be difficult at any age. If one or both are still in the throes of the adolescent identity crisis, it will be doubly hard.

Sometimes we're both so angry we can't even talk. I have a quick temper and he's very patient. Sometimes that aggravates me — that I can't get him mad. And it upsets him when I yell.
It's hard because he works from 3 P.M. to midnight, and when he's gone, I'm cleaning or washing. But he's understanding, dependable, fun, and gets along well with my family. Even when we argue, we sometimes end up laughing at the dumb things we said. (Lynn, married two years ago at 16 to Roberto, 19)

Intimacy suggests sharing of problems. Teenagers were asked, "If you have a problem, to whom do you talk?" Not many reported sharing problems with a boy/girlfriend. They were more likely to go to another friend or to a parent. In fact, only two in five of those already living with a partner said they would share problems with their mates.

If you have a problem, to whom do you talk?

"Girl/boyfriend or husband/wife"

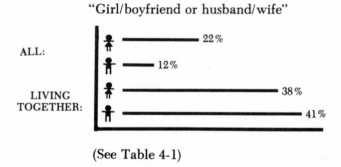

(See Table 4-1)

Counselor Helps With Communication

Very few would confide in a teacher, counselor or minister, but Yvette, married at 17 to Vince, 19, thinks a counselor saved her marriage:

We used to fight about everything. I thought if we were fighting so much, Vince must want a divorce, but we didn't talk about it. Then I was surprised to find he went over to the college to talk to one of the counselors about how we could get along better. When I found out I thought, "He really cares."

I talked with his counselor, too, and then we both talked together. Vince was telling everything that day. I usually tell Vince when I don't like something he does, but when I'd ask him what he didn't like about me, he wouldn't tell me. But that day with the counselor he said he didn't like this and he didn't like that. . . no big thing, just little things that bothered him and that mostly I could do something about.

The counselor said, "When you get mad, do you not even say 'Goodnight'?" We told him, yes, sometimes we didn't talk for a week. He said, "Don't ever do that. Every time you have a fight, settle it before you go to bed. Give him a kiss and say, 'I'm sorry. If you want to fight again, we'll do it tomorrow.' "

It's working. When he gets mad, I say, "Vince, I'd like to talk to you about something." If he says, "No, I don't want to talk," I tell him we have to talk. Then he may tell me what he didn't like and I'll say I'm sorry and I'll try not to do it again.

I think it's a good idea, talking with somebody. Not with your parents — sometimes your parents help but not usually. If I tell my mom I had a fight with Vince, she'll say, "Don't fight with him. It's your fault." That's not what I want to hear. You don't really have to tell your mom what's going on here. If I have a fight with Vince, she doesn't have to know about it.

If you want to keep your marriage, you have to work together real hard. You have to do it together.

Young women were progressively less likely to share problems with either a boyfriend/husband or their parents as they went from being pregnant to parenting an infant to being the mother of an older child. Instead, the mothers were more likely to talk with another friend or, for one in ten, to a teacher, counselor, or minister. (Table 4-3)

Do couples tend to be closer, to share more, during a pregnancy? After the baby is born, are they less close? Is there simply less time for sharing problems? Fewer problems to share? Counselors working with teenagers need to be aware of these possibilities.

Karolynn found a problem in her relationship very soon after she and Al were married. It was solved only after talking with both him and her parents:

Al thought of me as "his." That was funny — I was married to him now, I was his, and I was to do what he said, come and

go when he said. We got into a big fight and sat down and
talked with my parents. Finally he started seeing things my
way and the way my family was.

We were at my parents when it all came up, and it got so
bad that my mom had to step in. We had to talk it out — "We
feel this way and you feel that way." It was hard, but we did
talk it through.

We're the kind of people that if we can't communicate we
have to sit down and talk. I have always been that way
because if I don't, I'll hold a grudge for a long time.

Teenagers from the three religious groups showed little
difference from the total sample except for Protestants who
apparently share more problems with parents and friends. Very
few young people from any of the religious groups would discuss a
problem with a teacher, counselor or minister. (Table 4-4)

Handling The Arguments

More than four times as many (44 percent) of the "happy"
living-together partners share problems with their mates as do the
"unhappy" respondents, an indication of the value of good
communication within a relationship. (Table 4-5) Sharing the same
religion and/or belonging to the same ethnic group also indicated
more sharing of problems between partners. (Table 4-6)

Sharing problems with one's partner may be an indication of the
development of intimacy. But what happens if these problems
erupt into arguments between the two? How do these young people
expect to work out the inevitable disagreements bound to occur in
their relationships?

Until he saw the counselor, Vince represented one in ten of the
males when he didn't do anything about his problems. Slightly
fewer young women take this approach. Almost two-thirds of the
women and half the men would tell their partners they're upset.

If you are upset with your partner, what do you do?

"Tell him/her I am upset"

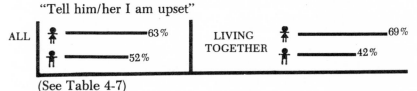

(See Table 4-7)

Young people living together are more likely to tell their partners they're upset — although one-tenth of the women and one-fifth of the men said they wouldn't do anything. Young people living together were less likely to leave because of an argument, but for some, this clears the air.

> *We argue. Sometimes I have to talk to him about something I have to get through to him. Occasionally we don't talk to each other for awhile, and he'll go to bed or I'll go down to my friend's. Then the next day one of us says, "I'm sorry."*
>
> *But we don't fight that much which I like. I don't want to be fighting with somebody all the time. He always says, "Lucia, we aren't going to be like our parents. I don't want to be like them." My mom has gone through two divorces, my dad is on his second, and Arnie's mom and dad are getting divorced. We want our marriage to last. (Lucia, married at 17 to Arnie, 18)*

> *When I'm upset, I tell him and then leave. I think it through, then come back and talk about it. (Esther, married at 16 to Bill, 17)*

Older teenagers are more likely to tell their partners they are upset and are less likely to leave than are younger respondents. (Table 4-8)

If you are upset with your partner, what do you do?

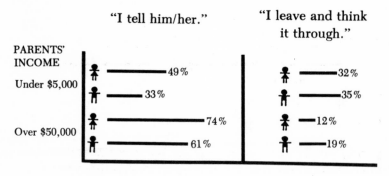

(See Table 4-9)

Teenagers whose parents earn more than $50,000 per year are
much more likely to tell their partners they are upset than are
young people from homes with an annual income of under $5,000.
As the parents' income goes up, young people are much less likely
to leave when they're upset. Apparently communication goes better
with money.

Communication patterns vary not only with socio-economic level
but also among ethnic groups. Anglo women were most likely to
tell a partner if they were upset — 70 percent made this response.
In contrast, only 29 percent of the Black males gave this answer,
but more Anglo, Asian, and Native American males agreed. One-
third of the Black teenagers, males and females, said they would,
when an argument occurred, leave and think it through. Fewer
young people from the other ethnic groups made this response.
Black respondents were also more likely than other young people to
answer "Don't do anything." (Table 4-10)

Couples living together but who did not share the same religious
beliefs were less likely to tell the partner if s/he was upset than
were couples with the same faith. They were more likely to leave
in the event of an argument. Partners representing different ethnic
groups also followed this pattern, but to a lesser extent.

If you are upset with your partner, what do you do?

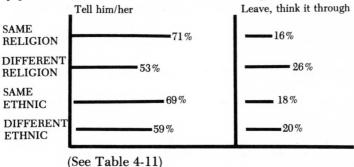

	Tell him/her	Leave, think it through
SAME RELIGION	71%	16%
DIFFERENT RELIGION	53%	26%
SAME ETHNIC	69%	18%
DIFFERENT ETHNIC	59%	20%

(See Table 4-11)

Who Has The Last Word?

For real intimacy to develop between two people, open
communication is essential. Trust, respect, and caring provide a
good foundation for this kind of sharing, and this implies an equal
relationship between the two partners.

But some young people, one-fifth of the males and one in twenty females, think the husband should have the final word in an argument. Very few women and almost no men would give the wife this privilege. Obviously if one partner feels s/he has more right than the other to close an argument, communication won't be truly open. (Table 4-12)

While Catholic and Born-again Christian males' responses did not differ much from the overall sample, one-fourth of the Protestant males said the man should have the last word. Almost no Protestant females agreed. (Table 4-13)

About one-fourth of the Hispanic and Black males also said the man should have the last word. One-third of the Asian males agreed. The sample of Asian males, however, included only 15 individuals. Fewer Anglo and Native American teenage men said the man should have the final say. (Table 4-14)

The most relevant factor in the responses to this question was the income of the respondents' parents. Percentage of males and females thinking the man should end the argument ranged from 11 percent (women) and 30 percent (men) whose parents' income was less than $5,000 per year to 3 percent of the women and 15 percent of the men from homes with incomes over $50,000. The same drop in percentages occurred among those (very few in any group) who felt the woman should have the final word. More and more teenagers, as their family income was higher, felt the whole question did not matter. (Table 4-14)

Ann, married ten years ago at 16 to Charlie, 19, offers guidelines for handling arguments. Trust, respect, and caring are important parts of her guidelines:

> *I feel the most important part of any relationship is a very good sense of trust and communication. Being able to listen and to understand what your partner is trying to say, to be able to talk things out and, if not agree, at least compromise. I think before anyone decides to get married, they should honestly talk about their values and feelings instead of finding out afterward.*
>
> *Most of our arguments happen when we're tired and because we haven't communicated our feelings and thoughts fully to one another. We usually hold hands and never yell when we fight. Also, past mistakes are not brought up and there is no name-calling or personal putdowns . . . not an easy way to fight,*

*but a terrific way to remain assured we love one another and
only have a difference of opinion.*

Obviously Ann and Charlie prefer to talk things through
together. The majority of teenagers agree.

Summary and Conclusions

Many young couples would like to communicate better with one
another because they realize how important this is in the
development of intimacy. However, if either or both is still trying
to develop her/his own identity, being open and sharing with the
other person may be difficult.

When they had problems, few teenagers in the survey shared
them with partners. They were more likely to talk with other
friends or with their parents. Even among those married and/or
living with a partner, less than half shared their problems with
their mates.

More of these teenagers, when upset with his/her partner, would
tell him/her. Some, however, in such a situation, would either do
nothing or would leave.

More open communication appears to be the pattern between
couples whose parents' annual income is high as compared to those
from homes with very little money. Those from low-income homes
are more likely to walk away from an argument.

Learning to communicate well is not instinctual and teenagers
need help in learning these skills. If a couple enters their
relationship already aware of some of the techniques which lead to
good communication, they are more likely to be able to talk freely
with each other. Counselors and teachers can help them learn how
to express feelings through I-messages, how to listen to the partner,
then offer feedback to the message received, and other aids to good
communication.

Understanding the rules of "good" fighting often helps. They
need to realize that fighting fair does *not* include bringing up last
month's problems, putting down one's partner, or criticizing one's
mother-in-law!

These and other suggestions concerning communication are
included in *Teenage Marriage: Coping with Reality* (Lindsay,
1984). Other good references on this topic include *Marriage: How*

to Have It the Way You Want It by David Edens (1982); *Couples: How to Confront Problems and Maintain Loving Relationships* by Carlfred Broderick (1981); and *The Newlywed Handbook: A Refreshing Practical Guide for Living* by Yvonne Garrett (1981). All are written in an interesting manner likely to appeal to teenagers.

Good communication is an important part of a good relationship. If a teenage couple can talk freely with each other, they have made a good start toward the long-lasting relationship so important to them both.

Chapter 5

Is There Life After Sex?

> *Brian would never force me or anything, but
> sometimes I get the feeling that somebody has
> told all the men in the world that it's written
> in the marriage contract that women have to
> do it whenever men want it. I think there is an
> imbalance in it. Men seem to be able to turn
> off things that happen during the day while
> women, at least myself, worry so much that, if
> something goes wrong, it sticks with me and I
> can't simply roll over and have sex with him.
> It can be a problem. (Alyssa, married two
> years ago at 16 to Brian, 17)*

After watching TV soap operas and some of the current movies,
one might indeed wonder, "Is there life after sex? Or is sex all that
matters?" Today's adolescents have been bombarded all their lives
with these television shows and movies. Sexually explicit
commercials appear everywhere — on the TV screens in their
living rooms, on the billboards along the highway, in newspapers
and in magazines including those published especially for
teenagers.

Sex is portrayed as something wonderful — and of course it can
be. But occasionally in class a young wife will imply that in her

partnership, sex is not all she thinks it should be. One young
woman, mother of three children, gave a poignant reply to a
survey question, "Is sex an important part of your marriage?"
Crossing out the "Very important," "somewhat important," and
"not important" answers, she simply wrote, "I don't care for it."

Sex Is Part of Total Relationship

Young people need help in understanding that loving, caring,
satisfying sex may not always happen between two people. Sex
usually goes better if it is part of a total relationship.

> *We always have arguments when it comes to sex. Just
> because I don't want to give in, he says I don't love him. Our
> biggest problem is fussing at each other for crazy childish
> reasons. And I have to be home or always tell him where I've
> been. I don't have any freedom anymore. (Melinda, moved in
> at 16 with Greg, 17)*

Gary Yates, counselor at Children's Hospital, Los Angeles, has
helped many young couples improve their overall relationship with
each other. "I don't think it's necessarily true that a good sex life
makes for a better relationship," he commented. "I find that when
there is a decent relationship, a sense of commitment to one
another, the sex gets handled. It isn't the sex technique that makes
the relationship work. Instead, the quality of the relationship can
make the sex good."

When I was writing *Teenage Marriage: Coping with Reality*, a
book for teenagers, I called a friend in Nampa, Idaho, to ask for
advice on the sex chapter. Ellen Peach, family nurse practitioner,
Community Health Clinics, Inc., sees many teenagers in her
practice. She also leads community workshops in which she helps
parents learn to communicate with their children about sex. "I'll
ask my patients what they'd like you to cover," she said. "Call me
back next week."

When I called her back, Ellen reported, "You opened a veritable
Pandora's Box. In fact, you've changed my whole approach to
counseling!" As she had promised, she said to her patients, "My
friend is writing a book about teenage marriage, and she wants
advice as to what to include in the chapter on sex. What do you
think is needed?"

Every teenage woman with whom she talked that week spoke of problems in this area. They weren't finding their sex lives at all similar to the TV soap operas or the romance novels.

They described lack of interest in sex, pain with intercourse, and husbands who weren't very considerate. These were mostly young mothers of infants and they were usually exhausted — but they couldn't understand why they were no longer interested in sex.

"We talked about men having different expectations in sex than women, and about the importance of good communication between sex partners. I heard a lot about how babies can wreck a couple's sex life — both because the baby's always there and because the young mother is likely to find intercourse uncomfortable for awhile after childbirth," Ellen commented.

Teenage couples need to be aware of these possible difficulties. Both husband and wife need to be reminded *before* childbirth that sex may not be important to her for awhile. It might be pointed out to the young man that if he becomes deeply involved in sharing the care of their baby, his wife is likely not to become so exhausted — which in turn may help her be interested in sex sooner than she might be otherwise.

Sally, married at 17 and divorced two years later, remembers that period:

> *I know after I had Janie, it was at least five weeks before I had any interest in sex at all. When she'd go to sleep I'd get my naps. I was exhausted! My girlfriend got pregnant two weeks after she had her baby...I couldn't have handled that.*
>
> *We honestly didn't have a very good sexual relationship anyway. He was too forceful, not very loving or caring at all.*

Karolynn, still married after eight years, remembers the time seven years ago after she had their baby:

> *I went through that (no interest in sex) right after I had Clara. I was so afraid of getting pregnant again plus Al just turned me off and I would push him away. I started thinking I was going to get that way — frigid, you call it? You start feeling like your husband will go out and find someone else.*
>
> *It wasn't even right after the baby was born because Al knew I'd have to wait six weeks so he didn't hassle me. I don't know why, but all of a sudden I just didn't want to do it. We*

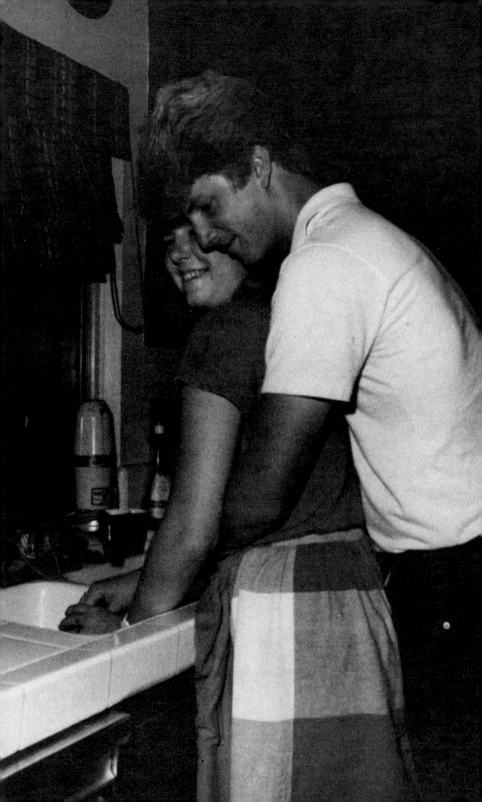

finally started talking about it and I was willing to give in. It's been pretty good since then. You've got to talk because otherwise you're lost!

"Sex Begins in the Kitchen" is the title of the corresponding chapter in *Teenage Marriage*. It is also the title of a book by Dr. Kevin Leman (1981: Regal Books), and was used with Dr. Leman's permission. The point of the chapter and of his entire book is that a couple's sex life is greatly influenced by the rest of their relationship. For most people, sex doesn't operate in a vacuum.

Kathleen described the growth of her interest in sex:

At first I never really liked it. Then after I got pregnant with him it kind of switched around. I think my problem when I didn't think sex was fun was when I was doing it because I thought I had to, not because I was in love. I think I still felt that way when we were first married. Then after awhile I felt real love for Henry, and we were more affectionate, and somehow there was more meaning to it.

Importance of Sex Within Marriage

Do teenagers think sex is an important part of marriage? Teenage men living with their partners placed less importance on sex within marriage than did the other young men.

Is sex an important part of marriage?

"Absolutely" + "Probably"

ALL:
    77%
    84%

LIVING TOGETHER:
    75%
    78%

(See Table 5-1)

Elise and Hector married mostly because she was pregnant. At first their sex life was not good:

Emotionally I felt like brother and sister, not husband and wife. That almost caused us to break up. I didn't like feeling like he was my brother. There wasn't much of anything, not even much companionship. I had a kid and he was mine, but Hector was working nights and he'd sleep most of the day. I was bored — we didn't have time together, didn't do anything together.

We had a big fight over that and he did leave for a few days. Then I did a dumb thing. I overdosed on aspirin. When he came home and found out he made me throw up. The next day we talked things out and he decided to spend more time with me and our son. That's helped our sex life too.

The woman doesn't have to feel it's her obligation — it's for her enjoyment and for mutual satisfaction. It's not a job — although sometimes it feels like it is.

In all ethnic groups men were more likely than women to consider sex an important part of marriage. The small sample of Asian men were most likely to maintain that sex is absolutely important in a marriage — 71 percent as compared to only 35 percent of Asian women. However, if the "Absolutely" and "Probably" answers are combined for this group, the difference almost disappears. The same type of difference occurs within the other ethnic groups, but to a smaller degree. (Table 5-2)

The higher their parent's income, the more likely was a teenage woman to think sex was absolutely important in a marriage — 56 percent of those whose family income was above $50,000 down to 36 percent of those in the lowest income group. No real pattern appeared among men when analyzed according to family income. (Table 5-3)

Not much difference in responses to this question appeared among the Catholic, Protestant, and Born-again Christian teenagers.

Women who had never been pregnant were most likely to think sex is an important part of marriage. At least 5 percent less of those who had had an abortion, were pregnant, or already had a child shared this opinion. (Table 5-4)

Respondents were also asked how much importance they placed on husbands and wives being good sex partners. Again, the men placed more importance on each spouse excelling in this area.

How important do you think it is for a wife to be a good sex partner?

"Very important" + "Somewhat important"

```
         ♀
WIFE     ♀ ————————————————————————●88%
         ♂ ————————————————————————●90%
```

How important do you think it is for a husband to be a good sex partner?

```
            ♀
HUSBAND     ♀ ————————————————————————●87%
            ♂ ————————————————————————●91%
```

(See Table 5-5)

Viewpoints on Premarital Sex

According to the media, many teenagers experience sexual intercourse at a very early age. Is everyone really "doing it"? Does "everyone" think this is all right? The survey responses indicate that many teenagers think so, although about one-fourth of the males and one-third of the females do not approve of premarital sex.

Young women already living with a partner, when compared with the total sample, were less likely to be opposed to premarital sex. One in five, however, disapproved although some of these young women were living with boyfriends without being married. (Table 5-6)

Do you think a couple should have sexual intercourse before they are married?

"Absolutely" + "Probably" + "It doesn't matter"

```
ALL                ♀ ————————————————————●67%
                   ♂ ————————————————————————●74%

LIVING             ♀ ————————————————————————●78%
TOGETHER           ♂ ————————————————————————●75%
```

(See Table 5-6)

A young woman in the nationwide survey who disagreed with the majority viewpoint commented on this question:

> *Do I think a couple should have sexual intercourse before they get married? If you're talking about a young couple still in high school, my answer would be "No." High school couples are still too young to know what's going on.*
>
> *Having sex is the easy part, but really loving someone with your heart is the hardest part. I know I won't have sex until I'm married.*

Rural women were most opposed to sex before marriage as compared to women living in the suburbs and in the cities. Males differ very little in these groups. (Table 5-7)

Born-again Christian women were most likely to consider premarital sex wrong. Protestant women were a little more likely to condone sex before marriage. Fewer Catholic males were opposed as compared to Protestant and Born-again Christian males. (Table 5-8)

The older teenagers were less opposed to sex before marriage than were those aged 14-16. (Table 5-9) Hispanic, Asian and Anglo women were less likely to approve sex before marriage than were Black or Native American women. (Table 5-10)

Comparing responses of young women who have had abortions with those who were pregnant or already parents is interesting. Only 16 percent of the 79 who had had an abortion were opposed to premarital sex, just half as many as in the total group. Responses of those who were pregnant and/or parents fell between these two groups. (Table 5-11)

Only one-third of the teenage women in this survey and one-fourth of the men think premarital sex is either absolutely or probably wrong. Many young people are having sexual intercourse before they marry, some at a very young age. Pregnancy too soon is a reality for many of these young people, and many conceive at home. Marnita, now the mother of three children, was married three years ago at 16 to Andy, 18. She remembers how and where it all started — and how her life has changed:

> *When I first started having sex with Andy, we would just go to my house and nobody was there. We'd be watching TV and all of a sudden we'd be in my room. Back then, we'd do it a lot*

but now it's only once or twice during the whole week —
partly because right now if little Andy hears us he'll get up and
crawl right between us.

Contraceptive Information Needed

The survey contained no questions about contraception.
However, young wives in our school sometimes are very unhappy
about unplanned pregnancy. Teenagers as a group have trouble
looking into the future, planning for what may happen. Over and
over pregnant teenagers say, "No, we weren't using anything. I
didn't think I'd get pregnant." Psychologically, this thinking is
similar to the idea some teenagers have that they can drive a car
too fast but *they* won't have accidents.

Young people not yet pregnant, whether married or not, need to
be reminded that one-fifth of all first premarital pregnancies
among teenagers occur in less than a month after the couples start
having intercourse — and half the pregnancies occur during the
first six months. (Planned Parenthood Federation of America, 1981)
If they decide to have intercourse, they must also decide either to
risk pregnancy or to use a reliable contraceptive consistently.

For a young couple with no income and still in school, an
unplanned baby can make life even more difficult. Contraceptive
services need to be available, services which are inexpensive and
easily accessible. Most important, teenagers need to know about
these services.

We were together just a short time when I got pregnant.
Nobody ever told me anything about birth control. I did get
the pill about two months later but I was already pregnant.

The schools should be doing more on birth control. In
Health it was only a three-day class, a double class with 65-70
kids. They have more involvement with drugs than with
pregnancy. I think it should be reversed. Teaching about drugs
is important but birth control is even more important. (Esther,
married at 17 to Art, 26)

Summary and Conclusions

Young couples may find their sexual relationship not as satisfying
as they would like, partly because of the different expectations men

and women often have in this area. Especially after childbirth, young women report lack of interest in sex, probably at least partly due to sheer exhaustion. A good book to offer teenagers on the subject of sex is *Teenage Body Book* by Kathy McCoy and Charles Wibbelsman (1979).

One-third of the women and a quarter of the men in the survey said they were opposed to sex before marriage. The others either think it's a good idea or it doesn't matter.

In spite of the wide acceptance of premarital sex among teenagers, contraceptive counseling is not readily available in many areas. The result is a steady rise in unplanned pregnancies, abortions, and premature parenthood among teenagers.

Schools and other social agencies must take a more active role in encouraging young people either to delay becoming sexually active or to be responsible in the use of contraceptives.

Yes, there is life after sex for teenagers. With lots of love mixed in with trust, respect, and caring, a young couple's sexual relationship can be part of a deeply satisfying marriage. But it must be part of their total relationship — sex *does* begin in the kitchen. . . and continues throughout the entire partnership.

Chapter 6

Who Does The Housework?

I work — I'm a waitress — and I'm in charge of keeping house and taking care of the kids. Sometimes I feel like I'm a slave. Ray seldom picks up the house and he never cleans it. Sometimes after I've left it all clean, I'll come home from work and it's a total mess. I told him if he'd just have the living room picked up I could at least walk in the door and be impressed. (Donita, married 7 years ago at 17 to Ray, 18)

Mopping floors and vacuuming the house aren't jobs most people enjoy. Traditionally these tasks have been delegated to women, a situation equal marriage proponents would like to see changed.

The good news is that many of the 3000 teenagers in the survey, men and women, *want* both husband and wife to work together on such tasks as cooking, washing dishes, cleaning house, washing clothes, mowing the lawn, and washing the car. From one- to two-thirds of these young women and one-fourth to more than half the young men don't want the traditional arrangement in which she cooks and cleans while he gardens and takes care of the car. They want to share these roles.

"In a good marriage, who should be responsible for the following tasks?"
                                   "BOTH HUSBAND AND WIFE"

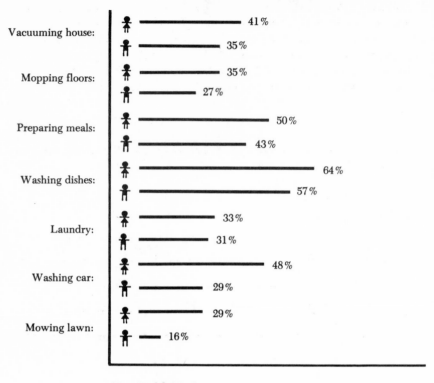

(See Table 6-1)

Similar results were obtained in the large "Monitoring the Future" surveys directed by Lloyd Johnston and Jerald Bachman and sponsored by the National Institute of Education (Herzog and Bachman, 1982). This was a study of high school seniors' sex role attitudes and the relationship of those attitudes to various plans for adult roles. The equal division of housework is the preferred arrangement among these seniors, according to Herzog and Bachman, and females want a "more equal" division than do males.

Traditional Roles Are Reality

While the good news is the fact that many teenagers, male and female, approve in theory the sharing of household chores, the bad

news is the *reality* described by eighty young women who
responded to the Teen Mother Program survey discussed in the
Introduction. Most of these women, aged 14-19 when they married
and/or moved in with their partners, reported being responsible for
all or most of the household chores. Between 79 and 89 percent did
most or, in the majority of cases, *all* the vacuuming, mopping,
dishwashing, and laundry. Their partners generally washed the cars
and mowed the lawn. Very few couples shared any of these tasks.

Teen Mother Program Alumnae Survey

*"In your first marriage or living-together partnership, who was/is
responsible for the following tasks?"*

"I AM" or "MOSTLY ME"

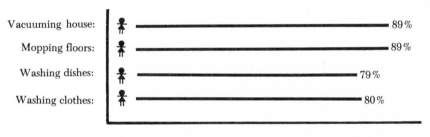

Vacuuming house:	89%
Mopping floors:	89%
Washing dishes:	79%
Washing clothes:	80%

(See Table 6-2)

Many of those who reported being responsible for all of the
housework also held paying jobs. About one-third were working
away from home at the time of the survey. All had young children.

Ideally, the person with the skills, the time, and the inclination
will do the work necessary to keep a home and family functioning.
Are these young couples following the traditional division of labor
because they want to and are satisfied with their work? Some
people would rather clean house and wash clothes instead of
working outside on the car and garden. Others prefer the latter. Is
it possible these young women do the housework themselves because
they want to? The young people I interviewed don't think so:

Alison became pregnant six years ago when she was 15. She and
Orlando quickly married, but she continued attending school and
graduated two years later. Since that time, she has had two more
children, and has been home taking care of their house and family.

She would like to have help from Orlando but knows insisting would only cause problems between them. She said:

> *Traditional roles? All the way! In fact, I told Orlando yesterday I'd love to switch roles so he could see how hard it is to keep house and take care of the kids. I suppose the woman should take care of the house and kids and I'll do anything to avoid a fight. I think that's the only way a marriage can survive.*
>
> *Of course Orlando always has his way but I'm so used to it that it doesn't bother me. My friends think I should stand up to him but I don't want to — I don't like to fight with him.*

The Teen Mother Program alumnae in the survey were asked specifically to describe the task-division in their *first* marriage or living-together partnership. Twenty-three of the eighty were no longer living with their first partners. Several mentioned being much happier in a second marriage and indicated the division of work at home was no longer in the traditional pattern.

Most teenagers want marriage to be forever. They don't want to jump from one partner to another. Perhaps if these young women had talked about their feelings before they married, if they had been able to discuss with their boyfriends an equitable arrangement for accomplishing necessary household chores, their partnerships would have had a better chance of survival.

Variations in Attitudes Expressed

In the nationwide survey, young women already living with partners gave about the same responses to the household chores questions as did women from the total sample. More young men in the living-together group, however, recommended that husband and wife share these tasks. (Table 6-3)

Ethnic groups varied less in their responses than might be expected. Asian males were less likely to expect their wives to do the vacuuming, mopping, and dishwashing although slightly more than half thought one's wife should be responsible for the cooking.

Black women expected the husband and wife to share the cleaning more than did women from other ethnic groups. Black men, on the other hand, were less likely to want to share these tasks than any group except Native Americans.

A higher percentage of Hispanic men and women said wives should cook and clean. An even greater percentage of Hispanic men and women thought the husband should wash the car and mow the lawn. (Table 6-4)

Born-again Christian teenage women are most likely to expect the wife in a good marriage to do the housework and the man to work outside. Protestant women are least likely to favor this plan.

Responses from young men from the three religions are quite different. More Protestant men expect their wives to clean house and wash dishes than do Catholic or Born-again Christian males. These Protestant teenage men, however, are *less* likely to think the husband should take care of the car and yard. More think these jobs should be shared by both partners. (Table 6-5)

Inner city and urban youths differed very little from suburban and small town/farm teenagers in their ideas on appropriate roles for husband and wife. One exception was that young women on farms and in small towns expect to be more involved in sharing gardening tasks than do teenagers from suburban and urban areas. This might be because gardening is likely to be a more important part of their lives if they live on farms or in small towns.

Analyzing respondents by parents' income shows differences. Generally, the higher the income, the more the teenagers advocate sharing household tasks. (Table 6-6)

Of the young people living together when they completed the questionnaire, 67 said their lives were easier than expected and 111 said living together was harder than they had expected. An analysis of their role expectations shows those who found life together harder than expected are more likely to think a good marriage involves more sharing of household tasks. (Table 6-7)

As mentioned before, the question was "In a *good* marriage, who should be responsible for the following tasks?" Apparently those with lower expectations were less likely to be disappointed in their relationships.

Housework Often Disliked

Many young wives are surprised to find the differences in their own thinking when compared to their mates' attitudes, judging from the comments of young women in our school. When class discussion turns to this topic, these young women say, "He thinks it's my job." "He says I don't clean house like his mother." "He expects me to pick up his clothes."

One young wife informed us that she simply refused to do more than her "share" of household tasks. "I'm not his slave," she said. Some of us admired her for her spunk — but her marriage ended in divorce a year later.

As a class assignment, a small group of teenage mothers (23) were asked, among other things, to describe something they intensely disliked doing. Each girl completed her short questionnaire by herself and did not exchange comments with her neighbors. The teacher offered no examples. Each young woman was on her own. In fact, the teacher expected such answers as "I hate doing homework" or "I can't stand getting up at 2 A.M. with the baby."

To the teacher's amazement, twenty — all but three — of these teenagers wrote "Cleaning house" or "Doing dishes" as their most disliked activity. Some of these same young women were among the group of 80 reporting a few months later that they were mostly responsible for these tasks. In these young partnerships, the women had obviously not *chosen* the traditional division of chores — but this was how they were living.

The difference, of course, in the results of the two surveys — the nationwide study and the Teen Mother Program alumnae survey — is basically in the questions asked. The teen mothers were asked to describe reality, the way things are for them. The 3000 teenagers answered a very different question: "In a *good* marriage, who *should* be responsible for..."

While many young men and women think that in a good marriage, husband and wife share homemaking chores, many very young couples are following the traditional plan. The wife does the housework and the husband works outside.

In the traditional marriage of one or more generations ago, the wife generally did not have a paying job. Homemaking *was* her job and she devoted full time to the many tasks necessary for keeping a home running smoothly. Her husband was busy earning the living and doing the necessary work on the lawn and car.

Suzanne, married at 16 to Bill, 18, approves with reservations:

> *It's not that I mind taking care of the house — I think that's pretty much the woman's job. I think the man should pick up after himself, but I think doing dishes and cooking dinner are pretty much her job. But I don't believe the woman should do all that and work, while the man doesn't do anything at home.*

*I think it's fair if the husband helps take care of the kids,
works, and helps out.*

Jurich (1984), in describing family developmental stages,
discusses the task of transforming a couple's early relationship into
a reality-based union. He points out that stress often develops when
a couple has a difficult time adjusting to one another's role
expectations. The above data support this concept.

Traditional Pattern Is Changing

Today many wives hold outside jobs. Many couples in urban
areas don't have lawns and gardens. Young people may not be able
to afford a car. The reality of the traditional division of labor in
this situation is a woman who is responsible for providing part of
the family's income while she continues to take care of the home
and a man who also provides part of the family's income but who
does not have other responsibilities within his family.

When this happens, it's not fair nor right nor rational. It is
simple exploitation of one individual by another.

Most people, however, are not deliberately unfair and
exploitative. Young men generally do not set out to take advantage
of their wives. Expecting her to do far more than her "share" of
household chores is not something that he intends to do — or even
admits he is doing. It is simply the way things are — which does
not make it right.

Is there a solution, a way for young couples to work toward an
equal relationship if that's what they want? Or even if it isn't what
they want, it may be a necessary goal because most young families
now need two paychecks in order to pay their bills.

Lots of discussing before marriage can help. If he thinks she
should mop the floors and cook all the meals while she thinks they
should share these tasks, they need to talk about it. If she thinks
she should not be involved in mowing the yard or washing the car
while he would like help, they should level with each other and
attempt some negotiating.

Negotiating may be harder after they are married. Esther and
Art had a problem, but they seem to have developed a workable
compromise:

*Art says I should have our house clean because I don't work.
Well, taking care of Joy is work. I clean up the house and she*

*pulls everything out again. Every time I think I have one mess
cleaned up, here comes another one.*

*That's Art's big thing, wanting his house clean. He could go
without dinner for a month if I would keep the house
immaculate. Part of our fights are because of the way I clean
— I don't do it to his expectations. I can pick up, but he would
rather have everything cleared away.*

*So now he cleans the entire house every weekend. He says,
"You do it five days, I'll do it two." So he does it two days the
way he wants and I do it five days the way I want. It works
for us.*

Summary and Conclusions

Many of the young people in the survey believe that in a good
marriage the husband and wife work together on such household
tasks as cleaning, cooking, washing clothes, and gardening. Few
wives find this to be a reality in their own lives, according to
results of a survey of alumnae of a teen mother program. Many of
these young women say they don't want to do all the housework,
especially those who also hold paying jobs.

Before starting to live together, young couples should discuss as
completely as possible all aspects of their relationship including
what each expects from the other in the handling of household
chores.

The questionnaire on which most of this research is based is
included in the Appendix and in *Teenage Marriage: Coping with
Reality.* If a young couple would complete this questionnaire
separately, then discuss their individual responses, each would at
least know how the other feels about these matters.

A "How would you feel if. . ." discussion is another good
technique. "How would you feel if I expected you to help me with
the dishes every night?" "How would you feel if I assumed you
would do the laundry while I cook supper?" Opinions and feelings
need to be shared before real negotiating can occur.

Housekeeping chores are a part of almost everyone's life. If two
people live together, they need to come to some agreement on how
and by whom these chores will be done. Hopefully, neither partner
will feel exploited by the other. Rather, both will work together
with love, respect, and caring to create the home environment they
need for a satisfying life together.

Chapter 7

Money — Reality Strikes Again

I was manager of a fastfood restaurant, working 65 hours and trying to go to school full-time before we got married. But school had to go. I had to pay bills and do other things. School got in the way. (Henry, married three years ago at 21 to Kathleen, 17)

Right now he brings home about $251 each week. Our rent is $350 and her formula is $23 a box. I go to the swap meet a lot and buy clothes for the kids.

He wants me to get a job so we can get a car and I've been trying to find one. I could work at MacDonald's or maybe Taco Bell. My mother-in-law would take care of the kids. (Marnita, married three years ago at 16 to Andy, 18)

Money problems "go with the territory" in very young marriages. . .and even in not-so-young partnerships. In our culture, the distribution of resources doesn't seem rational. An individual's highest earning power may come after the children are grown and gone. During the years of setting up housekeeping and handling the

many expenses of rearing children, the wage-earners are not likely
to be drawing high salaries.

This is especially true if those wage-earners were unable to
complete their education because of premature family formation.
Studies show these young parents are more likely to have unskilled,
low-paying jobs with little job security or chance of advancement.
(Nye and Berardo, 1973)

> *First, Brian was working at the pizza place, and then when
> we got together he got the second job at a theatre. When I got
> pregnant he got the third job in a clothing store.*
>
> *It was real stressful on him because before we got pregnant
> there were the two of us and it was half and half — we still
> went out, we still had fun, and we had the Corolla. Then
> when I got pregnant all that responsibility was especially hard
> on him. He took a beating physically — he had stomach
> problems and lost a lot of weight. We were doing all right
> mentally but I guess it took it out on him physically. (Alyssa,
> married at 16 to Brian, 17)*

For middle-aged couples, the two-paycheck marriage is often
a comfortable, satisfying situation. Housekeeping can be
relatively painless with the children gone, and essential
expenses may decrease. It is in the early years, when one
partner either must stay home with the children or pay for
responsible, loving childcare, that the income from two
paychecks is most needed.

Sudden Financial Responsibility

A young man suddenly financially responsible for a wife and
child is faced with a great deal of stress. He may react by
digging in, determined to handle these responsibilities.

> *Jed was a senior when we got married and he was working
> part-time. He has the same job — in an auto bodyshop, and he
> works all the time now. We had to pay all the baby's doctor
> bills, over $2000, so we had to stay here at my parents. But
> now we're getting back on our feet.*

I think he feels stressed. When we were first married, I don't remember him grinding his teeth, but a month or two ago I noticed it. Could that have something to do with him working so hard? (Phyllis, married at 16 to Jed, 17)

Or he may be defeated almost before he begins:

Glen's been drinking ever since I've known him. I was 13 and he was 17 when we started dating. He began drinking heavily after I got pregnant and he had a lot more responsibilities.

We always got along good at first except for his drinking. He got a better job and it really inspired him to do more, but I guess the responsibilities were real hard. People kept knocking him, and his parents expected money from every paycheck. We were barely making it as it was. Alcoholism is real hard to cope with when you're young. (Jill, married a year ago at 16 to Glen, 20. Now separated.)

Sometimes teenagers marry or move in together in order to escape the pressures at home. If she comes from a low-income home, and/or she has never had much spending money, she may think marriage will mean more income. Neither partner may be aware of the daily costs of living by themselves. The majority of teenage couples must start their life together within a parent's home or in a cooperative arrangement with other young people or relatives, often a difficult situation.

When we first got married we didn't even have a place to live. So Karolynn moved in with me and my parents. When I found out she was pregnant, I got a job and I'd go right from school to work. I couldn't even go out with the guys and play pool anymore. (Al, married eight years ago at 18 to Karolynn, 17)

Teenagers in the survey were asked if they thought getting married would change their financial situation. The majority agreed they would have less money:

How much do you think getting married at age 18 or younger would change your life as far as money is concerned?

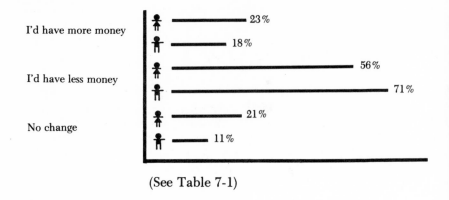

(See Table 7-1)

Fewer Black women (38 percent) felt marriage would mean less money. In fact, almost the same number of these young women said marriage would improve their financial condition. (Table 7-2)

Very little difference in expectations was shown among urban, suburban and rural youth, but parents' income did make a difference. Generally, the higher the parents' income, the more likely the teenager was to expect to have less money after marriage. On the low end of the income scale, about the same number of teenage women expected *more* money after marriage as expected less. While only 38 percent of these young women said they would have less money, 73 percent of those from the top income group felt this way. The pattern was similar for the males but less clear-cut. (Table 7-3)

Having "Enough" Money Recommended

Most teenagers think having "enough" money is "absolutely" or "probably" an important part of a good marriage. Less than 15 percent of either sex disagree with this concept. Viewpoints of the living-together group are similar. (Table 7-4)

Money was a problem a few times. Last year Larry was out of work for four months and I was working and making enough to support us. Sometimes he would say he was looking

*for a job, but instead he'd go out with his friends. But he
found another job and I don't have to work now.*

*Money does present a problem. You fight, and then when it
comes right down to it, you realize it's the money. Especially
when you're younger — a girl wants the clothes her girlfriend
has. But a lot of times you just can't. You each have to give in
a little. (Shauna, married at 17 to Larry, 19)*

Young people already living with a partner were asked if money
or the lack of it had been a problem in their relationships, and, if
so, if it was a bigger problem than expected. About one in five
replied "Always" or "Most of the time" to the first question while
more (45 percent of the women, 39 percent of the men) said it was
a bigger problem than expected. (Tables 7-5, 7-6)

*Ruben: Money. . .It's a problem, especially if you don't know
how to handle it or if your wife doesn't know how to manage.*

*Shari: We didn't have any bills until after we got married.
We didn't know what bills were until then, and we had a big
rent, and we had to buy a car and make those insurance
payments. It's hard. And sometimes you don't do the right
thing. I want to go out this week — and then we can't pay our
bills. (Shari, married at 19 to Ruben, 20. Divorced three years
later, six months after this conversation.)*

Almost half of the young people in the survey had lived with
their partners for less than six months, and the survey analyses did
not include a comparison of attitudes of these teenagers with others
who had been living with partners for a longer time. One might
assume the money problems, in many cases, would increase with
time.

*Right now we don't have any money. Jeff gets paid
tomorrow. He gets paid every two weeks and we run out the
last few days. We pay rent, car payments. We had On-TV but
we had to give that up. Jeff has a good job and that helps. But
I like to spend money — I like to go out and buy stuff for me
and Angela. That's a problem between me and Jeff, and I may
have to go out and get a job of my own so I'll have money of
my own. He says I'll just blow it. (Joni, married three years
ago at 16 to Jeff, 18)*

Many of the young people I interviewed talked in detail about their financial problems. In some of these young families, neither partner is working. He often doesn't have the necessary skills for getting and keeping a good job. If they have a child, the young mother is usually responsible for most of its care. Marge's mother discussed this problem:

> *His mother didn't want them to get married because he didn't have a job. But we said we could both help them. When the baby came, he still hadn't gotten a job. We got him one but he complained because it was a lot of work and it hurt his back, and he said he'd never get ahead. So he quit. He was going in late, playing games.*
>
> *So my husband had a very long talk with him. He told him he had to grow up, that he had a wife to support, and if he wasn't ready for that, he was free to leave. He said he'd look for another job. This went on for two years. (Mother of Marge, married at 16 to Marvin, 20. Separated two years later.)*

Most Recommend Joint Decisions

Four questions in the survey dealt with handling the money available: "Who should decide how the money is spent?" "Is it important that a husband and wife agree on how they spend money?" "Who should pay the bills?" "How important is it for the husband and for the wife to be a good money manager?"

Most of these young people, 91 percent of the women and 80 percent of the men, think both husband and wife should be responsible for deciding how to spend their money. Nearly all of them feel it is important for husband and wife to agree on financial decisions. Respondents living with partners felt the same way. (Tables 7-7, 7-8)

> *At first Al said it was his money because he earned it. If we were getting along good, he gave me money. If not...too bad. He'd say, "You had this money and now it's gone." Sometimes he'd try to act like my father. When he got that way, I'd say, "OK, Daddy." We finally worked it out. (Karolynn)*

Pregnant respondents were least likely to assign responsibility for money matters to both partners. Only 71 percent of these young women would do so as compared to 91 percent of the total sample of females. Instead, about one in ten thought the husband should make the decision, and another one in ten, the wife. Many of these young women were not living with their partners, however. (Table 7-7)

When a class of young mothers was discussing the money chapter in *Teenage Marriage: Coping with Reality,* several commented heatedly on their spouse's or boyfriend's practice of hanging on to the money. More than one complained, "He says he earns it and he spends it." Several insisted they had to ask for every penny they needed.

Teenage couples may find it hard to switch from being supported by their parents to being on their own while still very young. If she has always asked Dad for whatever she wants, she may find it tempting to try the same method with her husband. One student said, "I want a new dress for Easter — and he says we don't have the money, but I told him I have to have it. I always had a new dress for Easter before."

This young woman was 16 when she moved in with her boyfriend, 19, and his parents. Until recently he had been depending on his family for financial support. The money he earned he usually spent on his car and himself. But now suddenly he is responsible for supporting not one, but, very soon, three people on a very low income. This couple needs to develop skill in handling money, and they need to learn how to share responsibility for budgeting their income carefully.

Combining and sharing resources is important in most partnerships. This is often difficult for both men and women. When asked how they would handle their own paychecks when they start working, one or two of the young women in the class discussion replied, "That will be mine. I won't need to share with him."

Others in the conversation reminded them that sharing income goes both ways. Arlene said:

> I think at the beginning that was the main problem. I had a part-time job at school, and when I got my check, I said that was my money. So then Dale would say the same thing about his check. We fought about it for a long time, but no more. I guess we finally got it through our heads that it's our money, not mine or his.

> *If we don't agree, we try to talk it through. Usually what we*
> *do is one week he'll get something for himself, and the*
> *following week me and Chrissi will get something.*
>   *There for awhile he would want a lot of things and I would*
> *want a lot of things. So at the end of the week when he got his*
> *paycheck he would get $15 and I would get $15 to do whatever*
> *we wanted without the other one asking, "What did you do*
> *with it?" That worked pretty well. (Arlene, married three years*
> *ago at 18 to Dale, 18)*

In the nationwide survey, more women than men would have
both partners paying bills. Those living with partners were more
likely to give this responsibility to the woman. (Table 7-9)

> *When he gets paid we put the money out and we say this is*
> *for this, that's for that, and whatever is left over, we save. Yes,*
> *I know how much money he earns down to the hour. I would*
> *think there wouldn't be any trust if you didn't know. Trust is*
> *pretty important. If you can't trust him you can't be sure it*
> *will really work. (Phyllis)*

More of the Born-again Christian youth think the husband
should pay the bills — 15 percent of the women and 20 percent of
the men.

Importance of Money Management Skills

How important is it for a wife to be a good money manager? For
a husband to handle money wisely? Respondents were asked to rate
the value of this trait for each partner. Most said it was either very
or somewhat important.

About three-fifths of both men and women said it was very
important for the husband to be a good money manager, and
another third agreed this was somewhat important. Agreement was
not so widespread, however, on whether or not a wife also should
have this skill. About half the women said this was very important,
but fewer men agreed. An additional two-fifths of both men and
women said this was somewhat important. (Tables 7-11, 7-12)

Maura and George were married when she was a senior in high
school. George was three years older. They lived with her parents
for awhile, but that didn't work well. While they were there, her

mother helped handle their money, mainly by insisting they save regularly. When they finally moved out, Maura discovered that George wasn't at all good at handling money. She commented:

> *I thought moving out might help but it's gotten worse. A lot of our arguing is over the money. I have to make sure I get it to pay the bills because he's not too responsible.*
>
> *We fight about the money because sometimes we have the money and sometimes we don't. I have a checking account but George doesn't. Some day perhaps he'll have one. That's one of the big things we fight about, but if I don't do it, it won't get done.*

Pregnant respondents' views were almost the same as those of the total sample of women. Young mothers, however, placed more importance on both partners being good money managers. Almost 60 percent of the pregnant women thought it was very important for the husband, but less than half considered this important for the wife. Those mothers whose children were at least six months old placed just as much value on the woman's money management skills as on the man's. (Tables 7-11, 7-12)

Sharon, happily married for ten years and the mother of four commented:

> *We usually agreed on managing the money, but I've changed a lot. I used to listen to everything Frank said. I thought he was always right about money management — it was easier that way. But recently when he says, "Don't spend too much on this or that," I'll say, "Well, I have to buy it. We need it." Now I don't listen so much to what he says.*
>
> *I think I thought one person should be in charge of the money, and that I never was very good at it. I thought he was better and it didn't bother me. We usually discussed it, but if we disagreed, he usually said he was right. But that's changed. I don't accept that anymore.*

Young men already living with partners were less likely to think they needed to handle money well. More of these men thought it was a little more important for wives to be money-wise.

> *At first Andy sometimes wanted to spend the money he made — he'd buy more clothes than I could have, and he couldn't*

believe how much diapers and formula cost. But he changed.
He's paid on Thursday, and when he gets home I'll have
figured out how much money goes for bills and we each pay
part of them. If we don't work on our bills, they just pile up.
When we lived in Ventura, my telephone bill got too high, but
ever since then, we've worked it out. (Marnita)

Who Earns the Money?

Obviously young couples must have some money in order to be
able to make decisions about spending that money. The survey
asked several questions concerning who should earn the money.

One-third of the men, both in the total sample and in the living-
together group, said the husband should be responsible for
supporting the family. Only half of these men said both spouses
should share this responsibility, while two-thirds of the women felt
both should provide income. (Table 7-13)

When we were dating he said no wife of his would ever
work but now he's changed his mind. Now he says, "You're
going to have to get a job in a couple of years." It's OK with
me. (Alyssa)

If his/her family's annual income is over $50,000, only about 40
percent of the respondents think the husband should earn most of
the money. In low-income families (under $5,000 annually), almost
half the women and even more of the men insist the husband
should provide the income. Yet it is these families who most need
two paychecks in order to eat and pay the rent. (Table 7-14)

If their wives want to get jobs, half the men said this would
absolutely be all right, and an additional third, probably all right.
Less than 5 percent thought they would disapprove. (Table 7-15)

Arlynne and Cameron were married while she was in tenth
grade. Three years and two children later, Cameron has a steady
job and their marriage apparently is going well. When asked,
Cameron maintained he had no strong feelings about whether
Arlynne gets a job or stays home with their children. Arlynne
commented:

He didn't want me to work — that is, he didn't think I
should. Then he asked, "Well, is it important to you to do

*that?" Actually, I don't really want to work. Lots of people
think they don't want to be stuck at home with the kids but I
don't mind.*

*I do think if a girl hasn't graduated, she should. You never
know when you might have to go to work. Like with us, I have
skills, and if he gets laid off, I know I can find a job. I think
that's important because you never know how much you may
need it.*

According to Department of Labor figures, women still earn only
59 cents for every dollar a man earns. Women with high school
diplomas are likely to earn less than men who dropped out of
school in tenth grade. In most two-paycheck families, the husband
earns more than the wife does.

This pattern may change as more women enter the professions
and/or become more career-minded generally. Many older men
might find it threatening to have their wives bring home the bigger
paycheck. Some might consider this a threat to their masculinity.

In reality, the gap between men's and women's earnings is not
likely to change very rapidly. In the majority of families, the
husband will continue to earn the higher salary. In time, however,
the number of women earning more money than their husbands is
likely to increase. Do teenage men expect to have a problem if this
happens within their own marriages? Apparently the majority do
not.

Two out of five said it would be absolutely all right with them if
their partners earned more money, and another 29 percent said
probably. Some didn't know how they'd feel, but 14 percent
admitted they didn't like the idea. (Table 7-16)

Two-Paycheck Marriages Anticipated

About 80 percent of these young women expect to work until
they have children and after their children are in school. Only
about one in twelve said she didn't intend to do so. Teenagers
living with their partners were a little less inclined to work until
they have children — about 60 percent said they expect to have
jobs during this time. These young women, of course, are already
in this period or have passed on to the mothering stage. (Tables
7-17, 7-18)

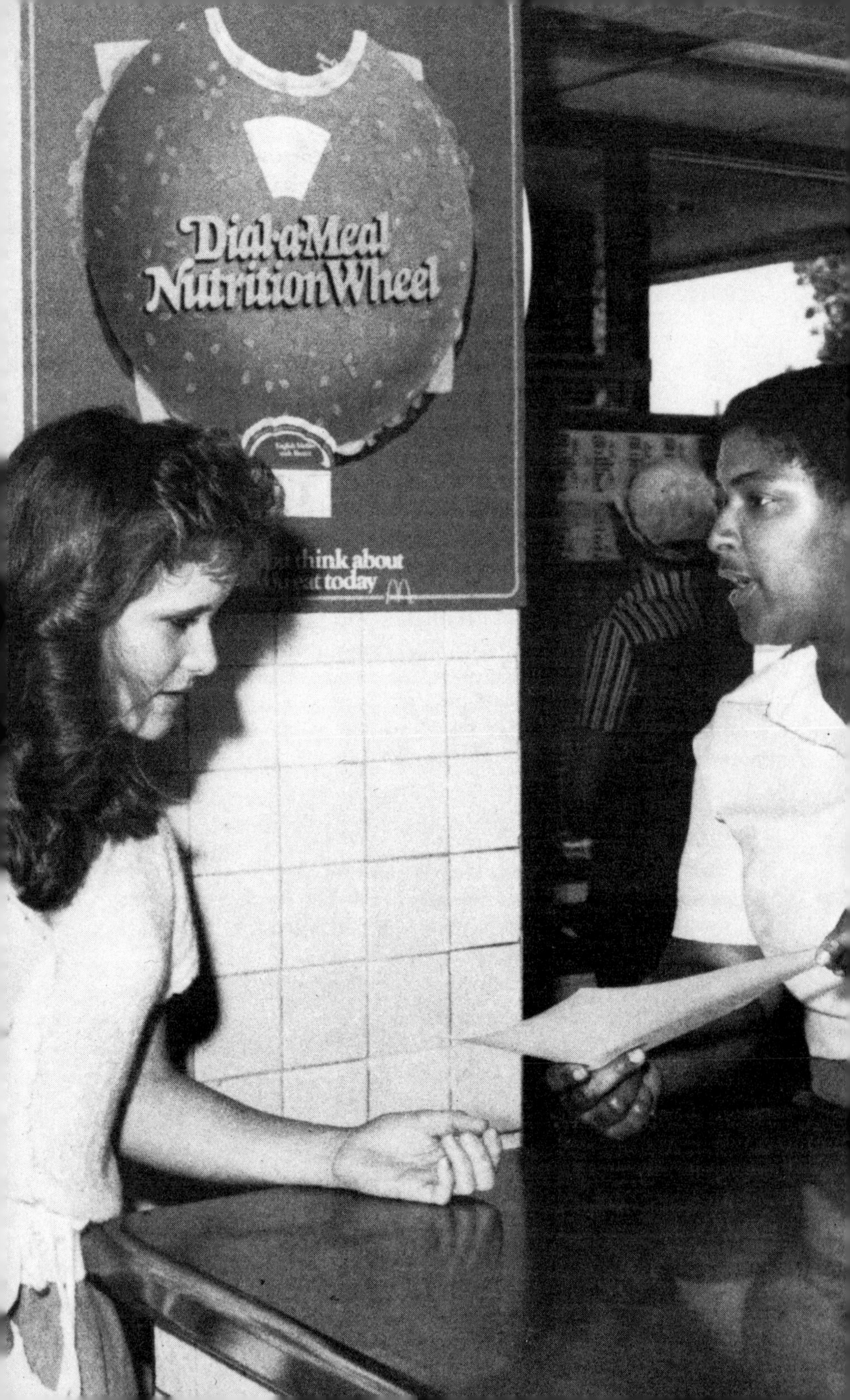
Dial-a-Meal
Nutrition Wheel
think about
eat today

*Frank was without a job once for a short time and that's real
upsetting. You see your savings go down and you think, "Here
comes a bill — how are we going to pay it?" That was when I
realized I needed a job. I'd be working now if we hadn't had
this last baby. We didn't expect him. Being a one-income
family is difficult. (Sharon, married at 16 to Frank, 18)*

Working while they have children under two years of age is
another thing. A majority (59 percent) of the total said they don't
expect to have jobs during this period. About one in three expects
to go to work while her children are small. More (41 percent) of
those living with partners said they expect to be working at this
time. (Table 7-19)

*I worked for about five weeks after Hank was a year old.
Then I quit. I don't plan on working again until my last child
is at least two. I didn't feel like a mother when I was working.
Sometimes he'd wake up at night and I'd be too tired for work.*
*Now we're getting a house, and not having any spending
money could hurt us. So I'll be baby-sitting other kids to help
out. (Kathleen, married three years ago at 17 to Henry, 21.
They have two children.)*

Teenage men were less likely than women to expect wives to
work while their children are small, only about one in eight of the
total sample. However, almost one-fourth of the males living with
their partners expect their wives to have jobs during this time.
(Table 7-19)

Before a couple has children and after the children are in school,
men, like women, are more likely to expect wives to work away
from home. Roughly 40 percent gave this answer, another 40
percent said it didn't matter, and the rest wouldn't expect it.
(Tables 7-17, 7-18)

George and Maura's son is 15 months old. George has a steady
job, but like other young couples, they have money problems.
When asked if he thought Maura should get a job, he said:

*I feel we should start pulling together. The baby can always
go over to her mom's or my mom's. I think she should be
working. We need the money.*

Although very few of the men were completely opposed to their
wives working, a few did not like the idea. Laurette's decision not

to marry Rob was based partly on his feelings concerning women
and jobs. She knew she would need a paying job and that he
wouldn't agree:

> *If I had married Rob, he wouldn't have let me go to school
> or get a job. Things are so expensive I knew we'd both need to
> work. Besides, I think people often have a better relationship
> when both are working and they see their kids together at
> night. They have more in common.*
>
> *Sometimes a husband says, "She just doesn't excite me any
> more." How can she excite him when she doesn't have anything
> to talk about? He says, "What did you do today?" and she'll
> say, "Well, I watched 'General Hospital' and Luke and Laura
> just split up." I think nowadays the wife has to work.*

Househusband Versus Housewife

Two questions phrased almost the same elicited widely different
responses: Males were asked, "Would it be all right with you if
your wife chose to stay home instead of getting a job?" Women
were asked, "Would it be all right with you if your husband
wanted to stay home while you get a job to support your family?"
About three-fourths of the men said it would be all right if their
wives stayed home and they worked. About three-fourths of the
women said the reverse would *not* be all right.

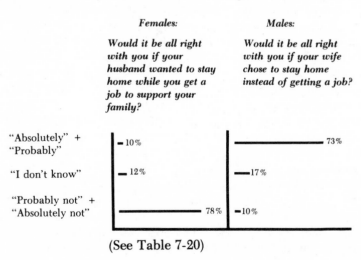

	Females:	Males:
	Would it be all right with you if your husband wanted to stay home while you get a job to support your family?	*Would it be all right with you if your wife chose to stay home instead of getting a job?*
"Absolutely" + "Probably"	— 10%	— 73%
"I don't know"	— 12%	— 17%
"Probably not" + "Absolutely not"	— 78%	— 10%

(See Table 7-20)

These percentages should not be surprising. Someone has to support the family, and in our culture, we tend strongly to think this is the man's responsibility. If the man's talents and preferences are in the job world and the woman prefers being the homemaker, wonderful. But what if the reverse is true? What if he would like to take care of the home while she works? Should he, too, have this opportunity if she can earn enough money?

Many women in this survey want to share the housekeeping and parenting roles with their husbands. Generally they are also willing and expecting to share the burden of financial support of their families. Perhaps some day a significant number of men will be able to choose to stay home, keep house, and parent children while their wives support them — just as more and more women now are able to choose to work away from home.

The flaw, of course, in the above plan is that in fewer and fewer families can either the husband or wife choose not to be an income producer. Many of the young men in the 73 percent who said it would be all right if their wives didn't work will find a second person's paycheck necessary for survival.

Summary and Conclusions

Most young couples face financial difficulties when they marry and/or start living together. The majority of teenagers in the survey understand they are likely to have less money if they marry before age 18. Most of them feel that having "enough" money is important in a marriage, and about two in five of the living-together respondents had found the lack of money to be more of a problem than they had expected.

Nearly everyone in the survey said it is important for the wife and husband to make joint financial decisions, but some of the interviewees described problems in this area.

A minority of these young people believe financial support is the husband's responsibility. Half of the men and two-thirds of the women believe the husband and wife should share this task. Teenagers from low income families were more likely to believe earning money is primarily the husband's responsibility.

About 80 percent of the women expect to work while they have children in school, but only one-third plan to work while their children are under two years of age. Men were even less likely to expect their wives to work while their children are small.

Many young people who marry while they are teenagers will not be able to prepare for a well-paying career. If they have a child to support, their expenses will escalate and lack of suitable childcare may keep the young mother at home. If she must get a job, she may find she's qualified only for work at a fast food restaurant, and that her salary there barely covers the cost of the babysitter.

Teenage Marriage: Coping with Reality (1984) offers young people guidelines for setting up a budget in order to make good use of the funds they have. Emphasis is placed on the importance of developing a spending plan which "fits" the people involved rather than attempting to follow a model budget set up by someone else. It is important that they negotiate agreement on priorities.

Financial problems faced by most teenage couples are severe and can be devastating to a relationship. *All* young people must be encouraged to obtain job skills and to prepare for a career. Most will need to produce income throughout most of their lives, and the more skills they develop, the more choices they will have. Most of us appreciate choices.

Chapter 8

Three-Generation Living

It was difficult living at his mother's. We lived there about two months and I couldn't handle it. I didn't feel married there — I felt like they adopted me. She would do the cooking, she would do the housework, she would do the laundry. I had to get out of there. He said we couldn't afford to move, but we moved.

I wanted responsibility as a married woman but you can't change it because you can't have two meals cooking, me cook for mine and her for hers. I guess you could share it but we didn't. She would even pick up our laundry before I could get to it. I wanted to be a family on our own. When you're married, you have to start learning responsibility. (Kathleen, married three years ago at 17 to Henry, 21)

This is her first grandchild, and he is spoiled. She likes to tell me what to do, how to dress him, what to feed him, when to feed him, how to give him a bath. Sometimes it bugs me.

*A couple of times we've gotten into some
real good fights. He was teething and I knew
it. My mother-in-law tells me, "The baby's
real sick, you should take him to the doctor." I
told her, "It's not that I don't want to take
him, but you guys act like he's dying and I
know he's all right." So Joel and I took him
out in the car and he fell asleep by the time
we got around the corner. We got something
to put on his teeth and he was better. (Estella,
married at 18 to Joel, 20.)*

Many couples of all ages have excellent relationships with his
parents and hers, but most would rather live separately. For a
young couple building their new relationship together, living with
his or her parents can be a real detriment to the bonding process
within their new partnership. Nevertheless, many very young
couples have no other choice.

Teenage couples seldom can afford to rent an apartment by
themselves. For most, any thought of buying their own homes must
be pushed aside. In the survey, in fact, 80 percent of the young
people already living with a partner did not start their lives
together by moving out by themselves. Roughly one-third lived
with his parents, one-third with her parents, and the others either
with other relatives or friends.

Most people find it hard to cope with combining two families
within one household. Many of the parents of these young couples
may have thought their years of parenting teenagers were almost
over — and then another one moved in. Not only did they make
room for the new son- or daughter-in-law, but in many cases, for a
new grandchild as well.

The following discussion focuses on the attitudes and feelings of
the young people. To be fair, the attitudes and feelings of their
parents should be included. Unfortunately, they were not part of
this research.

"No" To In-Law Living

In spite of the fact that two-thirds of these young people started
their lives together by living with his or her parents, almost half

reacted negatively to the question about this situation. Within the total sample of young people, most of them not yet married or living with their partners, even more, almost two-thirds, were opposed to living with parents after marriage.

How do you feel about a young couple living with either his or her parents?

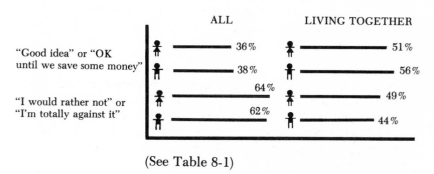

(See Table 8-1)

Married teenagers were less likely to approve of living with parents than were the young people living together without being married. Of the latter group, three in five thought this was a good idea or OK until they could save some money, while less than two in five of the married respondents agreed. (Table 8-2)

How do you feel about a young couple living with either his or her parents?

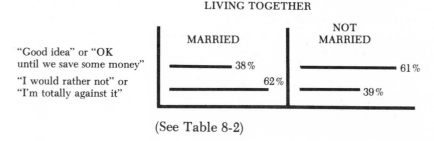

(See Table 8-2)

A major exception among the ethnic groups was the Asian males' response. Within this small sample 80 percent would approve living with parents at least until they saved some money, and 27 percent, far more than any other ethnic group, thought this was a good idea. Asian women, however, generally did not agree. (Table 8-3)

Protestant women were less likely to be favorable toward living with parents after marriage than were either Catholic or Born-again Christian women. Among these groups, the Born-again Christian men were most opposed to living with parents.

The higher the income of their parents, the less likely were teenagers to feel positive about living with them after marriage. However, this shift in attitudes was not steady from one group to the next. (Table 8-5)

Relationships with Parents Explored

Teenagers who already have a poor relationship with their parents would probably find it especially difficult to continue living with them after marriage. In the survey, teenagers were asked about their feelings toward their mothers and their fathers.

More than one-fourth of the women and one-fifth of the men in the survey said their relationships with their mothers were fair, poor, or they had no relationship. Almost twice as many teenagers, males and females, said their relationships with their fathers were poor as compared to their feelings about their mothers.

How is your relationship with your mother?

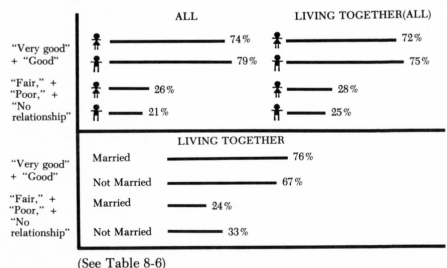

(See Table 8-6)

How is your relationship with your father?

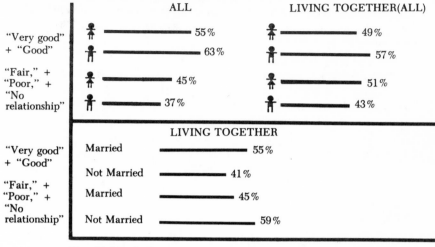

(See Table 8-6)

A much higher proportion of the teenagers living with a partner but *not* married reported negative relationships with both parents — one-third with their mothers and more than half, 59 percent, with their fathers. For some of them, this may partly explain their early move-in with partners. . . a chance to get away from an unhappy situation at home. Information is not available, however, as to the number of these young people either still living with their own parents or the number who had moved into a partner's home.

Teenagers already married, on the other hand, reported slightly closer relationships with their parents than did the total sample of females. Young women occasionally comment on the fact that marriage has improved their relationships with their mothers:

> *One thing I missed when I was growing up was more time with my mother. Right now we're closer than we've ever been. We do a lot of things together and we talk a lot. I wish we'd done that before. (Arlynne, married at 16 to Cameron, 17)*

Analyzing respondents' feelings about their parents according to their parents' income shows no pattern concerning their mothers. However, males and females are more likely to report a good relationship with their fathers as their parents' income rises. Only

41 percent of the women and 46 percent of the men whose parents earned less than $5,000 per year reported a "good" or "very good" relationship with their fathers while 66 percent of the females and 65 percent of the males whose parents earned more than $50,000 per year did so. (Table 8-7)

Much of the difference is probably explained by the fact that 26 percent of the women and 17 percent of the men from the low-income group reported *no* relationship with their fathers. Only 5 percent of the women and 7 percent of the men in the wealthier families gave this report. These wealthy young people were also more likely to have lived with both parents all their lives — three-fourths of the women and two-thirds of the men had done so as compared to half of the young people from the low-income homes.

Young Mothers Comment

The realities of teenage partners living with his or her parents were described by Teen Mother Program alumnae in the spring of 1984. Eighty-two young women married or living with boyfriends while teenagers participated in a survey in which they commented on their relationships. (See Appendix for questionnaire.)

Sixty-three (77 percent) together with their partners had lived for a time with his or her parents or, in one or two cases, other relatives. They were asked, "If you lived with parents, how did you feel about this?" All but six replied with descriptive comments, a far greater response than for any other open-ended question in the same survey.

Three-fourths of the comments were negative, and the others evenly divided between middle-of-the-road and positive comments such as "It was OK but it was a lot better living with just my husband" and "We live with his parents. They were wonderful people who helped us tremendously." The following are representative of the 43 negative comments:

> *It's very uncomfortable because you have to do what they say. I didn't like living with his parents. His mom put me down all the time.*

> *I hated it. I did it only because we had no place to stay after he got out of the Army.*

I didn't like it. His parents tried to dominate our lives. I had to give him a choice either to rent us our own place or I'd leave.

We were under a terrible strain and very unhappy.

It was too crowded and there was very little privacy. It was hard to talk to each other because you didn't know who was listening.

I hated living with his parents. They really made me feel like I owed them something. They're SO nosey, such busybodies. Besides that they were wonderful people.

I didn't like it. There was always more conflict and unwanted advice.

I hated it. If you want to be happy, don't live with them.

It doesn't work because you can't live with family. It affects your relationship a lot.

IT WAS AWFUL!!!

Sometimes It Works

Phyllis and Jed have been married more than a year and they are still living with her parents. She has mixed feelings about the situation, but knows that, because of heavy medical bills, they must stay there for awhile.

It's been hard this year because I don't do a lot of the things a wife does because my mom does the cooking. I clean everything but it's not our home. It's nice in a lot of ways, but I feel kind of bad when people want to come over. I don't really like to invite my friends over and impose on my parents.
It does work pretty well...I think it has a lot to do with my mother knowing she's not my baby's mother. I think a lot of times it doesn't work for other couples because the grandmother tries to take over. They still ask me if they can give her something and if I say "No," they don't do it.

When Jed and I fight, they stay out of it, too. If I'm mad, they don't get involved. They don't take sides.

Jed and my dad do things together. My dad helps coach the men's softball team that Jed is on. Our coed team is all my aunts and uncles and Jed is the coach.

Their living arrangement is working for several reasons. Both couples apparently pitch in with the house and yard work. Her parents are not overly involved with their grandchild, and, perhaps best of all, Jed and his parents-in-law really like each other.

Alyssa, Brian, and Alyssa's parents are also coping fairly well:

This first year we've had our ups and downs. It gets a little tense around here — we're four different people wanting four different things. It's nobody's fault — it's just hard having two families do their thing in the same house.

Most of the time we don't exactly let things go, but we don't comment every time somebody says something or does something we don't like. We don't cause a scene because it's usually not worth it.

My mother works 2:30-10:30. I cook dinner every night and I do most of the housework during the week although my mom does a lot in the mornings before she goes to work.

Arlynne's mother handled the situation well:

We lived with my mom for awhile. She didn't do anything with the baby. I really thought she would try to take over and tell me I was wrong in whatever I did, but she let me take all the responsibility. The first week after the baby was born I could hardly move and Cameron had to get out of bed and bring her to me. One night my mom said, "I know you're having trouble. Do you want me to take her?" I said "Yes," and she did. I appreciated that.

Help — Too Much Or Too Little

Parents who have already reared their children often want to give advice on childcare to their live-in son or daughter. The young parents are not likely to appreciate this "help." Other young wives are frustrated because they don't feel needed. They want to "keep house" but find his/her mother is taking care of everything.

Privacy may be nonexistent in a crowded household, a situation difficult for most couples to handle. Estella explained:

> *We have no privacy. Like sometimes I want to wear tight shorts and my husband will say you can't do that because all the boys are here. If we want to be alone in our room, somebody will knock at the door and say, "What are you guys doing?" We don't have any privacy at all. We can lie down on the bed and watch TV and his three sisters will be with us or his brothers.*

Some young women spoke of moving in with parents-in-law and feeling as though they were expected to act as maids to the rest of the family. One mentioned a 14-year-old sister-in-law who "never does anything while I'm supposed to clean the house and cook dinner." This young wife was 16, only two years older than her sister-in-law, but in the eyes of her mother-in-law, she was an adult with adult responsibilities. That's hard for an adolescent to understand.

A 16-year-old in anyone's home may find it easy to feel "like a slave" while a mother-in-law may be determined not to take on the work of caring for another "child." Good communication and compromise are essential. A contract set up before move-in time could prevent frustration later for everyone concerned.

David J. Rolfe, Ph.D., family life educator, has often worked with young couples and their parents in setting up a pre-marriage contract. Dr. Rolfe, who is now studying at Wycliffe Hall, Oxford, England, explained that he has the young couple, together with their parents, sit down and work through the contract. "You can tell by the way they work at it whether or not they'll make it as a couple and as an extended family," he commented. Dr. Rolfe's contract outline first appeared in *The Family Coordinator* (1977) and is reprinted here with his permission:

OUTLINE FOR PRE-MARRIAGE CONTRACT[1]

This contract outline is designed specifically for couples who will be living with one or the other set of parents after the wedding. Many of the topic areas apply to couples who either have a child, or expect one to be born in the first year of marriage.

To be effective, the couple planning to be married, with both of their sets of parents can get together and sort through plans on each of the topic areas. This may take a couple of hours to complete.

It is suggested that one person volunteer to take precise notes of the discussion, such that the final document is clearly understood by all concerned.

1. Financial — Source and amount of income, amount of rent (to be paid parents), how often and when this is to be paid. Specify exactly what is included in rent payment.

2. Schooling — How far are both people expected to go in school; how will they make arrangements to fit in their schooling, part-time work and babysitting? What are the grandparents' responsibilities in helping the couple do this?

3. Care of Baby — Indicate who is going to take care of the baby and, if the baby's grandparents are to be called upon to do babysitting, how much advance notice they need.

4. Medical Coverage — What provisions will be made to cover the medical expenses, doctor visits, medication, etc., both for the baby and its parents.

5. Timing of Wedding — The possible alternatives are to have the wedding immediately; just before delivery of the baby; or sometime after delivery. In addition to indicating the emotional personal preference, try also to specify the intellectual reasons in terms of schooling, finances, medical, etc., which make the emotional decision also a good, logical one. Decide where the wedding will be held, which clergyman or judge will perform ceremony, guests invited; who will pay for what.

6. Religion — If there are any religious differences in the families, indicate how the differences will be bridged and how this may affect the baby. Suggest possible baptismal plans, if any.

7. Household Duties — In this category can be included responsibilites for cleaning the house; when laundry and ironing are to be done; who will pay the bill for dry cleaning; when the couple can use the kitchen to make their own snacks; dishwashing; which meals will be eaten with the family, which will be eaten alone, etc. This area can also include who will do the grocery shopping and when; who will fix school lunches; and take out the trash.

8. Bathroom — If the house has several bathrooms, this area may be unnecessary for the contract; however, if there is only one bathroom some indication of who gets to use the bathroom when, who is responsible for cleaning up, scrubbing out the toilet and setting out fresh towels, will be helpful.

9. Yard Duties — This area includes lawn mowing, snow shoveling, maintenance of garden plot, installation or storage of storm windows, etc.

10. Automobile — If the couple own a car or have use of a car, explain who will be responsible for making car payments, paying insurance premiums, and generally covering the cost of gasoline, repairs and cleaning.

11. Rights of Grandparents — In this section will be covered such things as how the grandparents' privacy will be respected; curfew, if any; arrangements for skipping meals; being late for meals; where to entertain friends; plans for parties and serving liquor. Suggest what social plans are acceptable for the first Thanksgiving and Christmas following the wedding. Specify amount of time to be spent with each set of grandparents to avoid one set feeling less favored. Don't forget also to indicate how the privacy of the new parents will be safeguarded!

12. Changes — Suggest how changes can be made in this contract as circumstances alter.
13. Signature — Contract will be signed by the couple and both sets of parents. If someone doesn't feel ready to sign, then the contract needs revision.

Some Live With Friends

Living with parents and siblings is hard, but for many young couples, a necessity. Some young people avoid these problems by moving in with friends. This, too, is likely to be difficult.

Annie and Jose typify the young couple with no money who must endure fairly grim living conditions during the early part of their marriage. Now, three years later, they are still together, live in a fairly nice apartment, and are glad those early months are only memories:

At first we were sharing an apartment with another couple and his brother — a two-bedroom apartment. Jeanne didn't work, but the three men did and I was going to school. When they came home from work, they'd turn the music up real loud. They wouldn't clean the house — I had to do it. When I came home after a weekend away and found maggots under the rags because they didn't clean the kitchen at all, I flipped.

I remember one time I was washing the dishes, and I went in about every ten minutes to check on Kim. One of those times she was screaming her head off and I couldn't hear her because the music was so loud.

They were always fighting — it was our furniture, and they would break things. When we moved out they took half of our stuff. I didn't think I would run into a problem but I did and I didn't like it at all.

Then we lived in a tiny one-bedroom apartment with no bathroom. Jose was out of work and it was all we could afford.

It was a little room on top of the garage, and the people living down below kept their back door unlocked so we could use their bathroom and put things in their refrigerator. We stayed there about a month, and from there we went back to my mother's house for about two weeks. She was upset with Jose because he wasn't working and he wasn't looking for work.

Jose didn't like California and he wanted to move to Colorado. We finally did go there, and he got a job about two months later. He's been working ever since at the same place. We're doing okay now.

More Choices Today

Young couples today may have more choices than their parents and grandparents did. If they want to live together, they may get married or they may not. Either way, they may move out by themselves and try to make it on their own, often with very little income, or they may continue living with his or her parents.

The data mentioned earlier which show unmarried couples much more positive about living with his or her parents than were married couples offer insight into the current living-together phenomenon. It suggests a basic difference between very young couples and those who are older.

Older unmarried couples who live together often explain that they want to keep their independence, that they want no legal ties. "We're together because we want to be, not because a piece of paper says we have to be here," they insist.

With these very young couples, the situation appears to be quite different. If they believe they "must" be with their partners but they aren't ready for marriage, living with parents may be necessary. The result too often is two people still being treated like children when they supposedly are taking on adult responsibilities. This may be true, of course, whether or not they are married. The above statistic, however, indicates more acceptance of this dependency on the part of the young people not yet married.

Summary and Conclusions

Almost 80 percent of the young people in the survey already living with partners started their lives together by living with his parents or

hers or with friends. Most of these young people did not want to move
in with in-laws, but they felt they had no other choice.

Many of the young people complained about their situations, but
others spoke of arrangements which, while not what they might
prefer, were working. Lack of privacy, over-supervision by parents,
and unfair division of household chores were among problems
mentioned.

An additional factor in these arrangements is the poor
relationships with parents reported by many of the survey
respondents. Combining an already-poor relationship with parents
with the move-in of one's partner may explain some of the
difficulties encountered in these extended families.

A pre-marriage contract, as set up by David J. Rolfe, Ph.D., can
help families set up guidelines for a successful living-together
arrangement.

Some young people who cannot afford to rent an apartment by
themselves move in with friends and share the costs. This, too, can be
very difficult. Dr. Rolfe's contract outline could easily be adapted to
fit this kind of situation, and could prevent problems later.

Each couple together with their families needs to consider
carefully all the ramifications of the living-together choice before
they make the decision to move in with his or her parents or with
friends. They need to face the fact of some conflict being
inevitable. If everyone involved can discuss together *before* the
move-in their expectations concerning division of work, privacy,
financial arrangements, house rules, and the other aspects of
communal living, their chances of coping well with an inherently
difficult situation will improve.

With lots of trust, respect, and caring on the part of all members
of the household, this arrangement can help a young couple
prepare for their future life together in a home of their own.

Chapter 9

Who Parents The Children?

Marriage isn't what you expect it to be. Right after he moved in it was all hunky-dory — it was just us two and I liked that. But after Joy was born I had to divvy up my time between Art and Joy and Art didn't like that. It got easier when Joy could get around, but those first six months were bad for everybody. Joy was a breastfeeder and she'd be up five or six times every night, every hour or two.

She likes her Daddy now — she didn't used to like him because Art wouldn't hold her at first. But now when Art comes home, Joy grabs his pantleg and follows him all over the house until he sits down and holds her.

Those six months were a rough time. I was bitchy constantly because I didn't have enough sleep. We fought often during that time. I'd start the fight, just be a little picky, than an argument, then a big fight. It was hard for both of us. (Esther, married at 17 to Art, 26)

In many teenage marriages, the wife is pregnant before the wedding. Sometimes the young couple decides to postpone marriage until after the baby is born while others rush into marriage soon after the pregnancy is discovered. Some, of course, are not pregnant when they marry, but may have a child during the first year or two after the wedding.

Knowing how to parent a baby is not instinctual among human beings. Jurich (1984) points out that the birth of the first child often causes strain within the family, especially if the family is lacking in personal and/or financial resources. Becoming a parent is a major change in anyone's life. For a 16-year-old, or even an 18-year-old, the changes may be overwhelming. If the young couple has been heavily into partying, or even deeply involved in school and/or church activities, lack of time and money will put limits on their commitments. They can continue some of their activities, but no longer can they be as spontaneous as they were.

> *Sometimes I do regret having my kids. I'm 23 years old and I feel like I'm 40. I feel I'm in a rut — the same thing every day, get up, get the kids ready, feed them, take them to the babysitter, go to work, go home and fix lunch for Hector, go back to work, pick up the kids, fix supper, clean up, put the kids to bed, mop the floors, finally go to bed. You get Saturday and Sunday off and you want to sleep but they won't let you. You have to get up and fix breakfast for them. I get tired — exhausted. (Elise, married at 18 to Hector, 20. They now have three children.)*

Parenting Starts With Pregnancy

Pregnancy is a tremendously important part of parenting. Teenagers' records for having healthy babies are not as good as are older women's. Teenage mothers are more likely to be anemic and have toxemia. A higher percentage of babies born to teenage mothers are premature and dangerously small at birth. They have a higher chance of being born with a handicap. Marriage does not prevent these problems.

> *Before I got pregnant I was into drugs, went out to parties, got drunk, smoked pot, but then I got pregnant and all of that stopped. Actually I would advise any teenager not to have a*

*baby because it's a lot of work and you don't have any freedom
any more. I love Katie but if I could change it, I would. When
I got pregnant I thought it would be the greatest thing, but it
wasn't. (Maura, married at 18 to George, 21)*

The good news is that *if* a teenager eats the foods she and her
baby need during her pregnancy, stays away from drugs, alcohol,
and cigarettes, and sees her doctor regularly, she has about as good
a chance of having a healthy baby as does an older woman who
follows good prenatal care guidelines.

For most teenagers, however, the foods she needs while she's
pregnant are quite different from her accustomed diet. Babies
don't do well on cokes and french fries. Teenagers need more of the
Basic Four foods, especially milk, than do pregnant adults because
the teenagers are still maturing physically. Avoiding drugs,
including aspirin and cold pills, alcohol, and cigarettes may also
require tremendous self-control for the teenage mother-to-be. Being
involved with other pregnant teenagers in a special school program
or other group counseling situation often helps.

Encouraging a pregnant teenager, married or unmarried, to
continue school is extremely important. The young mother needs
an education and she needs to learn job skills whether she is
married or not.

A side effect of school attendance is likely to be the delivery of a
healthier baby. Research completed by Sandra B. James in the Los
Angeles pregnant minor programs a few years ago showed that the
more days a young woman attended school during her pregnancy,
the more her baby weighed at birth. *(CACSAP Newsletter,*
September, 1979) Too-low birthweight is a problem for more than
10 percent of the babies born to teenagers in the United States,
according to the March of Dimes Birth Defects Foundation.
Changing one's eating habits is extremely hard, but special school
programs for pregnant teenagers usually provide milk and other
nutritious snacks and lunches for their young clients. Pregnant
teenagers who eat well throughout pregnancy generally deliver
healthy babies.

Seeing the doctor regularly throughout pregnancy is highly
recommended for all pregnant women. Statistically, the baby
whose mother receives good prenatal care has a much greater
chance of being born healthy than s/he would have otherwise. For
some teenagers, however, this may be difficult to achieve.

If she's not married when she becomes pregnant, she may not want to tell anyone. She may try to convince herself, "If I don't think about it, perhaps it will go away." If she's trying not to think about it, isn't telling her parents, perhaps not even her boyfriend at first, she's not likely to get to the doctor. In fact, she may have neither the money nor transportation for the visit.

A young marriage which starts with pregnancy is likely to be difficult for the young couple involved. If the young man is aware of the importance to his baby of its mother's food habits and her regular visits to the doctor, he can be a big help. Perhaps he will be willing to change his diet and other activities in order to make it easier for her to follow good prenatal care guidelines. It's his baby too.

Good resources written especially for pregnant teenagers, married or single, include *Teenage Pregnancy: A New Beginning* (Barr and Monserrat, 1978) and *Teens Parenting: The Challenge of Babies and Toddlers* (Lindsay, 1981). Other excellent materials can be obtained at no cost from the March of Dimes Birth Defects Foundation.

Are *Two* Parents Important?

Mothering a child brings into one's life joy, work, fun, exhaustion, learning, awareness. . . the list could go on and on. The word "mother" implies a continuing relationship. To mother a child suggests a partnership, although not an equal one, in which two people interact intensively during the first 18 years of the child's life. For many people, the relationship remains close throughout life.

To father a child often signifies the same kind of close, loving relationship between father and child — or it may mean something quite different. Used as a verb, it can simply refer to the act of impregnation. A widely-held stereotype of teenage fathers is that of the young male who thinks getting someone pregnant "makes him a man."

Many schools and hospitals across the United States offer special programs for school-age mothers and their babies but very few include the fathers. Some of the young fathers are not involved because they don't want to be. Others who might be interested are busily trying to support their families and may feel that is the extent of their responsibility.

Lack of fathers in school programs does not mean teenagers want to ignore fathers. Teenagers think it is important for a child to live with both of his/her parents. More than 80 percent of the females and almost 90% of the males in the survey agree with this concept. (Table 9-1)

This should not be surprising — unless we wonder why an even higher percentage did not say a child should "absolutely" live with both parents. Most societies, and ours is no exception, believe children are better off with two parents. However, about half the children in the United States today will spend part of their growing-up years in a one-parent home. Most of us aren't happy with that fact.

What is Dad's Role?

When Dad is around, what role does/should he play? In the traditional marriage, he is usually responsible for supporting his family financially while Mother takes care of the kids and the house. In an equal marriage, parents share financial responsibilities, housekeeping, and childcare.

Traditional versus equal *marriage* is one thing. Assuming a family can survive on one paycheck, and if both like the traditional arrangement, fine. It's entirely possible for both husband and wife to have satisfying and happy lives while he earns the money and she's in charge at home.

But parenthood is another thing. Even if she wants to take complete charge of the children while he is out there earning the money, the *children* may have different ideas. Having two loving and caring parents actively involved in one's growing-up almost has to be better than having only one.

Trina, married at 17, and Jake were divorced five years later. She feels part of the problem was his lack of fathering skills:

> *Being a good parent was hard for him because he had no role model. His father brought him and his brothers up by himself, and he was an alcoholic. When it came to having children, Jake just didn't know what to do. He still kind of talks baby talk with them and Sally is far beyond that.*
>
> *I had such a good father and knew what a father ought to be like. I was used to getting a lot of love from my big family, lots of brothers around, and Jake wasn't. I tried to talk with*

*him about it but he didn't understand. He could only think in
terms of possessions, money. Just communicating was hard
because if they have not had this, how do you even talk about
it? I think he wanted to be a good father but he just didn't
know how to go about it.*

Teenagers in the survey agree on the importance of the father's
involvement with his children. The vast majority want both mother
and father playing with, disciplining, feeding, and generally caring
for their children. Many of these young people expect husband and
wife to share housekeeping chores but even more stated that both
parents should be involved in childcare tasks.

In a good marriage, who should be responsible for the following tasks?

"Both Husband and Wife"

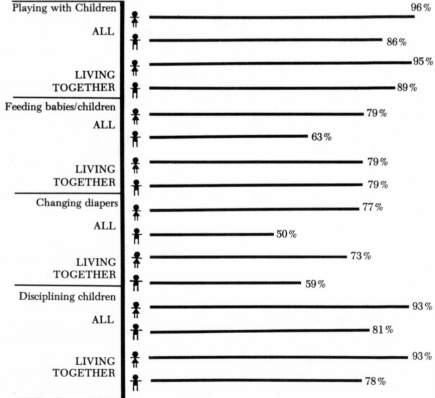

Playing with Children		96%
ALL		86%
LIVING TOGETHER		95%
		89%
Feeding babies/children		79%
ALL		63%
LIVING TOGETHER		79%
		79%
Changing diapers		77%
ALL		50%
LIVING TOGETHER		73%
		59%
Disciplining children		93%
ALL		81%
LIVING TOGETHER		93%
		78%

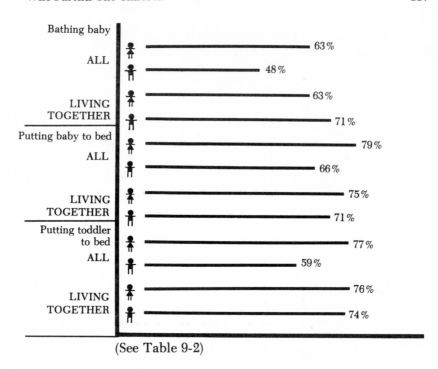

Bathing baby

ALL — 63%

48%

LIVING
TOGETHER — 63%

71%

Putting baby to bed

ALL — 79%

66%

LIVING
TOGETHER — 75%

71%

Putting toddler
to bed

ALL — 77%

59%

LIVING
TOGETHER — 76%

74%

(See Table 9-2)

From one-fourth to one-half of these young people thought the
wife should clean house, cook, and do the laundry and the husband
should mow the lawn and wash the car. (See Chapter 6.)
Obviously their attitudes toward childcare tasks are quite different.
More than three-fourths of the young women responding felt both
mother and father should share most childcare tasks. Fewer male
respondents, but still a majority, agreed.

Male/Female Attitudes Differ

The difference between the attitudes of teenage men and women
is interesting. Both in housekeeping chores and in caring for babies
and toddlers, women were more inclined than men to expect the
husband to be involved. The surprising fact is that in the total
survey, differences between the sexes are much greater in their
responses to childcare questions than to housekeeping items.

The average percentage difference between males and females
who think both spouses should vacuum, mop, cook, wash dishes,
wash clothes, garden, and wash the car is seven. Seven percent

more young women than young men, on the average, wanted these tasks shared. For the childcare questions, there is an average difference in the total group of more than 15 percent between male and female respondents. Fifteen percent fewer teenage men than women, on the average, think fathers should be involved in caring for their babies and children.

The push for equality brought about by the Women's Movement is making a difference. Judging from these figures, teenage men and women are moving from the traditional approach to homemaking toward an equal system. In the widely disliked household chore category, the change comes slowly, but in their attitudes, at least, men in this survey are not far behind women. (Their actions often do not match their attitudes. Refer to Chapter 6.)

When referring to attitudes toward childcare, however, the men are further behind. The biggest difference between the sexes concerns diaper-changing. Almost 40 percent of the young men think Mother should change the diapers while only 14 percent of the young women agree.

Arnie is one who doesn't "believe" in changing diapers, but he does want to be involved, according to Lucia:

He was saying that Derek doesn't really like to go with him and I told him, "Arnie, you have got to take him by yourself." So he's been taking Derek places, just the two of them without me, and now Derek goes to him a lot more. He meets Arnie when he gets home from work. They play hide and go seek and roll the ball back and forth, but he still won't change Derek. He's changed him just once since he was about three months old. He says that's the girl's job. (Lucia, married at 17 to Arnie, 18)

Attitudes among young people from urban, suburban, and rural areas were similar on the childcare questions. Among female respondents, age made very little difference, but among the young men, the 17- and 18-year-olds expected to be slightly more involved in childcare than did those aged 14-16.

Anglo teenagers showed the highest percentage of "Both" answers in almost every category, and Asian, the least. Hispanic men are sometimes described as macho, as not wanting to be involved in "women's work." More than 80 percent of the young men in this survey, however, thought both the father and mother should play with and discipline their children. Fewer, although

still a majority, thought a man should feed his baby and put his
children to bed. (Table 9-3)

To her regret, Cheryl's husband, Jesus, doesn't:

> *I think that if your husband doesn't like to help, it really*
> *gets to you sometimes. My husband doesn't help me at all with*
> *the baby. I mean he'll play with her a few minutes and that's*
> *all. He won't change her or feed her. He's no help at all.*

Young black men were more willing to change diapers and bathe
the baby than were other young men. Only one-third of the black
women, however, thought the father should be involved in bathing
baby. (Table 9-3)

Among the women, religious preference made little difference in
the attitudes held toward childcare roles. A higher percentage of
Born-again Christian males apparently want to be involved in
childcare — nearly three-fourths said fathers and mothers should
share the task of putting babies and toddlers to bed. About 60
percent favored sharing diaper-changing and baby-bathing as
compared to about 40 percent of the Catholic males. (Table 9-4)

Comparing attitudes of teenagers grouped according to their
parents' income shows a fairly steady increase in shared-role
thinking as the income becomes greater. In most areas, young
men's and young women's attitudes changed in the same direction
and to a similar degree.

Among women whose families' annual income was over $50,000,
88 percent thought Dad should help change the baby's diapers
while only 68 percent of the women from families with an annual
income of less than $5,000 agreed. Only half the men from the
wealthy families, however, agreed, very few more than those from
poor families. (Table 9-5)

As stated before, women in the entire survey averaged 15 percent
more "Both" responses to the childcare questions than did the men.
However, males from the top-income group, in all but the diaper-
changing question, offered more shared-role responses than did
females from the lowest income group.

Have these young people from upper-income homes experienced
the role modeling of more involvement in their own rearing from
their fathers? Or have their fathers, perhaps, been so busy earning
a living that they have not had much time for their children and
these young men want their own parenting experiences to be
different? To understand the reasons, further research is needed.

Discipline — Whose Task?

More than 90 percent of the young people in the survey think it is important for husband and wife to agree on how they discipline their children, but this does not always happen. Seventy-seven Teen Mother Program alumnae responded to the following question:

Teen Mother Program Alumnae Survey

"Do you and your partner agree on how to discipline the children?"

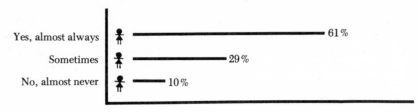

Estella already had a child when she and Joel were married. She is not at all happy with Joel's approach to fathering:

> *He hasn't had patience with her at all. Janet would cry and Joel would say, "Shut that kid up." That's why I think we're having only two. Joel wants another boy, but I tell him no. I tell him, "You can barely handle these two and you want another one?"*

Among many parents, spanking is considered an acceptable method of discipline. Others call it hitting and think it's wrong for big people to hit little people. When these two viewpoints collide within a family, finding solutions is difficult.

Young parents interviewed for this book often spoke of disagreeing on this subject. Glenna and Jeffrey's daughter is only one year old, and Glenna disagrees with Jeffrey's methods:

> *This is already a problem. Jeffrey wants to spank, but I don't go about it that way. I more or less show Babs and try to explain to her, verbally or through eye-contact. But I don't think*

*spanking, hitting, especially yelling does it. Jeffrey yells and
spanks and that just scares Babs and she doesn't learn that way.*

Alyssa and Brian, parents of one-year-old Erin, understand the
importance of agreement between parents on the discipline issue:

*We agree. We've worked out how we discipline her. Usually
we make her sit in the chair if she does something that takes
more than a "No." Whoever tells her "No" has to let her get
down. She can't go back and forth between us.*

Summary and Conclusions

Many teenage couples are pregnant when they marry and/or start
living together. Babies delivered to teenage mothers are more likely
to be born with health problems, but good prenatal care for the
young mother greatly improves her chances of having a healthy
baby.

Continuing their education is extremely important for both
parents. Some schools offer special programs for pregnant students,
but few provide any special services for the young fathers.

Most of the teenagers in the survey feel it is important for
children to be reared by both of their parents, and for both parents
to be truly involved in all aspects of childcare. Comparing the
responses from teenage women and men, however, shows 15
percent fewer young men recommending that Father be involved in
childcare tasks.

Nearly all of these young people think parents should agree on
how they discipline their children, but in the Teen Mother
Program alumnae survey, almost 40 percent of the young mothers
said they and their partners did not always agree in this area.

Agreeing on discipline is an important part of parenting. Even
more important is having both parents deeply involved in all
aspects of child-rearing. Teen fathers should be included in
childcare classes whenever possible. Offering special services only
to young mothers implies that fathers do not need to be as involved
as mothers in parenting their children. If a young father is ignored
during pregnancy and if he is not expected to be deeply involved in
childcare immediately after birth, he is likely to decide parenting is
primarily the mother's role. These young fathers need help, too, if
they are to take their share of responsibility for the young families

they have helped create. The father and mother who share the diaper-changing and the baby-bathing from the beginning will have a more closely-knit family than they ever will if only Mother or Father takes care of the children.

If both parents work, equal sharing of household tasks as well as childcare seems only fair. If Mother is "only" working at home, she may be responsible for most of the housework. But if she is also chiefly in charge of caring for the children, Dad will miss out on an important part of fatherhood. If he is not truly involved in all aspects of his children's care, he will find it difficult to build a close relationship with them. Both he and his children may feel cheated. If Dad is involved, everybody wins.

Chapter 10

Teenagers and Jealousy

I'm used to guys being jealous to an extent but everything bugged Matt about the opposite sex talking to me. I have a lot of male cousins and we stayed close. I get along better with the boys in my family than the girls. We're always talking, always keeping in touch.

I went back to Ontario for awhile to stay with my cousin and my cousin brought me back and Matt immediately thought that was my boyfriend. He doesn't know the older guys in my family, and so I guess he thought they were going to set me up out in the streets with their friends. So I had to stop talking to them.

Then I had guy friends out here. They pulled away because they thought he'd be bugged. We could go somewhere together and people would just walk past me and speak, and Matt embarrassed me every time. It could be some guy I had been going to school with, and he would turn around and say, "Don't speak to my wife." We would end up fighting in the mall. I couldn't stand it. (Audrey, married at 17 to Matt, 18. Separated one year later.)

Jealousy is a tremendous problem with many teenagers. Opening a class discussion on jealousy opens the floodgates for complaints. Harrowing tales are shared of boyfriends who won't "let" their partners go out with girlfriends, who get upset if she visits her mother or goes shopping by herself.

Boyfriends have come to the doorway of our Teen Mother Program to check if any boys are there. A girl may get hysterical if she sees her partner talking with another girl.

Seventy-one young mothers, alumnae of this program, responded to the question, "Is jealousy a problem in your partnership?" Almost half (48 percent) said it was. Their written comments included:

> *He feels I should only have him and no friends, male or female.*

> *Sometimes we both get mad because we don't want somebody of the opposite sex looking at the other one.*

> *He picks out my clothes. At first he didn't want me to come to school because of the guys.*

> *He doesn't like me to talk to his friends.*

> *He always got mad at me if someone in the car next to us was looking at me. He'd slap me and ask what I was looking at — when I didn't even know the other guy was looking at me.*

Importance of Self-Esteem

A major task of the adolescent is working out his/her identity. As stated before, according to Erik Erickson, the ability to form an intimate relationship depends on first developing one's own identity. (1963)

Good self-esteem comes easier if one has achieved a firm identity. The lack of positive self-esteem is often behind jealousy. If she doesn't feel good about herself, she will doubt that he really will stay with her. If he lacks self-esteem he can't believe she can talk with, perhaps be a close friend of, another male, and still continue to be with him.

Trust is difficult for many people, and the lack of trust often begins with a deep fear of being abandoned in early childhood.

Lack of trust in his/her mate causes pain for people of all ages.
Extreme jealousy can wreck a relationship.

> *There used to be a lot of jealousy when we first started going
> together. He was real possessive but now I can go out and he's
> not accusing, "Was there guys there?" After we had Derek he
> started trusting me.*
>
> *You just have to get them to trust you. If there's no trust in a
> relationship, sometimes I don't think it's worth it. I didn't like
> it when he was jealous. He was getting to where he was even
> telling me what to wear. If guys looked at me in this one
> outfit, he wouldn't want me to wear it again.*
>
> *Now he sees his friend acting just like he did. When I tell
> him he used to be that way, he says, "I can't believe it. You
> mean I was that bad?" I say "Yes," and he says, "I can't
> believe it. That's sick, being that jealous."*
>
> *He's more mature now, but he should be — he'll be 20 years
> old in December. He won't be a teenager much longer. (Lucia,
> married a year ago at 17 to Arnie, 18)*

Lucia's comment, "He was real possessive," is typical of many
teenagers. Jealousy and possessiveness are closely intertwined for
these young people. Not "letting" her go out with her friends is a
form of jealousy. Feeling overly possessive is often behind the
jealous feelings she has when he talks with other girls.

Anyone experiencing jealousy knows these feelings are real, no
matter what their source. If jealousy occurs because one's partner is
actually having an affair with someone else, denying those feelings
may not be healthy. But if a person is jealous every time his/her
partner looks at or talks with a person of the opposite sex, s/he
needs to work toward more acceptance of and trust in that partner.
Conquering this kind of jealousy is a positive step in most
relationships. Suggestions for teenagers working on this problem
are offered in *Teenage Marriage: Coping with Reality.*

"Looking" is Prime Cause of Jealousy

This survey does not deal with the question of whether or not
respondents have "real" reason to be jealous. Teenagers were
simply asked, "Would you be jealous if your partner..." Questions
focused on six areas of possible jealousy: looking at, talking with,

working with, attending school with, attending a concert with, and having a close friend of the opposite sex. Respondents could answer "Absolutely," "Probably," "I don't know," "Probably not," and "Absolutely not."

Tables 10-1 through 10-5 in the Appendix include complete data, but this discussion will center on those young people who said they would be either absolutely or probably jealous in the above situations. In other words, percentages given here of those who are jealous include teenagers who answered "Absolutely" and also those who responded "Probably" to these questions.

Differences in degree of jealousy between the sexes were not great. Most revealing were the numbers who said they would be jealous if their mates "looked at" members of the opposite sex. This would bother the *majority* of these young people. Slightly more women and almost as many men would be jealous if their partners "looked" as would be if they had close friends of the opposite sex.

Would you be jealous if your partner looked at a member of the opposite sex?

"Absolutely" + "Probably"

(See Table 10-1)

"Looking" can be as threatening to many teenagers as an openly friendly relationship. As one young woman said, "Well, it depends on how he looks at her." She then mimicked her boyfriend's come-on look which she in no way wanted to share with another woman.

George, married two years ago to Maura, said:

> *Jealous? Yes! If a guy is totally staring or really giving her down-looks, I say, "Hey, buddy." Yes, I guess I am jealous.*

Maura is at least as concerned:

> *Jealousy? It's there. You know, if George looks at a girl or I find him flirting or she's flirting, I get jealous.*

> *He's jealous too. If I dress up nice he says, "Where you going?" Sometimes he says, "What are you looking at him for?" But I would never cheat. If I went out with other guys, I'd tell him — because he'd find out anyhow.*

Even more Asian youth, about two-thirds, were concerned about the "looking." Almost two-thirds of the Hispanic teenage women felt the same way. Otherwise, feelings among young people from the different ethnic groups were similar on the "looking" issue.

Three out of four Anglo men would be upset if their girlfriends or wives had close friends who were males. Only one-half of the Anglo women had similar feelings. Within each of the other ethnic groups, opinions of males and females were very close on this subject. (Table 10-2)

Annie, married three years ago at 16 to Jose, 17, talked about her feelings on this subject:

> *I have a friend who has been a good friend since I was in kindergarten, about the only friend who stuck by me after I got pregnant — but Jose doesn't understand that. He used to have a good friend who was a girl and I didn't mind. I won't give up my friend just because Jose is jealous.*

As might be expected, having one's partner attend a concert with someone of the opposite sex would be hard for most of these young people to handle although the percentage dropped among men already living with their mates.

Talking with the opposite sex was not as threatening to these young people although slightly more than a third of both sexes would be jealous if their partners did so. For those already living together, a few more felt this way.

> *When we met we knew each of us was a flirt, but we love each other and that's what counts. Jealousy is someone's insecurity. Sometimes you need to flirt with a man or woman to satisfy yourself that you're still attractive to the opposite sex. (Heather, married at 17 to Mike, 18)*

Suburban women and both men and women from rural areas are less jealous if their partners talk with the opposite sex than are either suburban men or urban youth of either sex. (Table 10-3)

More Hispanic and Black teenagers, followed closely by Asians, say they are bothered if their mates talk with people of the opposite sex. Fewer Anglos and Native Americans feel this way. (Table 10-2)

Jealousy and School Attendance

A young person presumably could avoid attending a concert with or having a close friend of the opposite sex. S/he might even be able to avoid "looking at" or talking with the opposite sex if s/he has a jealous partner.

But what about school? Time after time I've visited pregnant teenagers who told me their boyfriends or husbands didn't want them in school. As mentioned earlier, boyfriends come to school to see if any boys are in the classroom. Are these isolated instances, or does this actually cause a problem among many young people?

Of the 3,000 young people who responded to this survey, one-fifth of the women and one-fourth of the men said they would be jealous if their partners attended school with the opposite sex. (Table 10-1)

Even more of the Hispanic young people, about one-third of both males and females, had these feelings about school attendance. Of the small sample of Asians, two-fifths of the men and one-third of the women felt the same way. Anglo youth were least likely to be jealous of a partner attending school with the opposite sex, but even in this group, 14 percent of the women and 18 percent of the men would be jealous. (Table 10-2)

Suburban women and rural youth of both sexes would be less likely to be jealous of school attendance than would suburban males or urban men or women. (Table 10-3)

Marge and Marvin separated after being married two years. His jealousy was one of their major problems:

> Marvin didn't want me going to school at Western because there's guys there. If I got late my brother would bring me to school. If I would have asked Marvin he would have said, "No, don't go to school today." He thinks it's dumb that I like school.
>
> If a girl in the same kind of situation asked me, I'd tell her to tell her husband or boyfriend, "That's tough." She needs

that diploma and he helped her get pregnant so the least he can do is help her get her education.

Marvin wants us to get back together. He says he's getting a job, but at this point I really don't want to. Now that I look at it, I think it was because of his immaturity and his jealousy. There were so many things I could have done without him. I could have had typing and shorthand classes after school while I was pregnant, but he didn't want me to. I know I could have done it.

There are many reasons for the high rate of school dropout among pregnant adolescents and school-age parents. In addition to financial problems and lack of childcare, a mate's jealousy may be a big factor in the decision to quit school.

Many school districts across the country offer no special services for pregnant teenagers and school-age parents. Of those which do, the trend appears to be away from separate programs and toward integrating special services into the comprehensive high school. Offering special services in these schools gives these young people the opportunity to stay in their own schools and still receive the much-needed special services, certainly an advantage for some students.

However, an even better approach for school districts would be to provide both a self-contained class and the special services in the comprehensive school. If the goal is to keep young people in school — which translates into preventing future dependency on welfare for many of these young people — the school administrators must consider the culture in which these students live.

If one-fourth of all young men, and a much higher percentage in some groups, would be jealous if their wives or girlfriends attended school with males, many of these young women will simply quit attending regular classes. Those districts which offer a self-contained program as an alternative, however, are likely to find some of these young women participating — young women who otherwise would undoubtedly be school dropouts.

School policy makers, administrators, counselors, and teachers need to be aware of this phenomenon and plan their program offerings accordingly. Young people who drop out of school are less likely to be an asset to society than are those who continue their education.

Rosa and Roberto, both Hispanic, were married when she was only 15. She was not pregnant until the following year, and she continued school after her marriage. When she became pregnant, Roberto wanted her to stay home during her pregnancy, then changed his mind because of the special program. Rosa explained:

> *A long time ago Roberto was very jealous. Right now he's just so-so.*
>
> *A couple of years ago if I turned around and there was a guy standing there and I looked at him, Roberto would say, "What are you looking at? Do you like him?" I would tell him, "No, I was looking at something else."*
>
> *He used to get mad every single day and I didn't even have time to go shopping with my girl friends. Most of the time I was at school or at home. Most of the jealousy was when we were together. Sometimes I got real mad and sometimes I thought it was because he loved me.*
>
> *Now he trusts me and I trust him. If he didn't, he wouldn't let me go to school. At first he said I couldn't go to the Teen Mother Program, that I had to stay home while I was pregnant. But then he thought about it and decided, since there'd be no guys there, it was all right.*

Rosa returned to her home school after their baby was born, and graduated with her class. She plans to continue her education and have a career.

Working Often Provokes Jealousy

Almost exactly the same number of young women, both from the total sample and from the group already living with their partners, would be jealous if their mates worked with other women as would be bothered if they attended school with women. The men were even more likely to be jealous if their partners worked with men. Of the total sample, 27 percent said this would bother them, and a full third of those living with partners had this bias. (Table 10-1)

A high percentage of these young men expect their wives to hold paying jobs. (See Chapter 7.) They know two paychecks are required in many families simply to pay the bills. Hopefully, their jealous feelings will decrease as they mature and gain more positive self-esteem.

Whatever the category of jealousy, the responses of teenagers from different geographic areas, with different religious beliefs, and from various socio-economic groups were similar.

Pregnant Teens More Jealous

In all categories, pregnant teenagers are more jealous than are those who have never been pregnant. Comparing degree of jealousy among young women in different stages of parenthood generally shows less and less jealousy as they move from pregnancy to being mothers of infants to parenting older children. This is understandable when one considers the poor self-esteem evidenced by many pregnant adolescents. Poor self-esteem offers an excellent foundation for jealousy.

Would you be jealous if your partner looked at other girls?
"Absolutely" + "Probably"

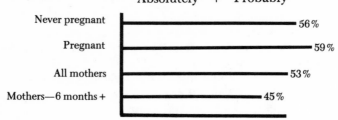

Never pregnant — 56%
Pregnant — 59%
All mothers — 53%
Mothers—6 months + — 45%

Would you be jealous if your partner talked with other girls?
"Absolutely" + "Probably"

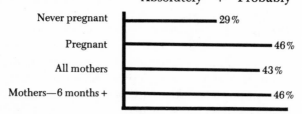

Never pregnant — 29%
Pregnant — 46%
All mothers — 43%
Mothers—6 months + — 46%

Would you be jealous if your partner worked with girls?
"Absolutely" + "Probably"

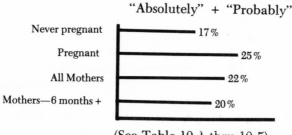

Never pregnant — 17%
Pregnant — 25%
All Mothers — 22%
Mothers—6 months + — 20%

(See Table 10-1 thru 10-5)

Would you be jealous if your partner went to school with girls?

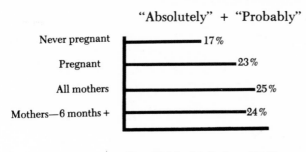

"Absolutely" + "Probably"

Never pregnant — 17%

Pregnant — 23%

All mothers — 25%

Mothers—6 months + — 24%

(See Table 10-1 thru 10-5)

Jealous? He was real jealous at first and then we learned to trust each other. I wasn't jealous because I couldn't stand that, but now I realize I could be. Jealousy is such a wasted emotion — it really is — you aren't hurting anybody but yourself. (Erin, married at 16 to Kelton, 18. Now divorced.)

A curious finding from the survey comes from comparing the attitudes held by young people married and/or living together who consider themselves "happy most of the time" with those who said they are "unhappy most of the time." Jealousy is generally considered a negative emotion, something which one tries to eradicate from one's personality. Yet those teenagers who say they are happy tend to be more jealous than those who are not happy!

In spite of the complaints many young people make about their partners' extreme jealousy, some of these teenagers must consider that jealousy a real sign of caring. "If he's jealous, he must really love me." This reality when coupled with the realities of the male/female world can create a tough situation for these young people. Al explained the phenomenon well:

When you first get married, you're real possessive. I know I was at first — like she's mine now and she should do what I feel is right for us. At first you think, this is my wife. You be careful.

You get really overpossessive and protective. You get the feeling you own her. We've been through that one — thinking I'm the father around here. It takes growing up and some time. You understand different things as you go along.

But after awhile you loosen up a lot. You grow up and you understand. (Al, married eight years ago at 18 to Karolynn, 17)

Summary and Conclusions

Many teenagers appear to be extremely jealous if their partners talk with or even look at people of the opposite sex. The majority of survey respondents said they would be jealous if their partners "looked," and one-third had the same feelings if they talked with members of the other sex.

Even school attendance causes problems for many of these teenagers. The result often is a pregnant teenager or a school-age wife who drops out of school because of her mate's jealousy. School counselors and teachers need to exert special effort to encourage these young people to stay in school. Districts which offer self-contained classes for pregnant and parenting teens may have better success in keeping these young people in school. Requiring students to attend a special program because of pregnancy or marital status is illegal but offering choices to students is good education practice.

The "cure" for jealousy many times is improved self-esteem on the part of the jealous person. The most important thing a counselor, teacher, parent, or anyone else can do for a teenager is help him/her develop positive self-esteem. Helping him/her get a good education and develop saleable job skills are valuable steps toward reaching this goal. In the process, the young adult is likely to find jealousy is no longer the problem it may have been.

Jealousy causes pain for many people, both adults and teenagers. Learning to control jealous feelings, to show trust, respect, and caring as part of their total love for each other is a major learning task for teenage couples. Anne, married two years ago at 18 to Quentin, 18, said firmly, "If there ever is jealousy by either one of us, then all trust is gone. Marriage can't be right if there isn't trust."

Anne is right. Trust and jealousy are not compatible, and trust is a basic ingredient of a good marriage. For many teenagers, building that trust is difficult.

Chapter 11

Teenagers And Spousal Abuse

There was a lot of hitting. It didn't start until I was in the middle of my pregnancy — that was when he started drinking heavily. He got to the point where he couldn't remember the next day, and he would drink and start hitting me. It got so bad sometimes I wouldn't get to school for awhile. Sometimes I asked for it because I'd talk back, but other times it was nothing.

One time I was feeding the baby, warming up his bottle, and Sherri was crying and Glen was yelling, "Get the baby, get the baby." I said I was warming up the bottle and he just went crazy. At first I didn't hit him back, but then I started to hit, too. You only put up with it for so long.

My father never hit me so I just wasn't used to it. I really didn't fight in school or anything. It hurt me the first few times more emotionally than physically. I never expected it, you know.

I didn't want to get married — I just wanted to see how it would work out, to see how he was turning, but my parents wouldn't

*accept me if I didn't marry him, so we were
married almost two years ago. My dad wanted
me to get married. He didn't know until two
weeks ago about the hitting. I never told
anybody because I was too ashamed. I really
loved Glen. (Jill, married two years ago at 16
to Glen, 19. Now separated.)*

Many Teenagers Accept Violence

People are not for hitting. However, about one-third of the
young men and one-quarter of the young women in the survey
tolerate spousal abuse under certain conditions. When asked how
they felt about husbands hitting their wives, they replied that it
was either "okay," "sometimes necessary," or "may happen when
he's angry or drunk." Even more of the young people already living
with a spouse gave one of these answers.

How do you feel about husbands hitting their wives?

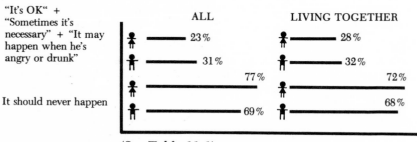

"It's OK" +
"Sometimes it's
necessary" + "It may
happen when he's
angry or drunk"

It should never happen

ALL   LIVING TOGETHER

23%   28%
31%   32%
77%   72%
69%   68%

(See Table 11-1)

In the total survey, a still larger proportion — one-third of each
sex — said it was either OK for a wife to hit her husband, is
sometimes necessary, or may happen when she's angry or drunk.
Of those already living with partners, this percentage jumped to 39
percent of the women and 43 percent of the men. (Table 11-2)

People hitting people is not right whether the hitter is male or
female. The fact of the male's greater size and strength, however,
means men can physically hurt women a great deal more than
women can hurt men. The reality is that one-third to one-half of
the women in this country are beaten at some point by their

husbands or lovers, but far fewer men are physically abused by women. (Walker, 1979) For these reasons, this discussion will focus on the attitudes toward and the reality of men abusing women.

For Many, Reality Involves Hitting

The above statistics are based on the attitudes of young people. The reality is that almost half the women in the survey who were already living with partners reported being hit by these partners at least once. One-fourth had experienced violence two or three times, and 8 percent, often.

Young men already living with partners admitted to inflicting even more violence. Thirteen percent, one in eight, reported hitting their partners *often.* Twenty-two percent said they had hit their partners two or three times, and a few others, once. (Table 11-3)

One young man I interviewed tried to explain why men hit women. He and Darla lived together for about a year and had a daughter. When I talked with him, Darla had moved back home with her mother, mostly because Manuel had beaten her several times. At that time she thought she would probably go back to him, but a year later they were separated with no plans to reunite.

Manuel talked first about his daughter, and about the problems he and Darla had while they lived with his family. When I asked about hitting, he replied:

> *Hitting. . . that's not good. As far as I know, though, some are driven into it, others just take advantage of them. But that's the way women are — just drive a man crazy. I guess if you're jealous it's more apt to happen. I guess that did it with us.*
>
> *But in my point of view, I think a girl is responsible for a man hitting her. A woman should know how a man is, know his ways, what he doesn't like, and what she could do is try to prevent it. The woman drives him to beat her up — his anger just makes him do that.*

We live in a violent society and these young people are very much a part of it.

Religious/Ethnic/Income Groups Compared

Young people from the different religious groups did not differ appreciably in their answers to "How do you feel about husbands

hitting their wives?" However, 72 of these young people lived with a partner who had a different religious belief while 277 shared the same faith with partners. The two groups differed very little in their realities — about half of each group reported being hit at least once by her spouse. But their opinions were quite different. Almost 20 percent more of the interfaith group accepted hitting. Nearly half said sometimes it's necessary for a man to hit his wife, or it may happen when he's angry or drunk. (Table 11-4)

The major difference geographically was among the 250 females and 57 males from the southeastern part of the United States. One-fourth of these young men said it is sometimes necessary for a man to hit a woman, and an additional one-fifth said it may happen when he's angry or drunk. Only 56 percent said it should never happen. (Table 11-5)

As their parents' income increased, young people's acceptance of hitting steadily decreased, especially among the women. Of those whose parents earned less than $5,000 per year, 35 percent tolerated hitting while only 12 percent did so among those with family incomes over $50,000. Men varied in their acceptance of hitting from 36 percent among the lowest-income group to 26 percent among the highest. (Table 11-6)

Spousal abuse cuts across all ethnic groups. Anglo youth were least likely to accept hitting, but fully one-quarter of these young men did so. Slightly more than half of the Black and Asian teenage men said it is either all right for a man to hit his wife, is sometimes necessary, or may happen when he's angry or drunk. (Table 11-7)

Violence During Pregnancy

Women are in most danger of being beaten while they are pregnant, according to Van Freemon who helped establish the Women's and Children's Crisis Center in Whittier, California. In fact, her research shows a woman who is pregnant is four times as likely to be beaten as is a non-pregnant woman. According to a Mott Foundation Report (1981), abuse is frequently faced by those who marry after they become pregnant.

Of the 51 fathers who completed the nationwide survey, almost half said it was either OK or sometimes necessary to hit one's wife or it may happen when he's angry or drunk. (Table 11-8)

Courtney, married three years ago at 15 to Tad, 22, is a large woman with a sweet face and nice smile. She dropped out of

school after their first baby was born. She stopped at school
recently to report the birth of their third child and to tell me, "If
you want to know about the shelters, I'll talk to you." She
explained that she had spent time recently in two homes for
battered women, but had returned home to her husband each
time. She hoped her story might help someone else avoid a
situation like hers.

A month later I visited her. Tad was there when I arrived, but
after a brief conversation, he left for work. Courtney talked about
her years with him:

> *Our problems mostly started before Veronica was born. Tad
> didn't want a second baby, and we got in a lot of fights after
> that — fist fights. Occasionally we would fight, but we were
> getting along so good until after she was born. That's when it
> all started. I had a bloody nose once in awhile but not broken
> bones.*
>
> *I went to the first shelter last year and I was there for a
> month. I didn't realize there would be so many women there.
> There's a lot of them. They really give you a lot of help, as
> much as they can. But 30 days is the longest you can stay, and
> that's not long. When I got out I stayed at my grandma's for a
> little while, then I came back here.*
>
> *Everything is fine when you first come back. It lasts for a
> week or two and then it starts all over again. And it's all for
> stupid reasons. You never fight about anything important.
> After that I went to another shelter and then I came back here.*
>
> *Everything was perfectly fine until about three weeks ago
> when I called the police to take me out of the house — but
> when they got here, I was afraid to press charges. After they
> left, we had a big fight and it put me in the hospital. What
> started the fight? He left his shoes on the floor and I tripped on
> them. I said "God, why did you leave your shoes in the middle
> of the floor again?" And that's what started that one. First he
> yells and I yell back, and then he hits and that's it.*
>
> *He's always sorry after he does it but that don't do any good.
> You never know when it's going to start. But they say once it
> starts it will never stop — not unless you go for counseling. He
> doesn't believe in counseling. Everything is my problem, not
> his. He says if I want to go to counseling, go ahead, but he
> won't go. He says he doesn't have a problem.*

Before he left for work, Tad, who didn't know Courtney would be talking about the violence in their relationship, shared his view of life with three small children. In doing so, he seemed to be alluding to the violence:

> *I think it's a wonderful life, having kids. Five babies would be no problem. Taking care of the house is no problem. She needs to be active. She thinks that everything is a lot of work but it ain't. She can do it in half an hour.*
>
> *I understand that taking care of the baby and being home, it's not easy. But working, it's not easy either. You have somebody who don't like you and they tell you they're going to fire you if you don't do this. You go to work and you have problems and you go home and you have problems. Here at home she can sit down and relax a little and then do her work. Nobody is pushing.*
>
> *I can't yell at Courtney no more because of things that happen between me and her but I make sure she knows what she has to do. She already has a little experience with what happens when she doesn't respect things like that.*

Courtney sees no way out of her predicament. She talks vaguely about going back to school but knows her husband would not help her. She would like to work in a daycare center but feels trapped. "Maybe when the kids are older..." she said.

Attitudes of Those Who Hit

In the total survey, 467 young men felt that husbands should never hit their wives while 205 teenage males said this was either OK, sometimes necessary, or might happen when he's angry or drunk. The two groups were analyzed separately in an effort to find differences between those who apparently condone family violence and those who don't. The young men who said it was either OK or sometimes necessary for a man to hit his wife, or it may happen when he's angry or drunk were more likely to make the following responses to survey questions:

1. They tend to have a poorer relationship with their parents but they are more likely to want to live with his or her parents after marriage. (Tables 11-9, 11-10)

2. When a couple has an argument, these men are almost three times as likely as the other group to say the man should have the final say. However, when these men are upset with their partners, they are much less likely to tell these partners how they feel. (Tables 11-11, 11-12)

3. They are more sexist in their attitudes concerning performance of household tasks and childcare. More of them feel wives should vacuum, cook, bathe and feed the baby, and do the laundry. (Tables 11-13, 11-14)

4. They were more concerned about problems occurring in interracial marriages. (Table 11-15)

5. Only three-fourths of these men expect their marriages to last the rest of their lives, and they are more likely to think marriage would tie them down. (Tables 11-16, 11-17)

6. About twice as many of this group as compared to the "no hitting" teenagers think a couple should have sexual intercourse before they marry. They were more likely to approve a man and woman living together without being married. (Tables 11-18, 11-19)

7. They feel it is less important for husband and wife to agree on how they spend money. (Table 11-20)

8. They are more likely to have firm ideas about their wives holding jobs. More said either "Absolutely" or "Absolutely not" to the questions about wives working. (Tables 11-21, 11-22, 11-23)

9. They are more troubled by jealousy in all the areas covered by the survey. (Table 11-24)

Support Groups Can Help

Mary Maracek is the Program Director of Respond, Inc., in Somerville, Massachusetts, a suburb of Boston. Respond, Inc., offers counseling, legal aid, support groups, and emergency shelter for battered women.

"The most important thing we can do to stop family violence is help people realize that beating and abuse are not all right under any circumstances, not when he's drinking, not when he's on drugs, not because his mother or father beat him," she pointed out. "That's when we begin to see some changes — when women who were trying to find excuses and reasons for the beatings finally realize there are no excuses. Only then are they able to let go of the guilt, the idea that if she were a better wife, he might not beat her."

Ms. Maracek talked about the need for teenage women to internalize this concept, to understand that violence is wrong. If the first time he grabs her and pushes her, she says "No," she is saying to him, "That's not OK. You have to make some changes."

"This puts the focus in the right place which is on his behavior," she explained. "The earlier this happens, the better."

Counselors with Respond, Inc., work closely with Emerge, a counseling agency in Boston for abusers. They find abusive men can change, but this is not likely to happen except through counseling. "There is hope for the man who wants to change. We find that men who are willing to open themselves up in counseling and learn to take a great deal of responsibility for their actions in the rest of their lives are able to change," explained Robert Wald, Program Developer for Emerge.

"Generally the men respond only to pressure from the women," he continued. "Our clients often have very little self-motivation, but if the woman insists he change, if she really will not take the abuse any longer and he knows she won't, only then is he going to change."

In Lucia's situation, court-mandated counseling helped:

One weekend about a year after we were together he hit me. We broke up, but we got together later that week. So the next week he hit me again and I had to go to the hospital. I couldn't understand how if he loved me he could hit me.

My dad pressed charges but after they arrested Arnie, I got my dad to drop the charges. They took him out of school which must have been pretty embarrassing for him. We were back together by then and seeing each other but we had to sneak.

They released him on the condition he would get counseling. So he went for a year, once or twice a week. He hasn't hit me since and we've been together for five years this October, ever since I was in eighth grade.

Summary and Conclusions

Almost one-third of the men and one-fourth of the women in the survey said it was either OK or sometimes necessary for men to hit their wives or it may happen when he's angry or drunk. Almost half the women already living with partners said they had experienced violence from their mates.

Attitudes of young men who indicated spousal abuse is all right under certain conditions were compared with those who don't think it's right, and a number of differences appeared. Those who are accepting of abuse tend to be less communicative with their partners and more sexist in their attitudes. They are less flexible in their feelings about wives working away from home, and they are more bothered by jealousy than were the other men.

Those who abuse women are not likely to stop unless they are involved in counseling. Sometimes through counseling they are able to change. If this doesn't happen, the women involved in abusive situations need help in getting out, in realizing the abuse is not their fault, and that they have a right to a better life.

A necessary part of this "right" is the ability to support herself and her children. Again, education and job skills are the root of the solution. Combining education, job skills, and positive self-esteem may provide the direction she needs.

The Battered Woman by Lenore E. Walker (1979) is an excellent resource on the subject of spousal abuse. Ms. Walker lists characteristics of men likely to beat their women and of women who accept being beaten. These characteristics are reprinted in *Teenage Marriage* (Lindsay, 1984)

Mary Maracek of Respond, Inc., is the author of a beautiful little book, *Say "No!" to Violence*, which stresses the fact that no one deserves to be hit, and that no one should remain in an abusive situation. The booklet is written directly to women who are victims of abuse. It is easy to read and would provide an excellent approach to a difficult subject in Family Living or other classes.

Included in the book is the following poem by Ms. Maracek which is reprinted with her permission:

i whisper to the wind

i whisper to the wind, "he beats me"
i say a prayer at night that he will go
i dare not speak the truth to others
my family, friends and children: they all know

they all whisper to the wind, "he beats her"
they say a prayer at night that he will go
they dare not speak the truth to others
their family, friends and children: they all know

we've created a conspiracy of silence:
no one tells the other what she knows
we all whisper to the wind "he beats her"
and say a prayer at night that he will go

Chapter 12

Divorce: The End Of A Dream

I got pregnant soon after my 16th birthday and married the father when I was a few months along. Norm was 18. At the time, I thought I loved him and I really thought the marriage would work. He was my first real heavy-duty boyfriend, and I was only in 10th grade. I hope my daughter uses her brain a little more than I did.

We were separated a few months after Shannon was born. We were living with my parents and they caught him beating me and kicked him out. The abuse started early but I didn't think it would continue. Once before the wedding he got violent with me but it was in the middle of planning the wedding and I didn't really realize what was happening. I was very upset but I didn't talk to anyone, told no one.

*I was young and scared but thought it
would get better when he could find a job and
keep it. I was wrong and my parents had
helped me by kicking him out. I didn't
actually divorce him for two more years
because I was too scared of him. I finally got
the courage to get the divorce but only after I
was living with another man. (Sue Ellen)*

Some teenage marriages survive. Some young couples are able to
develop their own identities and at the same time maintain a loving,
caring, and intimate relationship with each other. A long-lasting and
"successful" teenage marriage is described in the next chapter.

Hardship Can Destroy Love

Others are not able to cope together with the hardships of early
marriage. The financial struggles, the jealousy, living with in-laws,
too-early parenthood — all seem designed to undercut the love and
the romance within the relationship.

Sometimes the end comes quickly, and sometimes it takes several
years to decide the relationship cannot be continued. For some, the
decision to split is made with great difficulty. Others appear almost
flip about the whole thing. Divorce is seldom easy, but in our
society it has become acceptable. Over and over young people still
together have talked about the need to work through the problems
rather than walk out of the relationship.

Dora and Lee had a difficult time in the early years of their
marriage but appear finally to have developed a good relationship.
About five years after their wedding, Dora exhibited the "Lost
Adolescence Syndrome" described in Chapter 3:

*I felt cheated — I had to get out there and see what I had
missed by marrying at 15. I had to experience it, and I found out
I wasn't really missing anything. Once you get out there, there's
nothing but trouble — at least for me. It took me two months —
at first it was fun and exciting, and then it got boring.*

*The change in the kids was wild — you could see the hurt in
their eyes. Even their teachers noticed it. They lived with me
during the week and with their dad on weekends.*

*Then Lee and I went away for a weekend and really started
to talk. I moved back and it's been good ever since.*

*I came close to losing him and I thank God every day that
he stood by me. I think it all boils down to communication —
that was our main problem from the beginning. It took us a
good six years to work that out.*

A lot of pain, a lot of work, and a lot of maturity are packed
into this vignette. Dora and Lee didn't leap into divorce at the first
sign of trouble. They continued trying to improve the
communication between them and to work out their problems. The
trial separation convinced them that divorce was not the solution.

Just as the decision to marry should not be too quickly made,
neither should divorce be seen as an instant solution to the
inevitable problems of marriage. Sometimes counseling can help a
young couple sort out the rainbows and storms in their marriage.

The hardest part of counseling may be making the decision to
accept it. Sometimes caring others — teacher, parent, counselor —
can help young people understand that seeing a marriage counselor
for marital problems is much like seeing a medical doctor for a
broken leg.

Divorce Is Costly

If divorce is their decision, they may want it to happen as
quickly, cheaply, and simply as possible. *If* there are no children or
property, the procedure may be fairly simple. Generally, however,
getting a divorce is costly.

By the time a couple decides to divorce, communication between
them is likely to be almost non-existent. However, the more they can
resolve the problems of child support, custody, and property
settlements themselves, the less they will spend on attorney fees. If
they have no money, they may be able to get help from their local
Legal Aid or Bar Association. Some communities have divorce clinics
which may be less expensive than going to a private attorney.

If the woman is afraid of her ex-husband, she needs to
understand that after the divorce is final, he has no rights over her.
He may have visitation rights with their child, but only through
court action "for good reason" could he have the custody
agreement reversed. If he is abusive, she can get a restraining order
from the courts which should keep him away from her.

Young mothers need to realize that even though the court may award child support to her, that support is frequently hard to collect. Follow-through in this matter by the courts is often ineffectual.

Catherine Monserrat, counselor at New Futures School, Albuquerque, New Mexico, works with young parents, some married, some living with boyfriends, and others still with their parents. "Professionals need to be aware, especially if they have not gone through a divorce themselves, of the anguish, the guilt, the pain resulting from a divorce," she explained. "Even if the relationship was bad, to divorce means the death of that relationship, the death of the live-happily-ever-after dream."

During the divorce I was really hurt and I would lie in bed and cry. I'd find myself wanting to pick up the phone and talk to Hugh because for three years of our lives before we had Janie we were best friends. Sometimes I just wanted to go over and talk to him like we used to. Even today two years later I find myself daydreaming and then wonder, what am I thinking of him for? (Sally, married at 17 to Hugh, 20. Divorced a year later)

"The guilt and the anger need to be resolved, and sometimes professional counseling is needed," Ms. Monserrat continued. "If the young person doesn't deal with these feelings, with the patterns in her own life which caused her to marry this person in the first place, she will very likely marry the same kind of person next time. But if she can, perhaps with help, think about the characteristics that caused this relationship to go sour, maybe she will not make the same mistake again."

Norm and I lived together less than a year. From then on, every relationship seemed to turn real sour, real sour. My mother has commented about me and a couple of my friends — that we always tend to go for the rotten ones, that we want to be mistreated. I don't feel that's true, but she makes those comments.

The thing is, with a lot of them, their real personality came out later. First of all, don't get into anything real heavy too soon. That's what I was doing for awhile. I guess I followed the storybook thing that you're supposed to fall in love and everything will work out, but that's not true life. Just don't rush it.

I've been married to Howard now for two years and it's working, I think, because we both want it to real bad. He's been hurt a lot in the past too, and we've just had it. We love each other and we want it to work out.

With the others, I don't think I thought much about it at first. When they started going sour I would think, but then it was too late. (Sue Ellen)

Moving from one bad relationship to another happens to many teenagers. The dating process helps a teenager learn what s/he wants in a partner. It helps young people solidify their values and their goals. But if a teenager settles into a marriage or a living-together arrangement too soon, this learning may be cut short.

Reliving Adolescence After Divorce

Michele discovered after her divorce she not only was experiencing the "Lost Adolescence Syndrome," but that, at age 23, she felt she lived through some of the stages of adolescence she had missed because of her early marriage:

When I got married at 18 I had to grow up real fast. I had a Cinderella idea of marriage but it turned out to be Cinderella in reverse. I ended up cooking and cleaning for 13 people. Martha was born that first year and we stuck it out for a long time, but after 5½ years, we were divorced.

It's very scary afterwards. You feel so alone and vulnerable, and it's very hard to keep your direction. I felt myself going through the stages of growing up then, the stages I would have had if I hadn't gotten married so soon. I could see myself doing it, but I couldn't help it. There's a point when you can't decide if you're really an adult or still an adolescent — whether you're 18 or 26.

I would think, "Well, I'm in the college stage" — the parties, the clubs, staying out until the wee hours of the morning, those high-spirited times. Then there was the post-college stage of getting serious about looking for a job and deciding what my future really would be. I knew I had to go through these stages in order to be satisfied with where I would end up. Fortunately I had good enough judgment that I was

able to continue taking the responsibilities I had — caring for
my child, maintaining a home, keeping a job.
   It was real strange, almost like the twilight zone, real
spooky. I almost felt I was living out a fantasy. (Michele)

Importance of Self-Sufficiency

Ideally, people who decide to divorce will not jump immediately
into another partnership. Especially if s/he married very young,
s/he may not have had time to learn to be self-sufficient. If each
can gain that self-sufficiency before starting the next serious
relationship, some of their current problems may evaporate. Young
women in our culture are more likely than young men to feel they
"have" to have a partner. If she can get her life going in a good
direction without depending on someone else, her next relationship
should be an improvement over the first one.

Sally's marriage turned into a nightmare soon after her wedding.
She was 17, a high school senior, and Hugh was 20. He shared
none of his income with her, drank too much and was physically
abusive. After six months of this treatment, she decided to take
charge of her life. She got a job, put her money in a savings
account, applied for subsidized housing, and generally worked
toward becoming self-sufficient. Soon after moving into the low-
cost apartment, she told Hugh to leave and she filed for a divorce.
Two years later she said:

   I couldn't live the way I was living. I had to do something
   for myself and for Janie. I didn't want her to grow up in that
   kind of life. That little girl is the best thing that ever happened
   to me and I want a good life for her. Almost everything I do is
   for her.
      Sometimes I sit back and am amazed at all I've been through
   these three years, and I just keep going. That gives me strength
   just to know that I'm getting further and further away from
   the life we had. Some of the girls I know who are in bad
   situations say to me, "But I'm so scared." I tell them, "You just
   have to do it. You can't be scared, you have to go ahead and
   do it." My girlfriend spends weekends with me sometimes with
   her little boy because she's afraid to get out on her own. Her
   husband drinks and she thinks she has to stay with him because
   she doesn't want to work and she doesn't think she can do

*anything else. I tell her she's got to either stay with him and
quit complaining or go out and get a job for her and Jason. I
tell her she has to set her goals and go on. Things happen and
you deal with it.*

Child Custody and Visitation Rights

A divorce, like a stone thrown in a pond, ripples out to affect
those around the couple — their parents, their friends, and
especially their child(ren). Teenagers need to realize that if they
have children, the partnership with the father (or mother) will
continue long after the divorce. Custody and visitation issues along
with planning for the kids in general are a big part of divorce.

It would be lovely if every child could live with two parents who
care for him and love him. That's not possible for many children.
A co-parenting arrangement may be next best. Sometimes the
father has custody, but in most cases today the mother is granted
custody and the father, visitation rights.

Both parents may want custody and may be able to share this
responsibility. *The Joint Custody and Co-Parenting Handbook* by
Miriam Galper (1980: Running Press) is a good resource to offer
these young parents.

In some cases, the parent with custody may not like the way the
other parent treats the child. Often young mothers talk about fathers
who don't show up for their scheduled visits. If she has encouraged
her child to feel good about his father, it's hard to explain why he
doesn't call or come over as promised.

> *Now he tries to play Daddy every other Sunday. I feel sorry for
> Janie because she's confused. She asks, "Why doesn't my Daddy
> call me? Why doesn't he live here?" I get angry if Hugh doesn't
> call. He's supposed to have Janie every Sunday according to the
> divorce. I'm trying to force a relationship between the two. As
> much anger as there is, I think she needs to grow up knowing her
> father. Everything that happened was between Hugh and me and
> I don't want to take it out on Janie. (Sally)*

Sally and Hugh separated when Janie was only a year old. Sally
describes him as a violent man who drinks too much, and she and
Hugh apparently have quite different values and goals. I question
the wisdom of "forcing" a relationship between him and his

daughter. His legal rights are one thing. If he has co-custody or specific visitation rights, and chooses to act on those rights, that certainly is his privilege. But if, as she reports, he seldom shows up for his appointments with his daughter, doesn't call her, and generally ignores her, why push it? Sally is wise not to put down Hugh when talking with Janie. But to go out of her way to continue the relationship between her child and the man she claims to dislike intensely doesn't seem rational.

Sally is now engaged to a man who, she says, loves Janie and is very involved with her. Perhaps Sally needs to remember that biological fatherhood is one thing. "Real" fatherhood involves caring for, loving, being involved with a child. When the "two" fathers are the same person, wonderful. If they are not, that may be OK too.

> *Before I married Bob, Helen would ask about her Daddy all the time. But now if her father doesn't come to see her, it's no big deal. She says every once in awhile, "My Daddy will come to see me, won't he?" But we have a home life now — a mother and father, a baby and Helen, and she's satisfied with that. If her Dad doesn't come over it's OK because Bob has taken over that role. She was four when we were married. Bob treats her as if she were his own. He disciplines her, loves her, does things with her. In fact, he does more things with her than Steve ever did. Helen loves to play miniature golf, then go to MacDonalds for a hot fudge sundae and Bob does that with her. Steve is more apt to take her to the park to play baseball with his friends, then go out for a beer and Helen doesn't fit into that too well. (Rosemarie, married at 16 to Steve, 16. Divorced two years later, then remarried.)*

If there isn't an "active" father in the picture, the mother may need help in finding other male role models for her child. If she is dating several men, she would be wise for her child's sake not to push the father role too soon. If a close relationship develops, her child will need to be an important part of that relationship.

When a parent remarries, the new spouse may want to ignore the fact of the other father or mother. Janice lived with Hank's father for a few months and then she and the baby moved back in with her parents. Three years later she married John. Gilbert has continued to see his son regularly. Janice commented:

John can't stand Gilbert and he doesn't want me talking to him. But if my son is spending every other weekend with this man, I want to know what's going on. We have to talk, but I don't flaunt it and I don't hide it. I call him when John is at work, and I usually mention it — "I called Gilbert today to see if he's taking Hank this weekend."

Some fathers are the primary caregivers and are granted custody of their children by the courts. Others who have visitation rights cherish those rights and do all they can to maintain a close relationship with their children even if they must live separately. Rebecca married Jack when she was 17, and they were divorced a year later. She is now married to someone else, but knows that Jack and Troy both want to have a strong relationship with each other. She supports that desire.

Troy's father lives out of state but he visits Jack's mother every two or three weeks. Jack sends him postcards and calls him. He thinks he's special because he has two daddies. They're real close. (Rebecca)

Summary and Conclusions

Some teenage marriages survive, but many couples divorce soon after the wedding or within a few years. The financial, emotional, and psychological costs of divorce are high, and the decision to separate should not be made quickly. Professional counseling may help a young couple work toward a better relationship within their marriage.

Strong feelings of disappointment, anger, and guilt are likely to surface after one is divorced. Some individuals, instead of dealing with these feelings, jump quickly into another relationship. There they often find the same kinds of problems they encountered in the former partnership.

The Lost Adolescence Syndrome (Jurich, 1975), the compulsion to return to the "carefree" life of the teenager, may be exhibited by a person who feels s/he missed out on this stage by marrying too soon. For some people, it is enough to have a taste of the insecurities and the disappointments often inherent in a search for what might have been. They return to their marriages with the determination to succeed with these relationships. Others, after divorcing, may find themselves retracing some of the stages of adolescent development, stages which they missed because of early marriage.

Counselors, teachers, and caring others can help young people deal with problems in their relationships. They can listen and be supportive. Guidelines for this approach can be found in *Scenes from a Divorce* by Neil Paylor and Barry Head (Winston Press, 1983). They can also provide practical advice on finding legal help and, if there are children, dealing with custody, visitation rights, and child support.

The mother generally, but certainly not always, is granted custody of the children in a divorce. The father usually has visitation rights and is expected to pay child support. In reality, many young mothers find child support difficult or impossible to collect. Some fathers show little interest in their children and seldom visit them after the divorce. Others take full advantage of their visitation rights to maintain a close relationship with their children.

When parents remarry, each needs to continue to be sensitive to their children's needs to retain ties with both parents.

Divorce is painful and it is never easy. Many couples who marry while very young find themselves and their partners growing apart. If they have made every effort possible to make a success of their relationship, and it is still a bad situation, divorce may be appropriate. However, it is *not* a quick or a good solution for minor disagreements. Whenever possible, trust, respect, and caring are a better approach.

Chapter 13

Staying Married

Nowadays they make it too easy to get divorced. A lot of my friends don't even try. They get tired of being married and they say to hell with it and forget it. It's hard, it's a struggle, but it's worth it. I put in too many years just to wash him out of my life — and of course I love him or I wouldn't be here. It's no piece of cake, that's for sure. (Dora, married 10 years ago at 15 to Lee, 18.)

This book, in an attempt to paint the realities of life as a teenage couple, has described financial difficulties, lack of communication, extreme jealousy, spousal abuse, and other problems so often a part of very young marriage. The high divorce rate among teenage couples has been mentioned again and again.

Most counselors, teachers, parents and caring others who are aware of the hardships facing young couples consistently advise against early marriage and early parenthood. This advice is appropriate. Attempting to build intimacy with another person before one has had a chance to develop one's own identity is a formidable task. Those who delay marriage at least until age 20 are likely to be ahead financially, emotionally, and psychologically.

But some very young teenagers do marry and manage to build a solid, loving, long-lasting relationship with each other in spite of the hardships. Those who care about teenagers need to be aware of these young couples inasmuch as they, too, are part of the reality of teenage marriage. They fit no pattern except that nearly all have surmounted many problems in their relationships just as many older couples have. They may have had dreams about living happily ever after, but they learned that they had to work hard at turning those dreams into reality.

Ann and Charlie's story, while unlike most others, is representative of teenage couples who manage to keep love alive as they work through their difficulties.

Like many other teenagers who rush into early marriage, Ann wanted desperately to escape from an unhappy situation at home. Her mother and father were divorced when she was 9. She adored her father, but her mother was awarded custody of Ann and her sister.

Within a year her mother was married to a man who, together with his 14-year-old son, moved in with them. Ann liked her step-father and enjoyed having a brother — until one night he raped her. She was so hurt and ashamed that for several years she told no one. Soon after the rape, her "brother" and his father moved out and she never saw them again.

Ann's mother started a home business and expected Ann to help her several hours each day. Ann intensely disliked this situation. She started high school and found it to be a miserable experience. Remembering that period, she wrote:

> *Nervously I started high school and hated it. I was so painfully shy and I wasn't popular. I thought I was ugly — I had braces on my teeth and the world's worst case of acne. I thought I would die. I didn't.*
>
> *I was almost 15 when my sister introduced me to Charlie.*

Soon after she met him, Charlie left her for a brief stint in the Army. They began to correspond and, over her mother's objections, started planning their future. When he was home on leave, Ann would cut school to be with him. Soon after he was discharged, they left in his van. She was 15. They ran out of money, were picked up by the police, and she was returned home to her mother's custody.

Ann's relationship with her mother continued to deteriorate, but by this time she was communicating with her father. He regained custody, then gave her permission to marry Charlie.

Ten years later I remembered how Ann, newly married, pregnant, and 16, had demonstrated her writing ability in my class. Her letters through the years have been descriptive and revealing of her life with Charlie. I decided that, rather than reconstructing the story of their marriage through interviews, I would ask Ann and Charlie to share their lives through her writing.

They agreed with the plan, and two weeks later I received her "memoirs" with the following note attached: "Thanks for asking me to contribute, but please don't use my name on it. Writing this has really helped me sort out how I feel about lots of things."

Story of a Teenage Marriage

Charlie and I were married at sunrise in the park near Charlie's home. Everybody was there — even my mom came. I found out later that she never expected us to make it.

Charlie had a job and we had a car. We weren't sure where we'd live, but we had each other. His grandmother had a little one-bedroom house and since she was in the convalescent hospital, it had to be rented. We got it for $100 a month, and Charlie's Grandpa Smith paid the first month's rent for us. It really needed fixing up, but we were more than happy to do it. We were finally on our own — together.

Shortly after our wedding I found out I was pregnant. We were so excited! Praise God! We were going to have a baby. I could hardly believe it, and Mom, well, she nearly dropped her teeth when she found out. Her prediction was that now I'd never finish high school and make anything of myself. That made me even more determined to show her. She'd have to take back all the awful things she'd said and I'd stay married no matter what. She wasn't going to run my life any longer! (I didn't realize it then, but that very statement was proof that she did have a great influence on me.)

We got heavily into debt. Charlie was making $80 every two weeks, and our rent was $100 a month. We bought an organ on time which cost us $88 a month. We could make it if we

didn't eat, or buy gas for the car, or have any other expenses. What a fix we were in!

I kept expecting the "happily ever after" to come waltzing into our lives, but it seemed always to be in the future, just beyond reach and just out of sight. We kept thinking that the baby, or a raise in pay, or things we bought, or perhaps something else would make our ever-after happy. Those things didn't do it. Our first year was full of adjustments. Yes, we fought and argued. Usually I'd end up feeling like it was all my fault, and I was to blame for our troubles.

Later on, we moved out of the tiny house to another community where we were able to rent a three-bedroom house on five acres. It was a real dump, but we were experienced by then at fixing things up, so we were excited about having it. We had our second son and he was cute and special. We had moments of happiness, but it never seemed to move in with us as we expected.

Life was full of hard times. Charlie lost his job. We were broke. With two kids to feed, I went to school on the CETA program and also worked the graveyard shift at a donut shop on weekends. I baked 1000-plus donuts those nights and it took me the better part of ten hours. I got paid $25 for the shift.

Our relationship was at an all-time low then. I was angry with him for not having a job and he was angry with me for being gone all the time or just too tired to be a wife to him. But things brightened up when Charlie got a job where he had good benefits and was paid well. We were still barely scraping by, but now we had some money to do it with! We got into debt with credit cards and too many short-term loans. We were in serious trouble.

To make things worse, our rented house went up for sale and we had to move. We couldn't qualify for a V.A. loan because we had too many bills. We didn't want to rent a place because if we did, we couldn't have fixed it the way we wanted. A loan from Charlie's dad saved us. We got our bills paid so we could qualify for a loan to buy a real fixer-upper across town.

There we had more trouble. I worked for awhile, then quit. The lawyer I worked for wouldn't let me take the day off when our littlest son was sick. No job, no matter how good it paid, was more important to me than my kids. It turned out to be the best because I was happier to be home and Charlie was *glad for me to be there, too. We were managing to get by on his salary.*

I wanted to have another baby. Our youngest was 3 and I felt it was time. We got pregnant after three months of trying, and during that pregnancy we nearly got divorced.

The End — Or The Beginning

We were just drifting apart, further and further every day. Charlie was working every available overtime shift and often on the weekends too. The boys never saw their father and I never got to talk to him. It seemed we weren't a team anymore — just roommates with extra privileges.

We had a big fight, only this time it involved my friend, my best friend who had been living with us for two weeks. We ran out of the house with the kids, fearing for our safety. I called Daddy and he came and got us. We all slept at his condo that night.

I went back to our house, but I filed for divorce with the help of Mom who gave me the $300 to get things started. I told her that she had been right all along. We just wouldn't make it.

I was still looking for our "happily ever after" and it just wasn't there. It was too hard to fight against the man I loved. Yes, I still loved him and I really did want to have the best marriage ever for us. The problem was I could tell that Charlie didn't.

When I filed, and he got served the papers, it hurt him. He cried. He didn't think I'd ever do that. He wouldn't touch me or talk to me or even look at me. He kept his distance. Neither one of us would leave the house. My lawyer said that I could lose it if I left and I needed a place to live with the kids. We both stayed — separate bedrooms and separate lives.

It was awful and I thought about taking my own life. The only thing that kept me from killing myself then was that I couldn't see Charlie raising the kids by himself. They needed to have me to love them and show them tenderness and caring. He had become hard and cold and unfeeling, even toward the kids.

Finally one day we talked. All day and far into the night. We both wanted the kids. He got mad when I said I wouldn't let him have them and he said he knew the baby I carried wasn't his. That stung. It hurt more than any pain I'd ever felt in my life. I'd never been with another man. The thought of it made me sick!

After yelling and getting angry and crying and trying to make some sense of everything, Charlie agreed to go with me to counseling if I'd stop the divorce. I did, and we saw a counselor for several months. Perhaps the counseling helped us realize that we both wanted our marriage to be the best. He really did love me, and I loved him, too.

Not long after that, Johnny was born. We had him at home. He was born into the waiting hands of his papa. What a thrill to see Charlie loving our baby instantly! Along with our sweet new baby came the problems and pressures of parenting three boys including a newborn. We'd had enough strain on our marriage and didn't want to risk any more. We decided our family was complete, so Charlie had a vasectomy, a decision we're beginning to regret.

There have been many times when we wondered why it took us so long to get to this point. It seems we needed the rough times to make it together. Now I can't imagine ever living without Charlie.

Our New Life Begins

We moved to the mountains and started building our own house with our own hands. We bought a trailer and were to live in it for six months until the frame and drywall of the house was done. That six months turned into 18 months.

We went through one of the worst winters ever in the San Bernardino Mountains. There were snow drifts up to ten feet in places, one of which was our front door. A trailer door opens out and we were stuck. The electricity was out, the propane ran out, the pipes froze, and the drains froze. We couldn't get out at all! We pushed and shoved and got the door open enough to get a spoon out and started scooping snow into a pan. Then when it was big enough for six-year-old Jimmy to get out the door, we put him out and said, "Dig!" We got out and hiked through the snow to the neighbor's house.

We are now living in the basement of our incomplete house. There is a tarp over the flat floor overhead and we hope that it won't leak this winter like it has the past two years. I wouldn't trade my tiny basement for any big city house in the world. We are happier now than we've ever been. I think the lessons we've learned have been good for us. I know now that no matter what, I will never leave the man I love.

Our marriage isn't the living-happily-after that I assumed would come all by itself. It's hard work, and because we work so hard at it, we truly appreciate the happiness we have. Loving is risky business. You can't really love unless you bare your soul. In doing this, you may be hurt, yet you may find a love and friendship with someone you never thought possible. What a joy!

We were in our ever-after all the time and didn't know it! It's up to us to make it happy, up to us to love even when we don't feel like it at the moment. Working hard together at life and loving and everyday things has made us pretty solid. I'm glad for the hard times. I know we've grown because of them.

Conclusions

Building a satisfying marriage is never easy. Starting that marriage at age 15 is something like running in a marathon with a bad knee. There is a lot of hurting along the way, but if one succeeds, it is all the more exhilarating because of the sacrifice involved.

Lack of money played a big part in Ann and Charlie's problems. But when Charlie finally started working hard to support his family, he almost lost them. He learned that making money was not enough.

When she was first married, Ann was mature for her age. However, Charlie was three years older, and for a long time, he was mostly in charge of their lives. As Ann developed her own identity, she became more assertive. This change in a partner, which happens in many marriages, is often difficult for the other person to handle.

With their divorce almost finalized, they decided to try again and in doing so, found a whole new life together. It takes a strong person to say, "I'm glad for the hard times. I know we've grown because of them." The prognosis for this marriage is good.

Chapter 14

Conclusions - How Can We Help?

In these chapters we have looked at teenagers' attitudes toward marriage. We have studied the realities in the lives of teenagers already married or living together. Many of the problems faced by these young couples are obvious. Solutions to these problems are not.

Needs of young couples may be categorized as preventive, social, and remedial, according to Reiner and Edwards (1974). Preventing too-early marriage and parenthood is a goal of parents, educators, social workers, and most of all, of some young people. But when teenagers do marry and/or become parents, access to such social services as low-cost housing, public transportation, job opportunities, family planning services, and quality childcare are essential for young couples trying to develop a quality lifestyle within their relationship. Professional marriage counseling can sometimes remediate an already-failing marriage.

Value of Self-Esteem

Basic to any kind of solution to the many problems faced by young people is the building of positive self-esteem on the part of each one. A person who truly feels good about him/herself is more likely to do well in school and to develop good entry-level job skills. Positive self-esteem is often the result of the good feeling of accomplishment.

A young woman with positive self-esteem may be less likely to become pregnant too soon. A young man who feels good about himself may be able to make more responsible decisions concerning his sexuality.

If they decide to marry or to live together, their chances of coping will be increased if each has a good sense of self-worth. They are likely to have less difficulty with communication, jealousy, sex, and other relationship problems.

Building self-esteem is a life-long process. From infancy to adulthood and throughout life, people need to value themselves. Parents and schools play an integral role in the task of helping young people develop positive self-esteem. This is without a doubt one of the most important tasks of parenting and of teaching.

Prevention of Too-Early Pregnancy

Even though many teenagers no longer feel pregnancy is a reason to get married, marriage often follows a teenage pregnancy. "We were going to get married anyway. Getting pregnant speeded up our plans," they explain. About half of all teenage brides are pregnant when they marry. If the marriage fails, the children are likely to suffer at least as much, often more than the parents do.

Adolescence, marriage, and parenthood were labeled the "triple crisis" by LeBarre and LeBarre (1968), a concept which provides a simple, yet accurate indication of the problems inherent in many teenage marriages. As mentioned so often in this book, the adolescent's search for identity is often not compatible with the search for intimacy. Add parenthood to the scene, and the difficulties are greatly increased.

When the wife is pregnant before marriage, there is not time for a comfortable marital sexual relationship to be established before the last stage of pregnancy. She becomes more dependent at the same time the husband is faced with the stress of providing financial support coupled with his own anxieties about approaching parenthood. (Reiner and Edwards, 1974)

To surmount these difficulties, each partner needs to form a strong individual identity while they work together to develop an intimate relationship. Even if they succeed while coping with the demands of parenthood, they still must face some basic issues.

Completing their education, then finding and keeping satisfying, adequately-paid jobs while dealing with the demands of daily living will undoubtedly be a challenge to the young couple.

As a society, we could prevent some of the tragedies resulting from too-early marriage and from unplanned pregnancy. First, family life education should be provided for all students from kindergarten through high school. As young people mature, they need to understand the responsibility involved in being a sexually developing human being.

According to the Alan Guttmacher Institute, eight out of ten Americans believe that sex education should be taught in the schools, and seven out of ten believe that information about contraception should be included. Yet only three states and the District of Columbia require sex education in the schools, and seven additional states encourage it. The other states, in which four-fifths of the country's teenagers live, either have no policy on this issue or they have policies which explicitly leave any decision concerning sex education up to the local school boards. In a Gallup Youth Survey, the majority of students aged 13 to 18 reported having had no sex education at school. Less than one-third said they were taught about contraception. (Planned Parenthood Federation of America, 1981)

The premise behind the lack of sex education in many areas is the idea that young people will become more sexually active if they are offered sex education classes. However, studies show that sex education does not increase sexual activity among the young people involved, but that it does cut down on the number of pregnancies experienced by these young people. The average age for initiation of sexual relations in this country is 16, and 18 percent of the boys and 6 percent of the girls aged 13-14 have had intercourse.

Delaying sexual activity until adulthood is a sensible aim, and abstinence must be an acceptable choice for teenagers. It is not realistic, however, to concentrate on abstinence as the complete answer. Teenagers are greatly affected by our culture's preoccupation with sex as exemplified in movies, on TV, in advertisements, and throughout the media, and abstinence is *not* the message.

Contraception alone will not solve the problem of adolescent pregnancy. Certainly some teenagers would continue to become pregnant even if contraceptives were free and readily available to everyone. But contraception *is* part of the solution, an important part. When access to contraception is limited for teenagers, the result is more pregnancies, not less sexual activity. Several high schools in the United States provide on-campus health services which include the dispensing of contraceptives, surely a rational approach to the realities of teenage sexual activity.

We expect young people to be responsible in their attitudes and actions in the area of sex. Not including this topic in a school's curriculum does not seem to be a responsible approach on the part of the school or the community. Schools have a responsibility to their communities to help young people become responsible citizens. Practical sex education should be an integral part of that responsibility.

Help for Pregnant and Parenting Teens

In addition, all secondary schools need to offer special services for pregnant students and teenage parents. These young people too often drop out of school only to become dependent on our social service system. School programs with good outreach as a component can make a difference in these young people's lives - and in reduced expense to taxpayers. Young parents who finish high school and learn job skills are far less likely to depend on welfare for financial support. The extra costs of special services, including the high cost of childcare on campus for students' babies, are more than offset by the contributions most of these young people will make as they become productive members of our society.

Almost one-fifth of the babies born in the United States each year are born to teenage mothers, and about half of these young mothers are under 18. These babies are the winners when their mothers and fathers are able to continue school, get good jobs, and feel good about themselves. Some schools across the country realize the importance of education to young parents and the difficulties facing these teenage parents if they attempt to juggle childcare, school, and job.

These schools provide special classes for pregnant students who prefer not to continue in their regular classes. Infant care is provided on some campuses so that after the baby is born, the young mother can continue attending school and at the same time, learn parenting skills.

The need for childcare for the children of school-age parents is basic. Good infant care is expensive, but more expensive to society and to taxpayers are the young mothers who must rely on welfare for support because they dropped out of school and are unable to get and keep good jobs.

Side effects of the provision of childcare services in the schools are the benefits to the babies. In a top-notch center, young parents learn the parenting skills they need in order to help their babies develop to their fullest potential. Burton White (1975) stresses the importance of the first three years of life. If young parents receive the help they need during this important stage in their babies' lives, their children may be better able to cope with school, with jobs, with life than their parents are.

Alumnae of the Teen Mother Program described in this book do not fit the pattern of young mothers depending on welfare for survival. A study of this group in 1979 showed 77 percent of 101 survey respondents had depended on welfare grants for support during pregnancy. From one to five years later, ten were still in school and receiving aid, but only 13 percent of the others were receiving AFDC payments. Those who were not were either working or living with a husband who was working or, in many cases, both were employed.

Information on providing services for pregnant adolescents and school-age parents may be obtained from the National Organization on Adolescent Pregnancy and Parenthood. Contact Toni Brown, President, NOAPP, 6813 Winifred, Fort Worth, Texas 76133.

Job Training Imperative for All

Half of the money spent for AFDC is granted to single mothers who had their first child while still in their teens. Many of these mothers did not expect to have to rear their children by themselves, and they were not taught to be self-sufficient. The sexism inherent in our society promotes the phenomenon of the dependent female who becomes pregnant and soon has a child to support, but who has no job skills. More stress is still placed on boys becoming job-ready, but it is imperative that girls receive as much encouragement as boys for developing saleable job-entry skills.

Even though more stress is placed on boys becoming job-ready, our society offers relatively few job opportunities for teenagers, male or female. The unemployment rate for Black teenage men is especially high. Those who find jobs are not likely to earn enough to support a family.

The current push toward academic excellence in the schools is commendable. Coupled with academic excellence, however, must be teaching which helps all young people make responsible decisions in the area of sexuality and which helps these young people become economically self-sufficient.

Summary and Conclusions

About 95 percent of the people in the United States marry sometime during their lives. Few young people in the nationwide survey recommend early marriage. Even when pregnancy occurs, the majority do not advocate marriage as a "solution." When they do marry, they want a lifetime commitment.

If a young person has good self-esteem, s/he will be more likely to be able to make wise decisions in all areas of life. Delaying marriage and parenthood until after adolescent development is completed gives young people more choices and generally a better chance at a satisfying life. They are less likely to settle into low-paying jobs with little chance of advancement. Those who delay marriage until they are adults are more likely to develop a long-lasting and caring relationship with their partners and to provide a better life for their children.

Teens Look at Marriage has presented a picture of teenagers' attitudes toward marriage and of some of the realities faced by teenage couples. The culture of these young people is a mixture of adolescent dependence and adult responsibility. Combining the two roles is never easy.

The rainbows, roles, and realities of teenage partnerships are many-faceted. Some young couples, with much trust, respect, and caring, will be able to develop a satisfying long-term relationship. They are to be commended.

Appendix

Bibliography

Barr, Linda, and Catherine Monserrat. *Teenage Pregnancy: A New Beginning.* 1978. New Futures, Inc., 2120 Louisiana NE, Albuquerque, NM 87110. Spanish edition available.

_____. *Working with Childbearing Adolescents: A Guide for Use with Teenage Pregnancy: A New Beginning.* 1980. New Futures, Inc.

Broderick, Carlfred. *Couples: How to Confront Problems and Maintain Loving Relationships.* 1981. New York: Touchstone Books.

CACSAP Newsletter. Is Infant's Birth Weight Related to Mother's School Attendance? September 1979, p. 10

De Lissovoy, V., and Mary Ellen Hitchcock. High School Marriages in Pennsylvania. *Journal of Marriage and the Family,* 1965, 27, 67-79.

_____. Concerns of Rural Adolescent Parents. *Child Welfare.* 1975, 54, 167-174.

Edens, David, *Marriage: How to Have It The Way You Want It.* 1982. Englewood Cliffs, NJ: Prentice-Hall, Inc.

Erickson, E.H. *Childhood and Society.* New York: Norton, 1963.

Galper, Miriam. *The Joint Custody and Co-Parenting Handbook.* 1980. Philadelphia: Running Press.

Garrett, Yvonne. *The Newlywed Handbook: A Refreshing, Practical Guide for Living Together.* 1981. Waco, Texas: Word, Inc.

Greene, Brenda Z. Addressing Teenage Pregnancy and Parenthood. *Updating School Board Policies.* 1984, 15, 1-3.

Herzog, A. Regula, and Jerald G. Bachman. *Sex Role Attitudes Among High School Seniors: Views about Work and Family Roles.* 1982. Ann Arbor, Michigan: Survey Research Center.

Howell, Frank M., and Wolfgang Frese. Adult Role Transitions, Parental Influence, and Status Aspirations Early in the Life Course. *Journal of Marriage and the Family.* 1982, 44, 35-49.

Jurich, Anthony P. *Crisis in America's Heartland: Family Crisis in Rural America.* Unpublished manuscript. 1984.

Jurich, Anthony P., and Julie A. Jurich. The Lost Adolescence Syndrome. *The Family Coordinator.* 1975, 24, 357-361.

LeBarre, M. and W. LaBarre. *The Triple Crisis: Adolescence, Early Marriage and Parenthood.* 1968. New York: National Council On Illegitimacy.

Leman, Kevin. *Sex Begins in the Kitchen — Renewing Emotional and Physical Intimacy in Marriage.* 1981. Ventura, California: Regal Books.

Lindsay, Jeanne Warren. *Teenage Marriage: Coping with Reality.* 1984. Buena Park, California: Morning Glory Press.

_____. *Teens Parenting: The Challenge of Babies and Toddlers.* 1981. Morning Glory Press.

Maracek, Mary. *Say "No!" to Violence.* 1983. Somerville, Massachusetts: Respond, Inc.

McCoy, Kathy, and Charles Wibbelsman. *The Teenage Body Book.* 1979. New York: Pocket Books.

McGinnis, Tom. *Your First Year of Marriage.* 1977. North Hollywood, California: Wilshire Book Company.

Moore, Kristin A., Sandra L. Hofferth, Steven B. Caldwell, and Linda J. Waite. *Teenage Motherhood: Social and Economic Consequences.* 1979. Washington, D.C.: The Urban Institute.

Mott Foundation. *Teenage Pregnancy: A Critical Issue.* 1981.
    Flint, Michigan: The Charles Stewart Mott Foundation.

Nie, Norman H., C. Hadlai Hull, Jean G. Jenkins, Karin
    Steinbrenner, and Dale H. Bent. *SPSS: Statistical Package for
    the Social Sciences,* 2nd edition. New York: McGraw-Hill, Inc.

Nye, F. Ivan and Felix M. Berardo. *The Family; It's Structure and
    Interaction.* 1973. New York: The Macmillan Company.

Paylor, Neil, and Barry Head. *Scenes from a Divorce.* 1983.
    Minneapolis: Winston Press.

Planned Parenthood Federation of America. *Teenage Pregnancy:
    The Problem That Hasn't Gone Away.* 1981. New York: The
    Alan Guttmacher Institute.

Reiner, Beatrice S., and Raymond L. Edwards. Adolescent
    Marriage — Social or Therapeutic Problem? *The Family
    Coordinator.* 1974, 23, 383-390.

Rolfe, David J. Pre-marriage Contracts: An Aid to Couples Living
    with Parents. *The Family Coordinator.* 1977, 26, 281-285.

Toews, John. Adolescent Developmental Issues in Marital
    Therapy. *Adolescent Psychiatry.* 1980, 8, 224-252.

Walker, Lenore. *The Battered Woman.* 1979. New York: Harper
    and Rowe Publishers, Inc.

Weeks, John R. *Teenage Marriages — A Demographic Analysis.*
    1976. Westport, Connecticut: Greenwood Press.

White, Burton L. *The First Three Years of Life.* 1975.
    Englewood Cliffs, New Jersey: Prentice-Hall, Inc.

Note: The annotated bibliography in *Teenage Marriage: Coping
with Reality* includes almost all of the above books together with
ordering information.

Research Data

Not all respondents in the nationwide survey answered every question. Therefore, each table which follows includes the actual number of young people who answered that particular question. Tables and bar graphs labeled "All" contain data from the complete sample of more than 3000 young people. Those labeled "Living Together," as implied, offer statistics taken from the responses of the 359 young people who were living with a partner at the time of the survey. All other tabulations of data, whether by ethnic group, religion, parents' income, or other category, refer to analysis of the total sample of young people. Any information specifically concerning the living-together group is so identified.

Comparison of attitudes of teenagers from different religious groups is based only on responses from Protestant, Catholic, and Born-again Christian youth. Responses of Jewish teenagers are not included because only 21 responded to the survey, and none are represented in the living-together sample. Neither do the religious group analyses include data from the responses of 522 youth who answered "Other" when asked to which group they belonged. Respondents who claim no religion were asked not to answer this question, and 334 females (11 percent) and 85 males (12 percent) gave no answer. However, both the "Other" and the missing answers were considered too vague to be useful for research purposes.

In the questionnaire, respondents were asked if they lived in the inner city, an urban area, suburb, town of 10,000 or less or on a farm. However, in the survey analysis, inner city and urban area youth are combined. Also combined are those living in towns of 10,000 or less and on farms. Thus the comparisons are made among urban, suburban, and rural youth.

The sample of Asian youth is small, 31 women and 15 men. However, these young people's attitudes are included in analyses of survey results. Again, as with the small sample of young men living with partners, one needs to consider the small sample when drawing conclusions from the research.

All survey data are listed in percentages.

For more information, contact Jeanne Warren Lindsay, c/o Morning Glory Press.

CHAPTER 1
Marriage — If, When, Why
Percentage Tables

Table 1-1A

What Do You Think Is The Best Age For Women To Get Married?

	ALL	
	F N = 2283	**M** N = 669
17 or younger	1.8	3.0
18-19	14.0	13.2
20-24	61.3	62.9
25-29	20.9	19.1
30 or older	2.1	1.8

Table 1-1B

What Is The Best Age For Men To Be Married?

	ALL	
	F N = 2309	**M** N = 684
17 or younger	.8	2.6
18-19	6.5	10.4
20-24	51.3	50.6
25-29	36.8	30.7
30 or older	4.7	5.7

Table 1-2

When You Get Married, Do You Expect It To Last The Rest Of Your Life?

| | ALL | | LIVING TOGETHER | |
	F	M	F	M
	N = 2328	N = 683	N = 327	N = 28
Absolutely	67.9	57.1	63.3	71.4
Probably	22.0	28.3	22.0	21.4
It doesn't matter	2.5	6.0	4.0	3.6
Probably not	6.6	5.9	9.5	--
Absolutely not	1.1	2.8	1.2	3.6

Table 1-3

Are You Happy With Your Partnership?

| | LIVING TOGETHER | |
| | F | M |
	N = 298	N = 24
Yes	53.0	58.3
Most of the time, yes	35.6	16.7
Most of the time, no	5.0	4.2
No	6.4	20.8

Table 1-4

How Do You Feel About A Man And a Woman Living Together If They Aren't Married?

| | ALL | | LIVING TOGETHER | |
	F	M	F	M
	N = 2340	N = 686	N = 324	N = 28
It's OK	40.0	56.1	53.4	50.0
OK if they plan to marry	26.7	25.2	31.8	32.1
OK but I wouldn't do it	15.7	6.4	6.5	10.7
I think it's wrong	17.6	12.2	8.3	7.1

Table 1-5

How Do You Feel About A Man And A Woman Living Together If They Aren't Married?

RELIGION

| | CATHOLIC | | BORN-AGAIN CHRISTIAN | | PROTESTANT | |
	F	M	F	M	F	M
	N = 854	N = 291	N = 392	N = 117	N = 302	N = 84
It's OK	42.7	57.4	26.0	47.9	35.8	51.2
OK if they plan to marry	28.5	27.1	27.8	25.6	26.2	20.2
OK but I wouldn't do it	17.7	6.2	17.9	6.0	17.5	14.3
I think it's wrong	11.1	9.3	28.3	20.5	20.5	14.3

Table 1-6

How Do You Feel About A Man And A Woman Living Together If They Aren't Married?

ETHNIC GROUP

	BLACK		ANGLO		ASIAN		NATIVE AMERICAN		HISPANIC	
	F	M	F	M	F	M	F	M	F	M
	N = 410	N = 58	N = 1343	N = 411	N = 30	N = 15	N = 115	N = 48	N = 405	N = 145
It's OK	34.6	50.0	41.7	56.9	43.3	40.0	52.2	72.9	35.1	53.8
OK if they plan to marry	32.0	24.1	23.3	23.6	26.7	33.3	22.6	22.9	34.1	29.0
OK but I wouldn't do it	16.6	10.3	14.7	6.3	10.0	6.7	15.7	--	18.5	6.2
I think it's wrong	16.8	15.5	20.3	13.1	20.0	20.0	9.6	4.2	12.3	11.0

Table 1-7

How Do You Feel About A Man And A Woman Living Together If They Aren't Married?

	URBAN		SUBURBAN		TOWN/FARM	
	F	M	F	M	F	M
	N = 1213	N = 264	N = 465	N = 234	N = 626	N = 184
It's OK	43.8	52.7	43.0	62.8	29.9	52.7
OK if they plan to marry	28.9	29.2	22.8	20.9	25.4	24.5
OK but I wouldn't do it	15.2	7.6	16.1	4.3	16.5	7.6
I think it's wrong	12.1	10.6	18.1	12.0	28.3	15.2

Table 1-8

How Do You Feel About A Man And A Woman Living Together If They Aren't Married?

	GEOGRAPHIC AREAS					
	N. CALIF.		NORTHWEST		SO. CALIF.	
	F	M	F	M	F	M
	N = 162	N = 29	N = 306	N = 49	N = 588	N = 285
It's OK	56.8	48.3	39.2	65.3	45.4	59.6
OK if they plan to marry	22.2	24.1	22.9	18.4	27.2	25.3
OK but I wouldn't do it	11.1	10.3	11.4	2.0	15.1	4.6
I think it's wrong	9.9	17.2	26.5	14.3	12.3	10.5

	GEOGRAPHIC AREAS							
	NM-TX		MIDDLE WEST		NORTHEAST		SOUTHEAST	
	F	M	F	M	F	M	F	M
	N = 316	N = 79	N = 519	N = 172	N = 237	N = 76	N = 247	N = 57
It's OK	42.7	65.8	32.8	52.3	43.9	56.6	24.3	35.1
OK if they plan to marry	27.5	22.8	30.6	27.9	25.3	27.6	27.5	22.8
OK but I wouldn't do it	19.0	5.1	18.3	9.3	14.3	6.6	17.8	8.8
I think it's wrong	10.8	6.3	18.3	10.5	16.5	9.2	30.4	33.3

Table 1-9

How Do You Feel About A Man And A Woman Living Together If They Aren't Married?

| | Never Pregnant | Had Abortion | Pregnant | Mothers | Fathers |
	N = 1240	N = 73	N = 443	N = 435	N = 51
It's OK	34.3	54.8	44.7	49.0	68.6
OK if they plan to marry	21.9	23.3	34.3	33.1	17.6
OK but I wouldn't do it	19.8	12.3	11.7	9.0	2.0
I think it's wrong	24.0	9.6	9.3	9.0	11.8

Table 1-10

When A High School-Age Girl Gets Pregnant, Should
She And Her Boyfriend Get Married?

| | ALL | | LIVING TOGETHER | |
| | F | M | F | M |
	N = 2267	N = 666	N = 322	N = 27
Absolutely	14.1	12.9	10.2	14.8
Probably	25.8	35.1	21.1	40.7
It doesn't matter	27.2	23.0	40.4	25.9
Probably not	24.8	22.4	17.4	11.1
Absolutely not	8.1	6.6	10.9	7.4

Table 1-11

When A High School-Age Girl Gets Pregnant, Should
She And Her Boyfriend Get Married?

| | Never Pregnant | Had Abortion | Pregnant | Mothers | Fathers |
	N = 1211	N = 71	N = 430	N = 419	N = 49
Absolutely	18.7	11.3	7.7	7.9	14.3
Probably	29.6	25.4	26.0	14.3	28.6
It doesn't matter	18.8	29.6	38.8	39.4	40.8
Probably not	27.0	15.5	18.6	25.3	10.2
Absolutely not	5.9	18.3	8.8	13.1	6.1

Table 1-12

When A High School-Age Girl Gets Pregnant, Should
She And Her Boyfriend Get Married?

| | URBAN | | SUBURBAN | | TOWN/FARM | |
| | F | M | F | M | F | M |
	N = 1173	N = 257	N = 449	N = 225	N = 608	N = 180
Absolutely	10.9	13.6	13.1	12.0	21.2	12.8
Probably	22.8	35.0	23.2	30.2	33.6	41.1
It doesn't matter	30.8	20.6	25.2	26.7	21.1	22.2
Probably not	25.8	22.6	29.4	24.4	19.6	19.4
Absolutely not	9.6	8.2	9.1	6.7	4.6	4.4

Table 1-13

When A High School-Age Girl Gets Pregnant, Should She And Her Boyfriend Get Married?

	CATHOLIC		RELIGION BORN-AGAIN CHRISTIAN		PROTESTANT	
	F	M	F	M	F	M
	N = 829	N = 284	N = 385	N = 111	N = 291	N = 83
Absolutely	13.5	10.2	16.1	13.5	10.0	13.3
Probably	23.9	38.4	27.5	37.8	28.2	25.3
It doesn't matter	27.7	23.2	24.9	19.8	26.8	22.9
Probably not	26.9	21.1	24.7	24.3	28.2	30.1
Absolutely not	8.0	7.0	6.8	4.5	6.9	8.4

Table 1-14

When A High School-Age Girl Gets Pregnant, Should She And Her Boyfriend Get Married?

	ETHNIC GROUP									
	BLACK		ANGLO		ASIAN		NATIVE AMERICAN		HISPANIC	
	F	M	F	M	F	M	F	M	F	M
	N = 392	N = 58	N = 1310	N = 397	N = 30	N = 15	N = 110	N = 46	N = 391	N = 142
Absolutely	11.7	3.4	14.8	13.4	16.7	6.7	8.2	15.2	15.1	16.2
Probably	19.4	22.4	27.7	34.5	30.0	46.7	26.4	34.8	26.3	38.0
It doesn't matter	30.1	31.0	25.0	22.9	20.0	33.3	34.5	23.9	29.7	19.7
Probably not	23.7	31.0	26.5	23.2	26.7	6.7	22.7	21.7	20.5	19.0
Absolutely not	15.1	12.1	6.0	6.0	6.7	6.7	8.2	4.3	8.4	7.0

CHAPTER 2
Making That Big Decision
Percentage Tables

Table 2-1

Do You And Your Partner Have Similar Interests?

	LIVING TOGETHER	
	F	M
	N = 309	N = 24
Yes	57.9	66.7
No	7.1	4.2
Sometimes	35.0	29.2

Table 2-2

Is A Lack Of Similar Interests Ever A Problem?

	LIVING TOGETHER	
	F	M
	N = 304	N = 21
Yes	14.5	14.3
Sometimes	40.1	33.3
No	45.4	52.4

Table 2-3

For How Long Have You Lived With Both Of Your Parents?

	ALL		LIVING TOGETHER ALL		LIVING TOGETHER MARRIED	LIVING TOGETHER SINGLE
	F	M	F	M	F/M	F/M
	N = 2305	N = 676	N = 325	N = 27	N = 163	N = 181
All my life	59.2	61.5	32.0	40.7	34.4	30.9
10-15 years	15.4	15.4	32.0	29.6	33.1	29.3
5-10 years	9.8	9.3	12.6	14.8	12.9	13.3
0-5 years	10.2	8.9	13.2	14.8	10.4	14.4
Never	5.4	4.9	10.2	--	9.2	12.2

Table 2-4

Do You Want Your Marriage To Be Much Like Your Parents' Marriage?

	ALL		LIVING TOGETHER	
	F	M	F	M
	N = 2324	N = 680	N = 327	N = 28
Absolutely	12.1	11.6	8.3	7.1
Probably	16.4	20.1	8.6	7.1
It doesn't matter	8.3	15.1	8.3	14.3
Probably not	18.2	19.9	15.0	14.3
Absolutely not	45.0	33.2	59.9	57.1

Table 2-5

Do You Want Your Marriage To Be Much Like
Your Parents' Marriage?

	ETHNIC GROUP									
	BLACK		**ANGLO**		**ASIAN**		**NATIVE AMERICAN**		**HISPANIC**	
	F	M	F	M	F	M	F	M	F	M
	N = 402	N = 59	N = 1340	N = 405	N = 30	N = 15	N = 116	N = 47	N = 400	N = 145
Absolutely	8.2	6.8	13.1	12.6	16.7	--	15.5	8.5	11.7	12.4
Probably	10.9	10.2	19.0	20.5	16.7	20.0	14.7	17.0	14.8	23.4
It doesn't matter	7.5	11.9	8.1	13.8	16.7	40.0	4.3	14.9	10.0	17.9
Probably not	17.7	30.5	18.0	19.5	6.7	20.0	16.4	14.9	20.7	18.6
Absolutely not	55.7	40.7	41.7	33.6	43.3	20.0	49.1	44.7	42.7	27.6

Table 2-6

Do You Want To Marry A Person From
Your Ethnic Group Or Race?

	ALL		**LIVING TOGETHER**		**LIVING TOGETHER IS EASIER**	**HARDER**
	F	M	F	M	F/M	F/M
	N = 2328	N = 681	N = 326	N = 26	N = 64	N = 110
Absolutely	28.9	24.8	28.8	26.9	42.2	23.6
Probably	30.0	27.9	22.1	19.2	20.3	21.8
It doesn't matter	36.5	41.9	44.2	46.2	31.3	48.2
Probably not	3.0	3.5	4.3	3.8	6.3	4.5
Absolutely not	1.5	1.9	.6	3.8	--	1.8

Table 2-7

Do You Want To Marry A Person Who
Has The Same Religious Beliefs As You Do?

	ALL		**LIVING TOGETHER ALL**		**LIVING TOGETHER EASIER**	**HARDER**
	N = 2328	N = 680	N = 326	N = 25	N = 65	N = 104
Absolutely	23.1	17.8	19.3	20.0	21.5	14.5
Probably	30.0	31.5	28.5	20.0	27.7	28.2
It doesn't matter	43.9	47.2	50.6	56.0	47.7	54.5
Probably not	2.3	2.6	.6	--	1.5	.9
Absolutely not	.8	.9	.9	4.0	1.5	1.8

Table 2-8

Do You Think Marrying A Person From A Different Ethnic Group Would Usually Cause Problems Within A Marriage?

	ALL		LIVING TOGETHER ALL		LIVING TOGETHER IS EASIER	HARDER
	N = 2328	N = 685	N = 328	N = 28	N = 65	N = 101
Absolutely	5.8	7.3	6.1	7.1	7.3	7.7
Probably	23.2	20.6	20.7	14.3	27.7	18.4
It doesn't matter	41.7	42.2	39.6	42.9	35.4	47.2
Probably not	23.6	22.5	24.4	10.7	20.0	18.9
Absolutely not	5.7	7.4	9.1	25.0	--	9.0

Table 2-9

Do You Think Marrying A Person With A Religious Faith Different From Your Own Would Cause Problems Within A Marriage?

	ALL		LIVING TOGETHER ALL		LIVING TOGETHER IS EASIER	HARDER
	F	M	F	M		
	N = 2321	N = 683	N = 325	N = 27	N = 65	N = 104
Absolutely	8.9	7.6	7.4	3.7	3.1	8.1
Probably	28.8	24.3	27.4	11.1	29.2	25.2
It doesn't matter	34.4	36.6	36.6	37.0	44.6	38.7
Probably not	23.4	24.9	21.6	11.1	12.3	21.6
Absolutely not	4.5	6.6	7.1	37.0	10.8	6.3

Table 2-10

Do You Want To Marry A Person From Your Own Ethnic Group Or Race?

ETHNIC GROUP

	BLACK		ANGLO		ASIAN		NATIVE AMERICAN		HISPANIC	
	F	M	F	M	F	M	F	M	F	M
	N = 407	N = 59	N = 1339	N = 407	N = 30	N = 15	N = 115	N = 46	N = 400	N = 145
Absolutely	28.5	11.9	34.4	33.2	16.7	13.3	17.4	19.6	16.2	11.0
Probably	28.0	16.9	30.8	31.0	10.0	20.0	26.1	28.3	32.5	24.1
It doesn't matter	37.8	59.3	31.0	31.4	60.0	60.0	51.3	43.5	47.0	60.0
Probably not	4.2	8.5	2.4	2.5	6.7	6.7	4.3	6.5	3.3	3.4
Absolutely not	1.5	3.4	1.4	2.0	6.7	--	.9	2.2	1.0	1.4

Table 2-11

Do You Want To Marry A Person From Your Own Ethnic Group Or Race?

| | URBAN | | SUBURBAN | | TOWN/FARM | |
| | F | M | F | M | F | M |
	N = 1205	N = 260	N = 465	N = 235	N = 620	N = 183
Absolutely	25.1	21.5	25.8	19.6	39.0	36.1
Probably	29.1	27.7	31.2	26.8	30.6	30.1
It doesn't matter	40.2	47.3	39.6	45.5	27.1	29.0
Probably not	4.0	3.1	2.4	5.1	1.6	2.2
Absolutely not	1.6	.4	1.1	3.0	1.6	2.7

Table 2-12
Do You Want To Marry A Person Who Has The Same Religious Beliefs As You Do?

RELIGION

| | CATHOLIC | | BORN-AGAIN CHRISTIAN | | PROTESTANT | |
| | F | M | F | M | F | M |
	N = 846	N = 290	N = 392	N = 118	N = 305	N = 83
Absolutely	22.3	20.0	39.0	27.1	28.5	36.1
Probably	30.6	28.3	30.6	30.5	32.1	33.7
It doesn't matter	42.4	47.2	26.5	35.6	35.1	28.9
Probably not	3.1	2.4	3.1	5.9	2.6	1.2
Absolutely not	1.5	2.1	.8	.8	1.6	--

Table 2-13

Do You Want To Marry A Person Who Has The Same Religious Beliefs As You Do?

RELIGION

| | CATHOLIC | | BORN-AGAIN CHRISTIAN | | PROTESTANT | |
| | F | M | F | M | F | M |
	N = 848	N = 287	N = 393	N = 117	N = 304	N = 83
Absolutely	22.2	17.1	36.1	24.8	16.4	20.5
Probably	36.0	36.6	32.1	34.2	32.6	31.3
It doesn't matter	40.0	43.6	28.8	37.6	48.4	45.8
Probably not	1.5	2.1	2.0	2.6	2.0	2.4
Absolutely not	.4	.7	1.0	.9	.7	--

Table 2-14

Do You Think Marrying A Person From A Different Ethnic Group Would Usually Cause Problems Within A Marriage?

	CATHOLIC		RELIGION BORN-AGAIN CHRISTIAN		PROTESTANT	
	F	M	F	M	F	M
	N = 847	N = 291	N = 394	N = 118	N = 304	N = 84
Absolutely	5.4	4.8	8.4	6.8	6.3	9.5
Probably	19.5	21.3	29.9	27.1	25.7	22.6
It doesn't matter	41.2	43.3	38.8	37.3	40.1	45.2
Probably not	27.7	22.0	17.8	23.7	23.4	20.2
Absolutely not	6.1	8.6	5.1	5.1	4.6	2.4

Table 2-15

Do You Think Marrying A Person With A Religious Faith Different From Your Own Would Cause Problems In Your Marriage?

	CATHOLIC		RELIGION BORN-AGAIN CHRISTIAN		PROTESTANT	
	F	M	F	M	F	M
	N = 846	N = 288	N = 393	N = 109	N = 303	N = 84
Absolutely	7.1	6.6	14.8	11.0	6.6	7.1
Probably	29.9	24.0	33.1	31.4	29.0	29.8
It doesn't matter	33.7	37.5	28.8	34.7	36.6	38.1
Probably not	24.0	25.7	19.6	15.3	24.8	22.6
Absolutely not	5.3	6.3	3.8	7.6	3.0	2.4

Table 2-16

If You Do Not Belong To The Same Church or Practice The Same Faith, How Has This Affected Your Relationship?

	LIVING TOGETHER DIFFERENT RELIGION F/M N = 54
No problem at all	51.9
It's a problem only to our parents	11.1
This occasionally causes a problem for us	25.9
It's a big problem for us	11.1

Table 2-17

If You Do Not Belong To The Same Ethnic Group,
How Has This Affected Your Relationship?

	LIVING TOGETHER DIFFERENT ETHNIC GROUP F/M N = 82
No problem at all	59.8
It's a problem only to our parents	18.3
This occasionally causes problems for us	20.7
It's a big problem for us	1.2

Table 2-18

Do You And Your Partner Have Similar Interests?

	Living-Together Group			
	Religious Beliefs		Ethnic Group	
	Same	Different	Same	Different
	N = 269	N = 70	N = 248	N = 87
Yes	63.9	40.0	61.3	54.0
No	4.1	15.7	5.6	10.3
Sometimes	32.0	44.3	33.1	35.6

Table 2-19

Do You And Your Partner Find It Easy To Communicate
(Talk, Share Feelings) With Each Other?

	Living Together Group			
	Religious Beliefs		Ethnic Group	
	Same	Different	Same	Different
	N = 270	N = 70	N = 248	N = 88
Yes	59.3	45.7	58.9	47.7
No	9.3	24.3	12.5	13.6
Sometimes	31.5	30.0	28.6	38.6

CHAPTER 3
Coping With Changes
Percentage Tables

Table 3-1

How Much Do You Think Getting Married At Age 18 Or Younger
Would Change Your Life As Far As Friends Are Concerned?

	ALL	
	F N = 2289	M N = 673
More friends	18.2	25.9
Fewer friends	22.0	20.4
Different friends	32.3	23.9
No change	27.5	29.9

Table 3-2

How Much Do You Think Getting Married At
Age 18 Or Younger Would Change Your Life As Far As
Recreation and Partying Are Concerned?

	ALL	
	F N = 2315	M N = 678
More parties	19.7	20.1
Less parties	53.0	58.8
No change	27.3	21.1

Table 3-3

How Much Do You Think Getting Married At Age 18 Or Younger
Would Change Your School Attendance?

| | ALL | | LIVING TOGETHER | |
	F	M	F	M
	N = 2260	N = 668	N = 312	N = 25
I'd drop out	6.2	12.7	9.0	16.0
I'd continue going to school	34.7	31.0	32.7	16.0
I would graduate	34.2	39.1	29.2	48.0
Marriage wouldn't change my attendance	24.9	17.2	29.2	20.0

Table 3-4

How Much Difference Do You Think Getting Married At Age 18
Or Younger Would Make In The Amount Of Free Time You Have?

| | ALL | | LIVING TOGETHER | |
	F	M	F	M
	N = 2330	N = 679	N = 324	N = 28
More	10.0	8.5	10.2	10.7
Less	73.2	79.8	63.6	50.0
No change	16.8	11.6	26.2	39.3

Table 3-5

Has Your Partner Changed Much Since You Were Married Or Started Living Together?

| | LIVING TOGETHER | |
| | F | M |
	N = 296	N = 23
No change	29.7	21.7
Some positive change	31.8	30.4
Much positive change	12.5	30.4
Some negative change	16.6	13.0
Much negative change	9.5	4.3

Table 3-6

Has Your Partner Changed Much Since You Were Married Or Started Living Together?

	Living Together Group			
	Religious Beliefs		Ethnic Group	
	Same	Different	Same	Different
	N = 259	N = 63	N = 237	N = 82
No change	30.5	17.5	29.5	25.6
Some positive change	33.6	30.2	34.2	26.8
Much positive change	15.8	11.1	16.9	9.8
Some negative change	13.1	25.4	12.7	23.2
Much negative change	6.9	15.9	6.8	14.6

Table 3-7

Compared To What You Expected Before You Started Living
Together, Is Living Together:

| | All-Living Together | |
| | F | M |
	N = 301	N = 23
Easier?	20.3	8.7
Harder?	33.6	39.1
About what you expected?	46.2	52.2

CHAPTER 4
Learning To Communicate
Percentage Tables

Table 4-1

Do You Think Communication With Your Partner — Or Lack Of
Communication — Is A Problem In Your Relationship?

| | LIVING TOGETHER | |
| | F | M |
	N = 306	N = 24
Yes	21.6	20.8
Sometimes	33.7	33.3
No	44.8	45.8

Table 4-2

If You Have A Problem, To Whom Do You Talk?

	ALL		LIVING TOGETHER	
	F	M	F	M
	N = 1388	N = 482	N = 207	N = 22
Nobody	9.8	21.8	11.1	18.2
Parents	26.4	24.7	17.9	9.1
Teacher, counselor, minister	3.6	5.0	5.8	9.1
Another friend	37.8	36.3	27.5	22.7
Boy/girl friend, husband/wife	22.4	12.2	37.7	40.9

Table 4-3

If You Have A Problem, To Whom Do You Talk?

	ALL PREGNANT F	MOTHERS F	MOTHERS- 6 MONTHS + F
	N = 370	N = 284	N = 161
Nobody	9.3	9.9	11.2
Parents	28.7	22.9	18.0
Teacher, counselor, minister	3.6	8.1	9.3
Another friend	24.7	30.3	36.0
Boy/girl friend, husband/wife	33.7	28.9	25.5

Table 4-4

If You Have A Problem, To Whom Do You Talk?

	CATHOLIC		RELIGION BORN-AGAIN CHRISTIAN		PROTESTANT	
	F	M	F	M	F	M
	N = 521	N = 208	N = 219	N = 87	N = 157	N = 52
Nobody	9.2	19.7	8.7	20.7	7.6	13.5
Parents	23.4	25.5	31.1	24.1	21.7	40.4
Teacher, counselor, minister	4.2	3.4	3.2	6.9	3.2	5.8
Another friend	38.4	37.5	33.8	39.1	51.6	25.0
Boy/girl friend or husband/ wife	24.8	13.9	23.3	9.2	15.9	15.4

Table 4-5

If You Have A Problem, To Whom Do You Talk?

	HAPPY N = 185	NOT HAPPY N = 29
Nobody	10.3	17.2
Parents	16.8	13.8
Teacher, counselor, or minister	5.9	10.3
Another friend	23.2	48.3
Boy/girl friend or husband/wife	43.8	10.3

Table 4-6

If You Have A Problem, To Whom Do You Talk?

		LIVING TOGETHER		
	Same Religion	Different Religion	Same Ethnic	Different Ethnic
	N = 277	N = 72	N = 258	N = 94
Nobody	8.1	22.4	13.5	7.1
Parents	15.6	16.3	16.7	17.1
Teacher, Counselor, Minister	6.9	6.1	3.8	10.0
Another friend	28.9	24.5	26.9	30.0
Boy/girl friend or husband/wife	40.5	30.6	39.1	35.7

Table 4-7

If You Are Upset With Your Partner, What Do You Do?

	ALL		LIVING TOGETHER	
	F	M	F	M
	N = 1672	N = 545	N = 251	N = 19
Tell him/her you are upset	62.7	51.7	69.3	42.1
Hit him/her	2.6	5.5	1.6	5.3
Leave and think it through	22.5	28.4	15.9	26.3
Tell a friend or parent but not your partner	5.1	5.0	3.2	5.3
Don't do anything	7.1	9.4	10.0	21.1

Table 4-8

If You Are Upset With Your Partner, What Do You Do?

	AGE			
	14-16		17-18	
	F	M	F	M
	N = 819	N = 236	N = 843	N = 322
Tell him/her you are upset	59.5	45.3	66.2	56.6
Hit him/her	3.1	6.8	2.1	4.5
Leave and think it through	23.2	32.2	21.7	25.6
Tell a friend or parent but not your partner	6.5	7.2	3.9	3.2
Don't do anything	7.8	8.5	6.0	10.0

Table 4-9

If You Are Upset With Your Partner, What Do You Do?

	PARENT'S INCOME									
	UNDER $5000		$5000-$10000		$10000-$20000		$20000-$50000		OVER $50000	
	F	M	F	M	F	M	F	M	F	M
	N = 221	N = 43	N = 285	N = 69	N = 389	N = 130	N = 387	N = 171	N = 104	N = 62
Tell him/her you are upset	48.9	32.6	56.8	34.8	68.9	52.3	71.3	62.6	74.0	61.3
Hit him/her	2.3	7.0	1.4	5.8	3.1	6.9	2.1	2.3	1.9	11.3
Leave and think it through	31.7	34.9	27.7	42.0	18.8	26.2	19.6	23.4	12.5	19.4
Tell a friend or parent but not your partner	7.2	14.0	6.7	4.3	4.4	6.2	3.6	3.5	2.9	--
Don't do anything	10.0	11.6	7.4	13.0	4.9	8.5	3.4	8.2	8.7	8.1

Table 4-10

If You Are Upset With Your Partner, What Do You Do?

ETHNIC GROUP

	BLACK		ANGLO		ASIAN		NATIVE AMERICAN		HISPANIC	
	F	M	F	M	F	M	F	M	F	M
	N = 314	N = 49	N = 933	N = 326	N = 17	N = 12	N = 74	N = 37	N = 305	N = 114
Tell him/her you are upset	42.7	28.6	70.5	55.5	58.8	58.3	51.4	62.2	62.6	48.2
Hit him/her	3.5	10.2	2.7	5.5	--	--	--	2.7	1.6	5.3
Leave and think it through	33.8	32.7	17.8	27.9	23.5	25.0	29.7	27.0	23.3	28.1
Tell a friend or parent, but not your partner	6.7	12.2	4.4	4.0	11.8	--	6.8	--	5.2	6.1
Don't do anything	13.4	16.3	4.6	7.1	5.9	16.7	12.2	8.1	7.2	12.3

Table 4-11

If You Are Upset With Your Partner, What Do You Do?

	Same Religion	Different Religion	Same Ethnic	Different Ethnic
	N = 214	N = 53	N = 195	N = 73
Tell him/her	71.0	52.8	69.2	58.9
Hit him/her	.9	1.9	1.5	1.4
Leave and think it through	16.4	26.4	17.9	20.5
Tell a friend or parent, but not your partner	2.3	5.7	2.1	6.8
Don't do anything	9.3	13.2	9.2	12.3

Table 4-12

When A Couple Has An Argument, Who Should Usually Have The Final Say?

	ALL	
	F N = 2330	M N = 676
Male	5.4	19.2
Female	7.2	1.5
It doesn't matter	87.4	79.3

Table 4-13

When A Couple Has An Argument, Who Should Usually Have The Final Say?

RELIGION

	CATHOLIC		BORN-AGAIN CHRISTIAN		PROTESTANT	
	F	M	F	M	F	M
	N = 851	N = 283	N = 391	N = 117	N = 304	N = 83
Male	4.5	19.4	9.2	16.2	3.3	26.5
Female	6.8	.7	8..2	2.6	5.6	1.2
It doesn't matter	88.7	79.9	82.6	81.2	91.1	72.3

Table 4-14

When A Couple Has An Argument, Who Should Usually Have The Final Say?

ETHNIC GROUP

	BLACK		ANGLO		ASIAN		NATIVE AMERICAN		HISPANIC	
	F	M	F	M	F	M	F	M	F	M
	N = 411	N = 59	N = 1337	N = 407	N = 31	N = 15	N = 113	N = 47	N = 402	N = 139
Male	8.3	23.7	4.3	16.7	6.5	33.3	4.4	14.9	6.2	25.9
Female	15.3	1.7	3.6	1.7	3.2	--	8.0	--	10.4	--
It doesn't matter	76.4	74.6	92.1	81.6	90.3	66.7	87.6	85.1	83.3	74.1

Table 4-15

When A Couple Has An Argument,
Who Should Usually Have The Final Say?

PARENT'S INCOME

	UNDER $5000		$5000-$10000		$10000-$20000		$20000-$50000		OVER $50000	
	F	M	F	M	F	M	F	M	F	M
	N = 278	N = 56	N = 383	N = 85	N = 581	N = 162	N = 552	N = 217	N = 148	N = 73
Male	10.8	30.4	6.3	20.0	5.0	22.8	4.9	15.7	2.7	15.1
Female	14.0	1.8	8.6	3.5	6.5	--	4.0	1.8	4.1	--
It doesn't matter	75.2	67.9	85.1	76.5	88.5	77.2	91.1	82.5	93.2	84.9

CHAPTER 5
Is There Life After Sex?
Percentage Tables

Table 5-1

Is Sex An Important Part Of Marriage?

	ALL		LIVING TOGETHER	
	F	M	F	M
	N = 2321	N = 681	N = 325	N = 27
Absolutely	48.6	61.8	48.0	51.9
Probably	28.9	22.3	26.8	25.9
It doesn't matter	10.8	7.2	10.5	3.7
Probably not	6.8	6.3	9.2	11.1
Absolutely not	4.9	2.3	5.5	7.4

Table 5-2

Is Sex An Important Part Of Marriage?

ETHNIC GROUP

	BLACK		ANGLO		ASIAN		NATIVE AMERICAN		HISPANIC	
	F	M	F	M	F	M	F	M	F	M
	N=405	N=58	N=1335	N=408	N=31	N=14	N=114	N=47	N=399	N=145
Absolutely	41.2	55.2	53.3	64.5	35.5	71.4	36.0	53.2	45.9	59.3
Probably	27.9	25.9	27.9	21.3	38.7	7.1	36.8	19.1	29.3	26.9
It doesn't matter	9.1	6.9	10.9	6.4	19.4	7.1	11.4	17.0	12.0	6.2
Probably not	11.6	8.6	5.1	5.9	6.5	14.3	8.8	4.3	7.0	5.5
Absolutely not	10.1	3.4	2.8	2.0	--	--	7.0	6.4	5.8	2.1

Table 5-3

Is Sex An Important Part Of Marriage?

PARENT'S INCOME

	UNDER $5000		$5000-$10000		$10000-$20000		$20000-$50000		OVER $50000	
	F	M	F	M	F	M	F	M	F	M
	N=277	N=56	N=379	N=87	N=578	N=163	N=552	N=217	N=149	N=75
Absolutely	35.7	55.4	48.3	51.7	52.1	64.4	54.7	63.1	56.4	65.3
Probably	29.2	23.2	31.7	26.4	28.0	20.2	27.9	23.0	28.2	26.7
I don't know	12.6	5.4	9.0	14.9	9.3	3.7	10.0	8.3	11.4	4.0
Probably not	12.6	14.3	7.4	4.6	6.7	9.2	3.8	4.6	2.0	1.3
Absolutely not	9.7	1.8	3.7	2.3	3.8	2.5	3.6	.9	2.0	2.7

Table 5-4

Is Sex An Important Part Of Marriage?

	Never Pregnant	Had Abortion	Pregnant	All Mothers	Mothers-6 Months +	Fathers
	N=1234	N=72	N=441	N=426	N=241	N=50
Absolutely	51.2	54.2	39.5	50.0	49.0	58.0
Probably	29.7	20.8	34.2	23.2	25.3	24.0
I don't know	10.5	5.6	10.2	11.3	10.4	10.0
Probably not	5.0	11.1	10.4	9.2	10.0	8.0
Absolutely not	3.5	8.3	5.7	6.3	5.4	--

Table 5-5

How important do you think it is for a wife to be a good sex partner?		How important do you think it is for a husband to be a good sex partner?	
ALL		**ALL**	
F	M	F	M
N = 2213	N = 636	N = 2247	N = 639
Very important			
54.1	63.4	51.9	59.6
Somewhat important			
34.1	26.7	35.4	30.7
Not important			
8.5	7.1	9.2	6.7
It doesn't matter at all			
3.3	2.8	3.5	3.0

Table 5-6

Do You Think A Couple Should Have Sexual Intercourse Before They Are Married?

	ALL		**LIVING TOGETHER**	
	F	M	F	M
	N = 2284	N = 675	N = 319	N = 28
Absolutely	9.6	24.7	11.9	25.0
Probably	13.1	14.4	13.2	3.6
It doesn't matter	44.7	34.8	53.0	46.4
Probably not	14.6	14.2	12.5	7.1
Absolutely not	18.0	11.9	9.4	17.9

Table 5-7

Do You Think A Couple Should Have
Sexual Intercourse Before They Are Married?

	URBAN		SUBURBAN		TOWN/FARM	
	F	**M**	**F**	**M**	**F**	**M**
	N = 1178	N = 253	N = 453	N = 235	N = 615	N = 183
Absolutely	10.3	22.9	9.3	24.3	8.8	27.9
Probably	12.9	12.6	14.3	14.9	13.3	16.4
It doesn't matter	49.0	37.2	43.3	34.5	36.3	31.7
Probably not	13.7	15.0	13.9	15.7	17.2	11.5
Absolutely not	14.2	12.3	19.2	10.6	24.4	12.6

Table 5-8

Do You Think A Couple Should Have
Sexual Intercourse Before They Are Married?

	CATHOLIC		BORN-AGAIN CHRISTIAN		PROTESTANT	
	F	**M**	**F**	**M**	**F**	**M**
	N = 831	N = 284	N = 387	N = 117	N = 297	N = 83
Absolutely	7.2	22.9	9.3	17.9	10.8	19.3
Probably	11.7	13.7	10.1	14.5	16.2	18.1
It doesn't matter	48.7	36.6	38.5	33.3	41.4	32.5
Probably not	16.5	16.5	16.8	17.1	17.5	13.3
Absolutely not	15.9	10.2	25.3	17.1	14.1	16.9

Table 5-9

Do You Think A Couple Should Have
Sexual Intercourse Before They Are Married?

	AGE			
	14-16		17-18	
	F	**M**	**F**	**M**
	N = 1126	N = 297	N = 1146	N = 378
Absolutely	9.6	20.9	9.7	27.8
Probably	12.9	14.1	13.4	14.6
It doesn't matter	41.3	32.0	48.2	37.0
Probably not	15.9	18.2	13.2	11.1
Absolutely not	20.3	14.8	15.6	9.5

Table 5-10

Do You Think A Couple Should Have
Sexual Intercourse Before They Are Married?

ETHNIC GROUP

	BLACK		ANGLO		ASIAN		NATIVE AMERICAN		HISPANIC	
	F	M	F	M	F	M	F	M	F	M
	N = 391	N = 58	N = 1324	N = 403	N = 30	N = 15	N = 110	N = 47	N = 392	N = 143
Absolutely	15.3	27.6	9.4	26.3	6.7	20.0	7.3	31.9	4.6	18.9
Probably	20.2	19.0	11.0	12.7	20.0	26.7	10.9	19.1	13.0	13.3
It doesn't matter	42.7	32.8	44.9	33.7	36.7	26.7	53.6	31.9	43.6	40.6
Probably not	10.0	12.1	15.3	15.4	16.7	13.3	11.8	10.6	18.4	13.3
Absolutely not	11.8	8.6	19.4	11.9	20.0	13.3	16.4	6.4	20.4	14.0

Table 5-11

Do You Think A Couple Should Have
Sexual Intercourse Before They Are Married?

	Never Pregnant	Had Abortion	Pregnant	All Mothers	Mothers- 6 Months +	Fathers
	N = 1220	N = 69	N = 433	N = 419	N = 239	N = 50
Absolutely	8.3	17.4	9.5	12.9	13.0	34.0
Probably	13.2	14.5	12.5	15.0	15.3	18.0
It doesn't matter	36.8	52.2	56.4	54.7	51.5	36.0
Probably not	16.8	8.7	14.1	11.2	10.9	10.0
Absolutely not	14.9	7.2	7.6	6.2	9.2	2.0

CHAPTER 6
Who Does The Housework
Percentage Tables

Table 6-1

In A Good Marriage, Who Should Be
Responsible For The Following Tasks?

	ALL RESPONDENTS	
	F	M
Vacuuming house:	N = 2340	N = 681
Husband	1.1	2.5
Wife	38.4	41.9
Both	40.7	35.5
Doesn't matter	19.8	20.1
Mopping floors:	N = 2339	N = 681
Husband	1.6	2.2
Wife	46.8	53.3
Both	34.8	27.0
Doesn't matter	16.9	17.5
Preparing meals:	N = 2320	N = 676
Husband	.8	1.8
Wife	37.5	40.8
Both	49.8	42.6
Doesn't matter	11.9	14.8
Washing dishes:	N = 2336	N = 682
Husband	1.5	3.1
Wife	24.2	27.7
Both	63.9	56.7
Doesn't matter	10.4	12.5
Washing clothes:	N = 3326	N = 684
Husband	1.8	2.5
Wife	55.7	52.0
Both	33.2	31.0
Doesn't matter	9.3	14.5
Washing car:	N = 2319	N = 678
Husband	32.0	49.1
Wife	.8	3.7
Both	48.5	28.9
Doesn't matter	18.7	18.3
Mowing lawn:	N = 2332	N = 679
Husband	56.8	71.0
Wife	.9	2.8
Both	29.0	1.9
Doesn't matter	13.3	10.3

Table 6-2
TEEN MOTHER PROGRAM ALUMNAE SURVEY

In your *first* marriage or living-together partnership, who was/is responsible for the following tasks?

Vacuuming:	N = 81	
	I am	63.0%
	Mostly me	26%
	He is	--
	Mostly him	1.0%
	Both of us	10%
Mopping:	N = 80	
	I am	61.2%
	Mostly me	27.5%
	He is	1.3%
	Mostly him	1.3%
	Both of us	8.8%
Washing Dishes:	N = 80	
	I am	51.3%
	Mostly me	27.5%
	He is	--
	Mostly him	1.3%
	Both of us	20.0%
Laundry:	N = 81	
	I am	63.0%
	Mostly me	17.0%
	He is	--
	Mostly him	1.0%
	Both of us	19.0%
Washing Car:	N = 80	
	I am	11.3%
	Mostly me	--
	He is	47.5%
	Mostly him	21.3%
	Both of us	20%
Mowing Lawn:	N = 70	
	I am	6.0%
	Mostly me	--
	He is	51.0%
	Mostly him	27.0%
	Both of us	16.0%

Table 6-3

In A Good Marriage, Who Should Be
Responsible For The Following Tasks?

	LIVING-TOGETHER GROUP	
	F	M
Vacuuming house:	N = 325	N = 28
Husband	.3	7.1
Wife	40.9	28.6
Both	42.8	53.6
Doesn't matter	16.0	10.7
Mopping floors:	N = 326	N = 27
Husband	1.8	3.7
Wife	49.1	44.4
Both	36.5	40.7
Doesn't matter	12.6	11.1
Preparing meals:	N = 322	N = 27
Husband	1.2	3.7
Wife	46.9	29.6
Both	43.2	59.3
Doesn't matter	8.7	7.4
Washing dishes:	N = 328	N = 28
Husband	1.2	3.6
Wife	35.4	25.0
Both	55.8	60.7
Doesn't matter	7.6	10.7
Washing clothes:	N = 326	N = 28
Husband	1.8	--
Wife	58.0	42.9
Both	34.0	50.0
Doesn't matter	6.1	7.1
Washing car:	N = 320	N = 26
Husband	36.6	30.8
Wife	1.2	3.8
Both	48.4	50.0
Doesn't matter	13.7	15.4
Mowing lawn:	N = 326	N = 27
Husband	62.9	51.9
Wife	.9	--
Both	26.7	33.3
Doesn't matter	9.5	14.8

Table 6-4

In A Good Marriage, Who Should Be Responsible For The Following Tasks?

ETHNIC GROUP

	BLACK		ANGLO		ASIAN		NATIVE AMERICAN		HISPANIC	
	F	**M**	**F**	**M**	**F**	**M**	**F**	**M**	**F**	**M**
Vacuuming house:	N = 413	N = 57	N = 1341	N = 409	N = 31	N = 15	N = 112	N = 46	N = 405	N = 145
Husband	2.4	7.0	.4	1.7	3.2	--	1.8	2.2	1.5	3.4
Wife	33.2	42.1	38.6	42.5	41.9	33.3	35.7	39.1	44.7	42.1
Both	47.7	36.8	39.1	35.5	41.9	33.3	42.9	41.3	37.⁸	33.8
Doesn't matter	16.7	14.0	22.0	20.3	12.9	33.3	19.6	17.4	16.0	20.7
Mopping floors:	N = 313	N = 59	N = 1342	N = 408	N = 29	N = 15	N = 113	N = 46	N = 407	N = 144
Husband	5.1	5.1	.6	2.0	3.4	13.3	3.5	4.3	.5	--
Wife	35.1	59.3	48.6	50.7	41.4	46.7	42.5	54.3	54.3	59.0
Both	46.0	22.0	33.0	28.9	27.6	20.0	35.4	17.4	29.7	27.8
Doesn't matter	13.8	13.6	17.8	18.4	27.6	20.0	18.6	23.9	15.5	13.2
Preparing meals:	N = 409	N = 56	N = 1333	N = 407	N = 28	N = 15	N = 113	N = 46	N = 401	N = 143
Husband	1.0	--	.6	2.0	3.6	6.7	.9	2.2	.7	1.4
Wife	41.6	44.6	33.6	34.6	39.3	53.3	36.3	37.0	46.9	57.3
Both	49.4	46.4	52.5	46.7	42.9	20.0	51.3	50.0	41.6	29.4
Doesn't matter	8.1	8.9	13.3	16.7	14.3	20.0	11.5	10.9	10.7	11.9
Washing dishes:	N = 412	N = 59	N = 1341	N = 411	N = 30	N = 14	N = 115	N = 46	N = 404	N = 143
Husband	3.2	--	1.0	4.4	6.7	--	.9	2.2	1.5	1.4
Wife	27.4	33.9	21.6	23.1	16.7	14.3	21.7	28.3	30.7	38.5
Both	61.2	52.5	66.1	59.4	60.0	64.3	70.4	52.2	58.7	53.1
Doesn't matter	8.3	13.6	11.3	13.1	16.7	21.4	7.0	17.4	9.2	7.0
Washing clothes:	N = 411	N =	N = 1340	N = 410	N = 31	N = 15	N = 115	N = 46	N = 402	N = 145
Husband	2.2	1.7	1.5	1.7	6.7	--	1.7	4.3	2.0	4.8
Wife	54.3	39.0	54.0	51.7	50.0	46.7	54.8	45.7	63.4	61.4
Both	37.0	39.0	33.7	32.0	33.3	26.7	33.9	34.8	28.1	24.8
Doesn't matter	6.6	20.3	10.8	14.6	10.0	26.7	9.6	15.2	6.5	9.0
Washing car:	N = 408	N = 58	N = 1334	N = 408	N = 28	N = 15	N = 113	N = 45	N = 403	N = 143
Husband	46.8	58.6	25.2	42.2	25.0	46.7	27.4	57.8	40.9	62.2
Wife	1.7	5.2	.4	3.7	--	6.7	1.8	2.2	.7	3.5
Both	38.0	19.0	53.⁵	34.6	46.4	20.0	54.0	22.2	42.2	20.3
Doesn't matter	13.5	17.2	20.8	19.6	28.6	26.7	16.8	17.8	16.1	14.0
Mowing lawn:	N = 413	N = 59	N = 1341	N = 408	N = 29	N = 14	N = 114	N = 46	N = 401	N = 143
Husband	70.0	64.4	48.2	67.9	62.1	71.4	53.5	71.7	71.8	81.8
Wife	1.9	1.7	.6	3.2	--	7.1	--	2.2	1.0	2.1
Both	19.9	25.4	35.6	16.9	24.1	7.1	31.6	13.0	16.7	10.5
Doesn't matter	8.2	8.5	15.6	12.0	13.8	14.3	14.9	13.0	10.5	5.6

Table 6-5

In A Good Marriage, Who Should Be
Responsible For The Following Tasks?

	CATHOLIC		BORN-AGAIN CHRISTIANS		PROTESTANTS	
	F	M	F	M	F	M
Vacuuming house:	N = 847	N = 289	N = 392	N = 116	N = 304	N = 83
Husband	1.4	3.1	1.0	1.7	.3	--
Wife	37.2	42.9	45.4	40.5	35.9	48.2
Both	41.1	34.3	35.7	35.3	41.4	36.1
Doesn't matter	20.3	19.7	17.9	22.4	22.4	15.7
Mopping floors:	N = 851	N = 288	N = 394	N = 118	N = 306	N = 84
Husband	.8	3.5	1.8	2.5	1.3	1.2
Wife	47.7	53.1	53.0	52.7	44.4	59.5
Both	32.2	26.0	31.0	30.5	35.9	28.6
Doesn't matter	19.3	17.4	14.2	15.3	18.3	10.7
Preparing meals:	N = 842	N = 286	N = 390	N = 116	N = 302	N = 83
Husband	.7	2.1	.3	--	.7	1.2
Wife	36.6	46.2	45.9	37.9	32.5	36.1
Both	49.6	34.6	42.3	52.6	56.3	54.2
Doesn't matter	13.1	17.1	11.5	9.5	10.6	8.4
Washing dishes:	N = 851	N = 287	N = 392	N = 118	N = 304	N = 84
Husband	1.9	3.8	2.3	2.5	1.0	4.8
Wife	22.9	27.9	28.6	24.6	18.1	32.1
Both	63.9	55.7	59.2	61.0	68.8	54.8
Doesn't matter	11.3	12.5	9.9	11.9	12.2	8.3
Washing clothes:	N = 848	N = 291	N = 394	N = 118	N = 304	N = 84
Husband	2.1	3.1	1.5	3.4	1.3	1.2
Wife	57.0	56.4	62.2	45.8	47.0	50.0
Both	32.5	26.5	28.9	35.6	38.8	38.1
Doesn't matter	8.4	14.1	7.4	15.3	12.8	10.7
Washing car:	N = 845	N = 287	N = 391	N = 116	N = 305	N = 84
Husband	30.9	53.7	36.6	50.0	27.2	40.5
Wife	1.2	2.4	.5	3.4	.3	4.8
Both	49.0	24.7	46.0	32.8	48.9	36.9
Doesn't matter	18.9	19.2	16.9	13.8	23.6	17.9
Mowing lawn:	N = 845	N = 288	N = 392	N = 117	N = 306	N = 84
Husband	60.7	73.6	58.9	76.1	45.4	65.5
Wife	.5	2.1	.8	2.6	1.6	2.4
Both	26.2	12.2	28.8	17.1	33.0	22.6
Doesn't matter	12.7	12.2	11.5	4.3	19.9	9.5

Table 6-6

In A Good Marriage, Who Should Be Responsible For The Following Tasks?

	PARENTS' INCOME									
	UNDER $5000		$5000-$10000		$10000-$20000		$20000-$50000		OVER $50000	
	F	M	F	M	F	M	F	M	F	M
Vacuuming house:	N = 280	N = 55	N = 384	N = 86	N = 582	N = 165	N = 550	N = 218	N = 150	N = 74
Husband	1.1	3.6	1.6	1.2	.7	1.8	.7	.9	.7	6.8
Wife	48.9	52.7	45.8	45.3	37.8	44.8	32.7	39.9	32.7	32.4
Both	36.8	29.1	37.2	43.0	39.7	31.5	44.0	38.1	46.0	35.1
Doesn't matter	13.2	14.5	15.4	10.5	21.8	21.8	22.5	21.1	20.7	25.7
Mopping floors:	N = 281	N = 55	N = 384	N = 86	N = 581	N = 165	N = 553	N = 217	N = 149	N = 74
Husband	3.6	3.6	2.3	2.3	.5	2.4	.7	1.4	1.3	4.1
Wife	53.7	65.5	51.8	54.7	49.1	53.9	43.4	53.9	36.2	43.2
Both	29.9	21.8	31.0	31.4	32.5	24.2	38.0	27.2	43.0	32.4
Doesn't matter	12.8	9.1	14.8	11.6	17.9	14.4	17.9	17.5	19.5	20.3
Preparing meals:	N = 281	N = 54	N = 379	N = 86	N = 577	N = 164	N = 545	N = 215	N = 149	N = 74
Husband	.7	3.7	.8	1.2	.3	1.2	.6	1.9	1.3	2.7
Wife	47.3	50.0	41.4	45.3	37.1	43.9	33.2	40.0	30.2	25.7
Both	44.8	40.7	46.4	43.0	49.7	39.0	52.3	41.9	59.7	56.8
Doesn't matter	7.1	5.6	11.3	10.5	12.8	15.9	13.9	16.3	8.7	14.9
Washing dishes:	N = 281	N = 56	N = 383	N = 86	N = 582	N = 164	N = 553	N = 218	N = 149	N = 75
Husband	1.4	--	1.8	3.5	1.0	1.8	.9	4.1	3.4	5.3
Wife	36.7	37.5	28.7	29.1	25.6	28.7	16.3	23.9	17.4	25.3
Both	53.7	58.9	60.8	57.0	60.7	55.5	71.1	59.2	72.5	53.3
Doesn't matter	8.2	3.6	8.6	10.5	12.7	14.0	11.8	12.8	6.7	16.0
Washing clothes:	N = 280	N = 55	N = 385	N = 86	N = 579	N = 164	N = 551	N = 220	N = 150	N = 75
Husband	2.1	1.8	2.1	2.3	1.4	1.8	1.3	2.7	3.3	4.0
Wife	60.0	52.7	59.5	52.3	57.2	53.0	50.6	53.2	52.7	48.0
Both	33.6	27.3	29.1	25.6	32.3	32.9	35.8	29.5	36.0	37.3
Doesn't matter	4.3	18.2	9.4	19.8	9.2	12.2	12.3	14.5	8.0	10.7
Washing car:	N = 282	N = 56	N = 381	N = 85	N = 577	N = 164	N = 547	N = 216	N = 145	N = 75
Husband	47.2	64.3	39.9	51.8	29.1	54.3	24.3	41.7	22.1	44.0
Wife	1.1	--	1.8	4.7	.5	4.9	--	2.8	--	5.3
Both	37.2	23.2	42.8	24.7	50.4	22.0	53.6	34.3	61.4	33.3
Doesn't matter	14.5	12.5	15.5	18.8	19.9	18.9	22.1	21.3	16.6	17.3
Mowing lawn:	N = 281	N = 56	N = 381	N = 85	N = 579	N = 165	N = 553	N = 216	N = 149	N = 75
Husband	70.8	78.6	64.3	70.6	52.7	67.9	50.5	70.4	56.4	74.7
Wife	1.4	--	.3	1.2	1.0	4.2	.7	3.2	.7	1.3
Both	19.2	10.7	24.4	18.8	32.1	17.0	32.5	14.4	30.9	18.7
Doesn't matter	8.4	10.7	11.0	9.4	14.2	10.9	16.3	12.0	12.1	5.3

Table 6-7

In A Good Marriage, Who Should Be
Responsible For The Following Tasks?

	Easier Than Expected F	Harder Than Expected M
Vacuuming house:	N = 65	N = 109
Husband	--	.9
Wife	44.6	33.0
Both	41.5	49.5
Doesn't matter	13.8	16.5
Mopping floors:	N = 65	N = 109
Husband	4.6	2.8
Wife	46.2	44.0
Both	32.3	42.2
Doesn't matter	16.9	11.0
Preparing meals:	N = 65	N = 109
Husband	--	1.8
Wife	50.8	48.6
Both	40.0	43.1
Doesn't matter	9.2	6.4
Washing dishes:	N = 65	N = 111
Husband	3.1	1.8
Wife	35.4	33.3
Both	52.3	56.8
Doesn't matter	9.2	8.1
Washing clothes:	N = 65	N = 110
Husband	1.5	2.7
Wife	58.5	60.0
Both	35.4	31.8
Doesn't matter	4.6	5.5
Washing car:	N = 64	N = 108
Husband	48.4	35.2
Wife	3.1	1.9
Both	39.1	51.9
Doesn't matter	9.4	11.1
Mowing lawn:	N = 65	N = 111
Husband	69.2	60.4
Wife	1.5	1.8
Both	20.0	30.6
Doesn't matter	9.2	7.2

CHAPTER 7
Money — Reality Strikes Again
Percentage Tables

Table 7-1

How Much Do You Think Getting Married
At Age 18 Or Younger Would Change Your
Life As Far As Money Is Concerned?

	ALL	
	F N = 2321	**M** N = 678
I'd have more money	22.9	18.1
I'd have less money	56.0	70.6
No change	21.1	11.2

Table 7-2

How Much Do You Think Getting Married At Age 18 or Younger
Would Change Your Life As Far As Money Is Concerned?

	ETHNIC GROUP									
	BLACK		ANGLO		ASIAN		NATIVE AMERICAN		HISPANIC	
	F	M	F	M	F	M	F	M	F	M
	N = 407	N = 57	N = 1338	N = 410	N = 30	N = 15	N = 113	N = 45	N = 398	N = 142
I'd have more money	38.1	26.3	19.2	16.8	3.3	26.7	18.6	24.4	21.9	13.4
I'd have less money	38.3	59.6	62.6	72.7	63.3	66.7	50.4	60.0	53.8	75.4
No change	23.6	14.0	18.2	10.5	33.3	6.7	31.0	15.6	24.4	11.3

Table 7-3

How Much Do You Think Getting Married At Age 18 Or Younger Would Change Your Life As Far As Money Is Concerned?

	UNDER $5000		$5000-$10000		$10000-$20000		$20000-$50000		OVER $50000	
	F	M	F	M	F	M	F	M	F	M
	N = 281	N = 55	N = 379	N = 86	N = 580	N = 163	N = 552	N = 219	N = 148	N = 74
I'd have more money	35.2	29.1	28.5	15.1	18.6	20.2	18.3	13.2	15.5	22.0
I'd have less money	37.7	60.0	48.8	68.6	61.4	71.2	64.9	72.2	73.0	63.5
No change	27.0	10.9	22.7	16.3	20.0	8.6	16.8	9.6	11.5	9.5

PARENT'S INCOME

Table 7-4

Do You Think Having "Enough" Money Is An Important Part Of A Good Marriage?

	ALL		LIVING TOGETHER	
	F	M	F	M
	N = 2315	N = 676	N = 326	N = 28
Absolutely	40.9	50.6	39.2	42.9
Probably	34.8	28.0	34.4	32.1
I don't know	10.1	7.8	9.8	3.6
Probably not	9.7	8.9	10.1	7.1
Absolutely not	4.5	4.7	5.8	14.3

Table 7-5

Has Money — Or Lack Of It — Been A Problem In Your Relationship?

	LIVING TOGETHER	
	F	M
	N = 303	N = 23
Always	9.9	--
Most of the time	11.9	21.7
Sometimes	40.3	39.1
Not often	22.8	26.1
Never	15.2	13.0

Table 7-6

Has Money — Or Lack Of It — Been A Greater Problem Than You Expected?

	LIVING TOGETHER	
	F	**M**
	N = 305	N = 23
Yes, much greater	10.5	8.7
Yes, somewhat greater	34.4	30.4
No	55.1	60.9

Table 7-7

In A Good Marriage, Who Should Be Responsible For Deciding How Money Is Spent?

	All		Living Together		Pregnant	All Mothers	Mothers- 6 Months +
	F	**M**	**F**	**M**	**F**	**F**	**F**
	N = 2339	N = 684	N = 323	N = 28	N = 440	N = 434	N = 245
Husband	1.8	9.4	1.9	7.1	8.3	1.4	1.6
Wife	4.0	5.7	6.8	7.1	11.7	7.8	8.2
Both	91.4	80.1	89.2	82.1	.71.2	87.1	86.5
It doesn't matter	2.7	4.8	2.2	3.6	8.8	3.7	3.7

Table 7-8

Do You Think It Is Important That A Husband And Wife Agree On How They Spend Money

	ALL		LIVING TOGETHER	
	F	M	F	M
	N = 2322	N = 680	N = 328	N = 28
Absolutely	82.1	71.6	85.1	78.6
Probably	14.3	20.7	11.9	10.7
I don't know	2.1	4.0	1.2	3.6
Probably not	1.0	1.8	1.5	3.6
Absolutely not	.5	1.9	.3	3.6

Table 7-9

In A Good Marriage, Who Should Be Responsible For Paying Bills?

	All		Living Together		Pregnant	All Mothers	Mothers- 6 Months +
	F	M	F	M	F	F	F
	N = 2344	N = 683	N = 326	N = 28	N = 444	N = 434	N = 246
Husband	8.7	15.5	8.9	14.3	8.3	7.1	1.6
Wife	8.4	14.5	13.5	17.9	11.7	10.6	8.2
Both	72.1	59.3	68.1	53.6	71.2	71.9	86.5
It doesn't matter	10.7	10.7	9.5	14.3	8.8	10.4	3.7

Table 7-10

In A Good Marriage, Who Should Be Responsible For Paying Bills?

	RELIGIOUS AFFILIATION					
	CATHOLIC		BORN-AGAIN CHRISTIAN		PROTESTANT	
	F	M	F	M	F	M
	N = 850	N = 289	N = 392	N = 117	N = 306	N = 84
Husband	7.4	16.3	15.1	20.5	5.9	14.3
Wife	9.8	13.8	7.9	12.8	8.5	14.3
Both	71.9	60.9	68.4	59.0	71.6	58.3
It doesn't matter	10.9	9.0	8.7	7.7	14.1	13.1

Table 7-11

How Important Do You Think It Is
For A Husband To Be A Good Money Manger?

	All		Living Together		Happy	Unhappy	Pregnant	All Mothers	Mothers- 6 Months +
	F	M	F	M	F/M	F/M	F	F	F
	N = 2271	N = 651	N = 325	N = 27	N = 292	N = 40	N = 431	N = 412	N = 230
Very important	60.0	61.1	60.0	48.1	62.3	42.5	58.7	63.1	66.1
Somewhat important	35.4	33.0	34.2	37.0	31.2	50.0	36.0	30.3	27.4
Not important	2.1	3.4	2.2	11.1	2.4	7.5	1.6	2.9	3.5
It doesn't matter at all	2.5	2.5	3.7	3.7	4.1	--	3.7	3.6	3.0

Table 7-12

How Important Do You Think It Is
For A Wife To Be A Good Money Manager?

	All		Living Together		Happy	Unhappy	Pregnant	All Mothers	Mothers- 6 Months +
	F	M	F	M	F/M	F/M	F	F	F
	N = 2239	N = 639	N = 327	N = 27	N = 294	N = 40	N = 425	N = 405	N = 230
Very important	51.2	44.8	58.3	40.7	59.5	55.0	48.9	58.8	67.0
Somewhat important	42.2	39.9	35.6	51.9	34.0	40.0	41.6	34.1	26.5
Not important	4.2	11.0	3.7	3.7	3.7	2.5	5.2	4.4	4.3
It doesn't matter at all	2.5	4.4	2.5	3.7	2.7	2.5	4.2	2.7	2.2

Table 7-13

In A Good Marriage, Who Should Be Responsible For Earning Money?

	ALL		LIVING TOGETHER	
	F	M	F	M
	N = 2328	N = 676	N = 318	N = 28
Husband	17.8	32.4	23.3	32.1
Wife	.7	2.1	.6	3.6
Both	69.8	51.8	66.7	50.0
It doesn't matter	11.6	13.8	10.4	14.3

Table 7-14

In A Good Marriage, Should The Husband Earn Most Of The Money?

PARENT'S INCOME

	UNDER $5000		$5000-$10000		$10000-$20000		$20000-$50000		OVER $50000	
	F	M	F	M	F	M	F	M	F	M
	N = 279	N = 54	N = 375	N = 86	N = 580	N = 165	N = 548	N = 215	N = 149	N = 73
Absolutely	26.5	27.8	21.9	31.4	18.8	24.2	13.3	26.0	14.8	16.4
Probably	21.9	29.6	26.4	15.1	19.1	22.4	25.2	22.3	26.2	27.4
It doesn't matter	43.7	38.9	43.7	51.2	54.1	50.3	54.9	48.8	51.0	47.9
Probably not	3.6	1.9	4.3	2.3	2.9	1.2	4.2	1.9	6.7	1.4
Absolutely not	4.3	1.9	3.7	--	5.0	1.8	2.4	.9	1.3	6.8

Table 7-15

Males — Would It Be All Right With You If Your Wife Wanted To Get A Job?

	ALL M	LIVING TOGETHER M
	N = 645	N = 27
Absolutely	50.9	55.6
Probably	29.1	29.6
I don't know	9.3	11.1
Probably not	2.9	--
Absolutely not	1.6	3.7

Table 7-16

Males — Would It Be All Right With You
If Your Wife Made More Money Than You Did?

	ALL M N = 643	LIVING TOGETHER M N = 27
Absolutely	39.8	51.9
Probably	29.1	14.8
I don't know	17.3	25.9
Probably not	9.2	--
Absolutely not	4.7	7.4

Table 7-17

MALES: Do you expect your wife to work outside your home until you have children?

FEMALES: Do you expect to work outside your home until you have children?

	All F	All M	Living Together F	Living Together M	Pregnant F	All Mothers F	Mothers- 6 Months + F
	N = 2226	N = 651	N = 307	N = 27	N = 426	N = 386	N = 213
Absolutely	36.3	11.1	28.7	11.1	23.0	26.7	32.9
Probably	42.5	34.1	32.9	25.9	39.4	37.6	36.6
It doesn't matter	12.7	39.8	22.1	40.7	19.0	22.5	22.1
Probably not	6.1	8.3	12.1	3.7	13.6	9.8	6.1
Absolutely not	2.3	6.8	4.2	18.5	4.9	3.4	2.3

Table 7-18

MALES: Do you expect your wife to work outside your home after
your children are in school?

FEMALES: Do you expect to work outside your home after
your children are in school?

	ALL		LIVING TOGETHER	
	F	**M**	**F**	**M**
	N = 2261	N = 646	N = 320	N = 27
Absolutely	33.6	11.0	41.9	14.8
Probably	50.1	31.6	44.4	40.7
It doesn't matter	8.8	41.5	5.9	29.6
Probably not	6.2	10.1	7.2	3.7
Absolutely not	1.3	5.9	.6	11.1

Table 7-19

MALES: Do you expect your wife to work outside your home while
you have children under two years of age?

FEMALES: Do you expect to work outside your home while you
have children under two years of age?

	All		Living Together		Pregnant	All Mothers	Mothers- 6 Months +
	F	**M**	**F**	**M**	**F**	**F**	**F**
	N = 2239	N = 648	N = 316	N = 26	N = 428	N = 410	N = 228
Absolutely	7.2	4.2	13.0	7.7	10.0	15.6	17.5
Probably	24.4	7.6	28.2	15.4	31.1	32.2	32.5
It doesn't matter	8.3	20.5	9.5	23.1	11.2	10.7	9.6
Probably not	40.8	41.0	30.4	26.9	31.3	28.5	26.8
Absolutely not	18.6	26.7	19.0	26.9	16.4	12.9	13.6

Table 7-20

(Males) Would it be all right with you if your wife chose to stay home instead of getting a job?

(Females) Would it be all right with you if your husband wanted to stay home while you got a job to support your family?

	ALL		LIVING TOGETHER	
	F	M	F	M
	N = 2213	N = 637	N = 311	N = 27
Absolutely	3.9	41.8	5.1	51.9
Probably	5.6	31.1	7.1	14.8
I don't know	12.0	16.6	10.3	25.9
Probably not	22.7	6.3	20.3	--
Absolutely not	55.7	4.2	57.2	7.4

Table 7-21

Males — Would It Be All Right With You If Your Wife Chose To Stay Home Instead Of Getting A Job?

Females — Would It Be All Right With You If Your Husband Wanted To Stay Home While You Got A Job To Support Your Family?

RELIGION

	CATHOLIC		BORN-AGAIN CHRISTIAN		PROTESTANT	
	F	M	F	M	F	M
	N = 810	N = 278	N = 379	N = 109	N = 285	N = 76
Absolutely	3.8	41.0	2.9	39.4	4.6	44.7
Probably	5.2	34.2	4.7	32.1	6.7	30.3
I don't know	12.1	14.4	9.2	20.2	13.7	18.4
Probably not	24.2	6.5	22.2	6.4	27.7	1.3
Absolutely not	54.7	4.0	60.9	1.8	47.7	5.3

CHAPTER 8
Three-Generation Living
Percentage Tables

Table 8-1

How Do You Feel About A Young Couple
Living With Either His Or Her Parents?

| | ALL | | LIVING TOGETHER | |
	F	M	F	M
	N = 2326	N = 680	N = 325	N = 27
Good idea	3.9	8.2	6.2	22.2
OK until we save some money	32.6	30.1	44.9	33.3
I'd rather not	50.8	47.5	40.6	33.3
I'm totally against it	12.7	14.1	8.3	11.1

Table 8-2
How Do You Feel About A Young Couple
Living With Either His Or Her Parents?

| | LIVING TOGETHER | |
	Married F	Not Married M
	N = 166	N = 180
Good idea	4.2	7.2
OK until we save some money	33.7	53.3
I'd rather not	48.8	33.3
I'm totally against it	13.3	6.1

Table 8-3

How Do You Feel About A Couple Living With Either His Or Her Parents?

	ETHNIC GROUP									
	BLACK		ANGLO		ASIAN		NATIVE AMERICAN		HISPANIC	
	F	M	F	M	F	M	F	M	F	M
	N = 410	N = 59	N = 1338	N = 406	N = 30	N = 15	N = 111	N = 48	N = 402	N = 144
Good idea	6.6	6.8	2.8	7.1	3.3	26.7	8.1	10.4	3.7	9.0
OK until we save some money	30.5	37.3	30.6	28.8	36.7	53.3	36.0	37.5	39.1	26.4
I would rather not	46.1	39.0	55.2	50.7	43.3	13.3	45.0	43.8	43.5	47.2
I'm totally against it	16.8	16.9	11.4	13.3	16.7	6.7	10.8	8.3	13.7	17.4

Table 8-4

How Do You Feel About A Young Couple Living With Either His Or Her Parents?

	RELIGION					
	CATHOLIC		BORN-AGAIN CHRISTIAN		PROTESTANT	
	F	M	F	M	F	M
	N = 850	N = 287	N = 392	N = 116	N = 305	N = 84
Good idea	4.4	8.0	4.6	8.6	2.6	6.0
OK until we save some money	34.9	28.9	31.6	23.3	26.2	36.9
I would rather not	48.2	49.8	49.0	50.9	58.7	44.0
I'm totally against it	12.5	13.2	14.8	17.2	12.5	13.1

Table 8-5

How Do You Feel About A Young Couple Living With Either His Or Her Parents?

	PARENT'S INCOME									
	UNDER $5000		$5000-$10000		$10000-$20000		$20000-$50000		OVER $50000	
	F	M	F	M	F	M	F	M	F	M
	N = 281	N = 56	N = 385	N = 85	N = 580	N = 166	N = 553	N = 220	N = 146	N = 73
Good idea	7.5	23.2	4.4	9.4	2.4	9.1	1.8	4.1	2.1	6.8
OK until we save some money	33.8	26.8	34.5	40.0	31.4	29.3	33.1	25.9	26.0	28.8
I would rather not	44.1	33.9	48.8	34.1	53.1	52.4	53.2	55.9	58.2	39.7
I'm totally against it	14.6	16.1	12.2	16.5	13.1	9.1	11.9	14.1	13.7	24.7

Table 8-6

How Is Your Relationship With Your Father?

	Living Together All		Living Together All		Married	Single
	F	M	F	M	F	M
	N = 2280	N = 672	N = 319	N = 28	N = 166	N = 176
Very Good	25.1	31.0	23.5	32.1	30.1	16.5
Good	29.6	32.3	25.4	25.0	25.3	25.0
Fair	22.6	18.2	21.0	10.7	19.3	22.7
Poor	10.4	8.9	9.7	7.1	8.4	11.9
No relationship	12.3	3.1	20.4	25.0	16.9	23.9

Table 8-7

How Is Your Relationship With Your Mother?

	UNDER $5000		$5000-$10000		$10000-$20000		$20000-$50000		OVER $50000	
	F	M	F	M	F	M	F	M	F	M
	N = 280	N = 55	N = 378	N = 86	N = 582	N = 166	N = 555	N = 219	N = 149	N = 73
Very good	42.5	52.7	40.7	53.5	41.1	36.1	43.6	39.7	43.6	45.2
Good	32.5	21.8	29.9	25.6	32.8	38.0	31.4	40.2	32.2	38.4
Fair	15.7	14.5	22.2	16.3	18.4	15.1	17.7	14.6	16.1	12.3
Poor	6.8	7.3	4.5	3.5	5.8	6.6	4.7	2.7	5.4	1.4
No relationship	2.5	3.6	2.6	1.2	1.9	4.2	2.7	2.7	2.7	2.7

PARENT'S INCOME

How Is Your Relationship With Your Father?

	N = 273	N = 52	N = 366	N = 84	N = 563	N = 161	N = 547	N = 219	N = 149	N = 75
Very good	19.0	34.6	22.7	26.2	23.1	27.3	28.7	32.9	31.5	32.0
Good	21.6	11.5	27.6	32.1	29.8	34.8	33.1	33.3	34.9	33.3
Fair	21.6	25.0	22.4	15.5	24.2	19.9	22.9	18.7	18.8	18.7
Poor	11.7	11.5	11.2	10.7	12.6	8.1	8.6	7.3	9.4	9.3
No relationship	26.0	17.3	16.1	15.5	10.3	9.9	6.8	7.8	5.4	6.7

CHAPTER 9
Who Parents The Children?
Percentage Tables

Table 9-1

Do You Think It Is Important For A Child To Live With Both Of His/Her Parents?

	All		Living Together	
	F	M	F	M
	N = 2428	N = 690	N = 328	N = 28
Absolutely	58.9	65.0	61.2	78.6
Probably	23.1	23.8	22.8	10.7
It doesn't matter	13.3	7.4	12.9	3.6
Probably not	3.1	2.8	1.8	3.6
Absolutely not	1.6	1.0	1.2	3.6

Table 9-2

In A Good Marriage, Who Should Be Responsible For The Following Tasks?

| | All | | Living Together | |
	F	**M**	**F**	**M**
Playing w/children	N = 2345	N = 673	N = 328	N = 28
Husband	.9	2.1	.6	--
Wife	.6	4.5	.9	7.1
Both	96.1	85.9	95.4	89.3
Doesn't matter	2.4	7.6	3.0	3.6
Feeding babies/ children	N = 2331	N = 678	N = 323	N = 28
Husband	.4	1.5	.3	--
Wife	14.9	25.1	14.6	14.3
Both	79.2	63.0	78.6	78.6
Doesn't matter	5.5	10.5	6.5	7.1
Changing diapers	N = 2332	N = 676	N = 326	N = 27
Husband	.6	.9	.6	--
Wife	13.7	37.9	19.0	29.6
Both	77.5	50.1	73.3	59.3
Doesn't matter	8.2	11.1	7.1	11.1
Discipline	N = 2331	N = 675	N = 324	N = 27
Husband	2.1	7.6	2.2	3.7
Wife	1.7	4.9	1.9	11.1
Both	92.7	80.9	93.5	77.8
Doesn't matter	3.5	6.7	2.5	7.4
Bathing Baby	N = 2337	N = 681	N = 326	N = 28
Husband	.5	.9	.3	--
Wife	28.8	37.3	31.6	14.3
Both	62.7	48.3	62.6	71.4
Doesn't matter	8.0	13.5	5.5	14.3
Putting baby to bed	N = 2332	N = 680	N = 327	N = 28
Husband	.6	1.2	.6	3.6
Wife	11.1	16.5	16.2	3.6
Both	79.2	66.2	75.2	71.4
Doesn't matter	9.2	16.2	8.0	21.4
Putting toddler to bed	N = 2318	N = 677	N = 323	N = 27
Husband	2.0	3.0	2.2	--
Wife	9.5	18.2	11.5	14.8
Both	76.8	59.5	76.2	74.1
Doesn't matter	11.7	19.4	10.2	11.1

Table 9-3

In A Good Marriage, Who Should Be Responsible For The Following Tasks?

ETHNIC GROUP

	BLACK		ANGLO		ASIAN		NATIVE AMERICAN		HISPANIC	
	F	M	F	M	F	M	F	M	F	M
Playing w/children	N = 414	N = 58	N = 1344	N = 405	N = 30	N = 15	N = 115	N = 46	N = 406	N = 140
Husband	2.2	1.7	.4	2.0	--	--	.9	2.2	1.2	2.9
Wife	1.2	5.2	.2	4.7	6.7	--	--	2.2	1.0	5.0
Both	93.5	84.5	97.5	86.7	90.0	80.0	96.5	80.4	94.8	86.4
Doesn't matter	3.1	8.6	1.9	6.7	3.3	20.0	2.6	15.2	3.0	5.7
Feeding babies/children	N = 411	N = 59	N = 1336	N = 406	N = 29	N = 15	N = 114	N = 46	N = 405	N = 143
Husband	.5	--	.2	2.0	3.4	6.7	--	--	.5	.7
Wife	19.2	20.3	12.1	21.4	13.8	26.7	14.9	28.3	19.8	36.4
Both	73.2	67.8	83.1	66.5	79.3	53.3	81.6	56.5	72.3	53.8
Doesn't matter	7.1	11.9	4.6	10.1	3.4	13.3	3.5	15.2	7.4	9.1
Changing diapers	N = 410	N = 59	N = 1338	N = 405	N = 29	N = 15	N = 115	N = 45	N = 405	N = 143
Husband	2.0	1.7	.3	.7	3.4	--	--	--	--	1.4
Wife	16.6	27.1	9.2	32.8	17.2	46.7	12.2	42.2	24.7	54.5
Both	73.4	59.3	82.7	54.3	65.5	33.3	80.0	48.9	65.9	37.8
Doesn't matter	8.0	11.9	7.8	12.1	13.8	20.0	7.8	8.9	9.4	6.3
Discipline	N = 407	N = 59	N = 1340	N = 404	N = 30	N = 14	N = 115	N = 46	N = 404	N = 143
Husband	3.4	8.5	2.1	5.7	3.3	7.1	.9	15.2	1.2	9.8
Wife	3.4	10.2	.9	4.2	10.0	7.1	.9	6.5	2.0	4.2
Both	87.5	74.6	94.3	82.7	86.7	78.6	93.9	71.7	93.8	81.8
Doesn't matter	5.7	6.8	2.7	7.4	--	7.1	4.3	6.5	3.0	4.2
Bathing baby	N = 412	N = 59	N = 1338	N = 408	N = 30	N = 15	N = 115	N = 46	N = 405	N = 144
Husband	1.0	--	.4	1.0	--	6.7	--	--	.5	.7
Wife	39.8	30.5	22.0	31.1	33.3	46.7	28.7	43.5	40.0	54.2
Both	52.9	55.9	68.7	52.5	46.7	20.0	66.1	47.8	53.1	37.5
Doesn't matter	6.3	13.6	8.9	15.4	20.0	26.7	5.2	8.7	6.4	7.6
Putting baby to bed	N = 411	N = 59	N = 1337	N = 407	N = 29	N = 15	N = 115	N = 46	N = 405	N = 144
Husband	1.7	1.7	.2	1.2	--	--	.9	--	.2	1.4
Wife	16.1	18.6	6.8	14.3	24.1	26.7	10.4	19.6	18.5	20.1
Both	74.2	66.1	83.8	69.3	65.5	46.7	76.5	65.2	71.6	60.4
Doesn't matter	8.0	13.6	9.1	15.2	10.3	26.7	12.2	15.2	9.6	18.1
Putting toddler to bed	N = 412	N = 59	N = 1331	N = 405	N = 28	N = 15	N = 115	N = 46	N = 401	N = 144
Husband	3.4	3.4	1.2	2.5	7.1	13.3	2.6	4.3	2.5	1.4
Wife	15.3	23.7	6.2	13.6	10.7	40.0	13.0	23.9	12.2	25.0
Both	68.7	59.3	81.6	64.2	67.9	20.0	70.4	54.3	72.8	53.5
Doesn't matter	12.6	13.6	11.0	19.8	14.3	26.7	13.9	17.4	12.5	20.1

Table 9-4

In A Good Marriage, Who Should Be Responsible For The Following Tasks?

	CATHOLIC		BORN-AGAIN CHRISTIAN		PROTESTANT	
	F	M	F	M	F	M
Playing w/children	N = 851	N = 284	N = 394	N = 114	N = 304	N = 84
Husband	1.2	2.8	1.0	.9	.7	3.6
Wife	.7	3.9	.8	4.4	.3	3.6
Both	95.7	86.6	97.0	89.5	95.4	83.3
Doesn't matter	2.5	6.7	1.3	5.3	3.6	9.5
Feeding babies/children	N = 850	N = 286	N = 393	N = 118	N = 303	N = 84
Husband	.4	2.1	.5	.8	.3	1.2
Wife	14.7	28.3	21.6	22.0	10.2	23.8
Both	79.3	59.1	74.3	67.8	82.2	64.3
Doesn't matter	5.6	10.5	3.6	9.3	7.3	10.7
Changing diapers	N = 851	N = 285	N = 391	N = 116	N = 302	N = 84
Husband	.5	.7	.5	1.7	.3	1.2
Wife	14.3	44.9	18.2	28.4	6.0	38.1
Both	77.2	41.8	75.2	60.3	81.8	52.4
Doesn't matter	8.0	12.6	6.1	9.5	11.9	8.3
Discipline	N = 849	N = 284	N = 396	N = 117	N = 303	N = 84
Husband	1.9	7.4	3.1	6.0	1.3	10.7
Wife	1.6	3.9	1.5	6.0	.7	4.8
Both	94.3	82.4	92.1	83.8	92.1	79.8
Doesn't matter	2.1	6.3	3.3	4.3	5.9	4.8
Bathing baby	N = 851	N = 287	N = 393	N = 118	N = 304	N = 84
Husband	.6	.7	1.0	.8	--	2.4
Wife	29.7	44.6	34.1	28.0	21.4	23.8
Both	62.6	40.1	58.0	58.4	67.4	56.0
Doesn't matter	7.1	14.6	6.9	12.7	11.2	17.9
Putting baby to bed	N = 850	N = 287	N = 391	N = 117	N = 303	N = 84
Husband	.7	1.4	.5	.9	.3	2.4
Wife	12.1	18.8	12.3	12.0	9.2	11.9
Both	78.2	63.1	78.8	76.9	79.5	67.9
Doesn't matter	8.9	16.7	8.4	10.3	10.9	17.9
Putting toddler to bed	N = 844	N = 286	N = 390	N = 117	N = 303	N = 84
Husband	2.1	3.1	1.5	5.1	2.3	--
Wife	10.0	21.3	10.5	9.4	6.3	10.7
Both	76.3	54.5	76.4	72.6	78.2	70.2
Doesn't matter	11.6	21.0	11.5	12.8	13.2	19.0

Table 9-5

In A Good Marriage, Who Should Be Responsible For The Following Tasks?

	PARENTS' INCOME									
	UNDER $5000		$5000-$10000		$10000-$20000		$20000-$50000		OVER $50000	
	F	M	F	M	F	M	F	M	F	M
Playing w/children	N = 280	N = 55	N = 385	N = 83	N = 582	N = 163	N = 555	N = 217	N = 150	N = 74
Husband	2.1	3.6	1.0	1.2	.7	1.8	.4	1.8	.7	4.1
Wife	1.1	3.6	1.0	6.0	.3	3.7	.2	5.5	--	2.7
Both	94.6	85.5	95.3	80.7	97.8	87.2	96.8	84.8	97.3	90.5
Doesn't matter	2.1	7.3	2.6	12.0	1.2	7.4	2.7	7.8	2.0	2.7
Feeding babies/children	N = 278	N = 56	N = 383	N = 85	N = 582	N = 162	N = 547	N = 219	N = 148	N = 73
Husband	--	--	.3	2.4	.2	1.9	.5	.9	.7	2.7
Wife	24.1	26.8	18.5	30.6	16.3	24.7	8.2	22.4	12.2	19.2
Both	70.5	60.7	74.4	56.5	79.2	64.2	85.7	64.4	85.1	71.2
Doesn't matter	5.4	12.5	6.8	10.6	4.3	9.3	5.5	12.3	2.0	6.8
Changing diapers	N = 279	N = 55	N = 383	N = 85	N = 580	N = 163	N = 551	N = 217	N = 148	N = 75
Husband	1.4	--	.5	2.4	.2	.6	.4	.5	.7	2.7
Wife	23.7	34.5	19.6	32.9	12.4	43.6	7.1	35.0	6.8	38.7
Both	67.7	47.3	71.8	49.4	79.3	46.6	83.1	53.5	87.8	52.0
Doesn't matter	7.2	18.2	8.1	15.3	8.1	9.2	9.4	11.1	4.7	6.7
Discipline	N = 281	N = 56	N = 380	N = 85	N = 581	N = 161	N = 551	N = 217	N = 150	N = 75
Husband	4.3	10.7	2.1	7.1	1.7	6.8	1.6	7.8	.7	6.7
Wife	3.6	7.1	2.1	3.5	1.0	8.7	.5	3.2	1.3	1.3
Both	87.2	71.4	92.9	81.2	94.1	78.3	94.9	81.1	94.7	88.0
Doesn't matter	5.0	10.7	2.9	8.2	3.1	6.2	2.9	7.8	3.3	4.0
Bathing baby	N = 280	N = 56	N = 382	N = 85	N = 577	N = 163	N = 553	N = 219	N = 148	N = 75
Husband	.7	--	1.0	2.4	--	1.2	.4	--	--	1.3
Wife	38.9	41.1	37.1	32.9	28.6	38.7	18.8	38.4	20.9	29.3
Both	55.7	41.1	55.5	49.4	63.3	48.5	69.3	47.0	75.0	56.0
Doesn't matter	4.6	17.9	6.3	15.3	8.1	11.7	11.6	14.6	4.1	13.3
Putting baby to bed	N = 277	N = 56	N = 382	N = 85	N = 579	N = 163	N = 551	N = 219	N = 149	N = 74
Husband	1.1	--	.3	2.4	.3	--	.2	2.3	.7	1.4
Wife	21.3	19.6	14.1	15.3	9.0	18.4	7.1	15.1	6.0	12.2
Both	71.5	64.3	76.7	67.1	80.7	60.7	82.2	68.5	88.6	77.0
Doesn't matter	6.1	16.1	8.9	15.3	10.0	20.9	10.5	14.2	4.7	9.5
Putting toddler to bed	N = 278	N = 56	N = 383	N = 84	N = 576	N = 163	N = 548	N = 218	N = 147	N = 73
Husband	4.0	3.6	2.1	3.6	1.0	3.1	2.0	1.8	2.0	4.1
Wife	20.9	19.6	10.4	14.3	6.9	22.1	6.4	16.5	5.4	12.3
Both	63.7	55.5	75.2	61.9	80.4	55.2	79.9	60.6	87.1	68.5
Doesn't matter	11.5	21.4	12.3	20.2	11.6	19.6	11.7	21.1	5.4	15.1

CHAPTER 10
Teenagers & Jealousy
Percentage Tables

Table 10-1
Would You Be Jealous If Your Partner:

		All		Living Together	
		F	M	F	M
		N = 2267	N = 637	N = 323	N = 27
Looked at the	Absolutely	21.0	19.9	22.3	14.8
opposite sex	Probably	35.1	33.3	30.7	29.6
	I don't know	11.4	16.0	11.8	3.7
	Probably not	26.0	24.2	26.9	22.2
	Absolutely not	6.6	6.6	8.4	29.6
		N = 2263	N = 637	N = 323	N = 27
Talked with the	Absolutely	12.4	9.3	19.8	18.5
opposite sex	Probably	22.7	26.1	22.6	18.5
	I don't know	15.9	18.8	18.0	14.8
	Probably not	38.0	36.1	29.7	22.2
	Absolutely not	10.5	9.7	9.9	25.9
		N = 2263	N = 639	N = 321	N = 27
Worked with the	Absolutely	6.2	8.0	9.0	18.5
opposite sex	Probably	13.1	19.4	13.4	14.8
	I don't know	16.0	23.3	12.1	12.5
	Probably not	43.1	37.9	43.0	37.5
	Absolutely not	23.7	11.8	22.4	12.5
		N = 2260	N = 635	N = 322	N = 27
Attended school	Absolutely	7.2	8.2	7.8	7.4
with opposite sex	Probably	12.2	15.4	14.9	14.8
	I don't know	12.1	18.1	9.3	7.4
	Probably not	41.0	41.7	41.0	25.9
	Absolutely not	27.4	16.5	27.0	44.4
		N = 2257	N = 636	N = 322	N = 27
Attended concert	Absolutely not	61.1	48.4	70.8	40.7
with opposite sex	Probably	24.0	30.8	15.5	25.9
	I don't know	6.2	9.9	6.5	7.4
	Probably not	4.5	6.6	4.0	11.1
	Absolutely not	4.2	4.2	3.1	14.8
		N = 2254	N = 627	N = 319	N = 26
Had close friend	Absolutely	25.6	27.4	29.2	19.2
of opposite sex	Probably	26.6	28.5	28.2	23.1
	I don't know	22.3	21.2	18.8	19.2
	Probably not	19.3	15.8	18.2	11.5
	Absolutely not	6.2	7.0	5.6	26.9

Table 10-2

Would You Be Jealous If Your Partner:

ETHNIC GROUP

	BLACK		ANGLO		ASIAN		NATIVE AMERICAN		HISPANIC	
	F	M	F	M	F	M	F	M	F	M

LOOKED AT MEMBERS OF THE OPPOSITE SEX?

	N = 389	N = 48	N = 1312	N = 384	N = 30	N = 15	N = 110	N = 42	N = 390	N = 140
Absolutely	21.9	22.9	20.2	19.8	20.0	13.3	17.3	14.3	22.6	20.7
Probably	30.8	29.2	35.4	32.3	43.3	53.3	36.4	38.1	38.7	34.3
I don't know	10.3	8.3	12.2	16.4	3.3	13.3	10.0	21.4	10.3	15.7
Probably not	24.2	27.1	27.1	26.0	26.7	13.3	28.2	23.8	24.1	20.7
Absolutely not	12.9	12.5	5.2	5.5	6.7	6.7	8.2	2.4	4.4	8.6

TALKED WITH MEMBERS OF THE OPPOSITE SEX?

	N = 386	N = 46	N = 1311	N = 386	N = 30	N = 15	N = 112	N = 42	N = 387	N = 141
Absolutely	21.2	15.2	8.2	7.0	10.3	6.7	10.7	7.1	17.6	14.2
Probably	24.1	28.3	20.5	23.3	30.0	33.3	23.2	19.0	28.9	32.6
I don't know	16.3	15.2	15.9	20.5	6.7	13.3	19.6	31.0	14.0	12.8
Probably not	26.9	32.6	44.7	38.9	43.3	33.3	34.8	33.3	31.8	31.9
Absolutely not	11.4	8.7	10.7	10.4	10.0	13.3	11.6	9.5	7.8	8.5

WORKED WITH MEMBERS OF THE OPPOSITE SEX?

	N = 388	N = 47	N = 1355	N = 387	N = 29	N = 15	N = 111	N = 42	N = 390	N = 141
Absolutely	8.0	8.5	4.0	7.0	10.3	6.7	6.3	4.8	10.3	10.6
Probably	14.4	25.5	11.5	16.8	31.0	40.0	16.2	26.2	14.6	21.3
I don't know	15.5	14.9	14.8	23.5	13.8	40.0	19.8	16.7	20.0	24.1
Probably not	34.5	40.4	48.2	41.1	27.6	13.3	36.9	35.7	39.5	32.6
Absolutely not	27.6	10.6	21.5	11.6	17.2	--	20.7	16.7	15.6	11.3

WENT TO SCHOOL WITH THE OPPOSITE SEX?

	N = 385	N = 47	N = 1313	N = 383	N = 30	N = 15	N = 112	N = 42	N = 390	N = 141
Absolutely	10.9	8.5	4.3	6.0	20.0	6.7	7.1	11.9	11.5	11.3
Probably	11.2	17.0	9.5	12.5	23.3	33.3	12.5	9.5	20.8	23.4
I don't know	13.0	10.6	12.0	19.3	6.7	13.3	17.0	26.2	11.3	15.6
Probably not	33.0	44.7	45.4	45.2	30.0	13.3	38.4	40.5	37.2	34.8
Absolutely not	31.9	19.1	28.9	17.0	20.0	33.3	25.0	11.9	19.2	14.9

ATTENDED CONCERT WITH THE OPPOSITE SEX?

	N = 386	N = 47	N = 1306	N = 413	N = 30	N = 14	N = 112	N = 42	N = 389	N = 141
Absolutely	60.4	44.7	59.4	46.2	53.3	28.6	56.3	50.0	69.2	57.4
Probably	17.9	23.4	27.2	32.7	20.0	42.9	21.4	28.6	21.1	27.0
I don't know	8.0	12.8	6.7	9.1	13.3	21.4	3.6	16.7	2.6	7.8
Probably not	5.7	8.5	4.0	8.3	10.0	--	9.8	2.4	3.3	3.5
Absolutely not	8.0	10.6	2.8	3.6	3.3	7.1	8.9	2.4	3.9	4.3

HAD CLOSE FRIEND OF THE OPPOSITE SEX?

	N = 386	N = 47	N = 1355	N = 380	N = 29	N = 15	N = 109	N = 41	N = 388	N = 137
Absolutely	29.0	27.7	22.0	25.8	31.0	33.3	22.0	19.5	33.8	32.8
Probably	26.2	25.5	26.4	28.4	31.0	33.3	27.5	31.7	27.8	28.5
I don't know	20.5	12.8	23.3	22.9	34.5	13.3	24.8	22.0	19.3	20.4
Probably not	16.1	19.1	22.8	16.1	3.4	13.3	15.6	22.0	13.4	12.4
Absolutely not	8.3	14.9	5.5	6.8	--	6.7	10.1	4.9	5.7	5.8

Table 10-3

Would You Be Jealous If Your Partner:

	INNER CITY/ URBAN		SUBURBAN		SMALL TOWN/ FARM	
	F	M	F	M	F	M
LOOKED AT THE OPPOSITE SEX?						
	N = 1166	N = 244	N = 453	N = 220	N = 612	N = 169
Absolutely	22.0	22.1	17.0	17.7	21.9	20.1
Probably	34.8	35.7	34.0	33.6	36.9	29.6
I don't know	10.9	16.4	10.6	17.3	12.7	13.6
Probably not	25.1	21.7	31.8	23.6	22.9	29.0
Absolutely not	7.1	4.1	6.6	7.7	5.6	7.7
TALKED WITH THE OPPOSITE SEX?						
	N = 1164	N = 241	N = 450	N = 222	N = 612	N = 170
Absolutely not	15.5	10.4	9.1	8.6	8.7	8.8
Probably	24.7	27.8	19.3	28.4	21.4	20.6
I don't know	14.8	20.7	16.2	14.9	18.0	21.2
Probably not	35.1	34.4	44.0	34.7	41.2	41.2
Absolutely not	10.0	6.6	11.3	13.5	10.8	8.2
WORKED WITH THE OPPOSITE SEX?						
	N = 1166	N = 242	N = 454	N = 222	N = 607	N = 171
Absolutely	7.4	8.7	4.4	7.7	4.9	7.6
Probably	13.5	18.6	11.5	18.9	13.7	21.1
I don't know	16.4	26.0	13.2	19.4	17.6	24.6
Probably not	40.8	36.4	45.2	40.1	46.1	38.0
Absolutely not	22.0	10.3	25.8	14.0	17.6	8.8
WENT TO SCHOOL WITH THE OPPOSITE SEX?						
	N = 1167	N = 240	N = 451	N = 221	N = 612	N = 170
Absolutely	9.9	10.0	4.0	8.1	4.4	5.9
Probably	14.3	17.1	9.3	16.3	10.0	11.8
I don't know	12.2	16.7	11.3	17.2	12.9	21.8
Probably not	37.3	42.5	41.3	37.1	46.4	47.1
Absolutely not	26.4	13.7	31.3	21.3	26.3	13.5
ATTENDED CONCERT WITH THE OPPOSITE SEX?						
	N = 1165	N = 241	N = 450	N = 221	N = 609	N = 170
Absolutely	63.9	49.0	54.4	47.5	60.4	48.8
Probably	20.2	34.4	30.0	29.0	27.1	28.2
I don't know	6.5	10.4	6.4	10.4	5.3	8.8
Probably not	5.0	4.6	4.7	7.2	3.6	8.8
Absolutely not	4.5	1.7	4.4	5.9	3.6	5.3
HAD CLOSE FRIEND OF OPPOSITE SEX?						
	N = 1159	N = 238	N = 451	N = 217	N = 609	N = 168
Absolutely	27.4	31.5	21.3	23.0	25.0	28.0
Probably	26.7	28.6	24.2	27.2	28.4	30.4
I don't know	21.7	22.7	22.8	22.1	21.5	17.3
Probably not	17.6	13.9	22.8	17.5	19.5	16.7
Absolutely not	6.6	3.4	6.0	10.1	5.6	7.7

Table 10-4

Would You Be Jealous If Your Partner:

		All Females N = 2267	Pregnant N = 429	All Mothers N = 410	Mothers- 6 Months + N = 227
Looked at other	Absolutely	21.0	24.7	22.7	19.8
girls?	Probably	35.1	34.5	30.0	25.1
	I don't know	21.0	9.6	11.2	15.0
	Probably not	26.0	23.1	26.3	29.1
	Absolutely not	6.6	8.2	9.8	11.0
		N = 2263	N = 428	N = 408	N = 227
Talked with other	Absolutely	12.4	22.0	17.9	16.3
girls?	Probably	22.7	24.3	25.5	22.9
	I don't know	16.1	15.0	16.7	19.8
	Probably not	38.5	28.5	30.9	30.4
	Absolutely not	10.5	10.3	9.1	10.6
		N = 2263	N = 430	N = 406	N = 226
Worked with	Absolutely	6.2	9.1	9.1	9.3
other girls?	Probably	13.1	16.3	12.8	10.6
	I don't know	16.0	17.4	16.5	19.5
	Probably not	43.1	36.3	40.1	39.4
	Absolutely	23.7	21.2	21.4	21.2
		N = 2266	N = 430	N = 409	N = 226
Attended school	Absolutely	7.2	10.5	10.0	9.3
with girls?	Probably	12.1	12.8	15.4	15.0
	I don't know	12.1	15.6	11.2	11.5
	Probably not	41.0	34.0	39.4	38.9
	Absolutely not	27.4	27.2	24.0	25.2
		N = 2257	N = 431	N = 407	N = 224
Attended concert	Absolutely	61.1	70.3	67.3	62.1
with girls?	Probably	24.0	16.0	15.2	15.6
	I don't know	6.2	5.6	8.1	11.6
	Probably not	4.5	2.8	4.9	4.9
	Absolutely not	4.2	5.3	4.4	5.8
		N = 2254	N = 429	N = 406	N = 226
Had close female	Absolutely	25.6	30.3	31.5	31.4
friend?	Probably	26.6	26.6	24.4	22.6
	I don't know	22.3	20.5	21.7	25.2
	Probably not	19.3	15.9	16.0	13.7
	Absolutely not	6.2	6.8	6.4	7.1

Table 10-5

Would You Be Jealous If Your Partner:

		HAPPY?	
		YES	NO
		N = 276	N = 35
Looked at a person of the opposite sex?	Absolutely	25.0	14.3
	Probably	30.4	37.1
	I don't know	10.5	11.4
	Probably not	26.4	28.6
	Absolutely not	7.6	8.6
		N = 275	N = 35
Talked with a person of the opposite sex?	Absolutely	19.3	14.3
	Probably	24.4	20.0
	I don't know	18.9	11.4
	Probably not	28.4	48.6
	Absolutely not	9.1	5.7
		N = 273	N = 35
Worked with a person of the opposite sex?	Absolutely	8.8	2.9
	Probably	14.3	11.4
	I don't know	13.6	11.4
	Probably not	41.4	57.1
	Absolutely not	22.0	17.1
		N = 273	N = 35
Attended school with opposite sex?	Absolutely	7.3	5.7
	Probably	15.4	14.3
	I don't know	10.3	2.9
	Probably not	41.4	54.3
	Absolutely not	25.6	22.9
		N = 273	N = 35
Attended concert with opposite sex?	Absolutely	71.4	51.4
	Probably	15.0	20.0
	I don't know	5.5	17.1
	Probably not	4.4	5.7
	Absolutely not	3.7	5.7
		N = 271	N = 34
Had a close friend of opposite sex?	Absolutely	31.0	23.5
	Probably	28.8	20.6
	I don't know	17.0	23.5
	Probably not	17.7	26.5
	Absolutely not	5.5	5.9

CHAPTER 11
Teenagers & Spousal Abuse
Percentage Tables

Table 11-1. How Do You Feel About Husbands Hitting Their Wives?

	ALL		LIVING TOGETHER	
	F	M	F	M
	N = 2324	N = 672	N = 318	N = 28
It's OK	.4	3.3	--	3.6
It's not good, but sometimes necessary	6.6	13.2	8.2	7.1
It's not OK, but may happen he's angry or drunk	16.2	14.0	19.5	21.4
It should never happen	76.8	69.5	72.3	67.9

Table 11-2. How Do You Feel About Wives Hitting Their Husbands?

	ALL		LIVING TOGETHER	
	F	M	F	M
	N = 2330	N = 681	N = 320	N = 28
It's OK	5.0	7.8	4.1	21.4
It's not good, but sometimes necessary	16.7	15.0	21.6	7.1
It's not OK, but may happen when he's angry or drunk	11.2	10.1	13.1	14.3
It should never happen	67.1	67.1	61.2	57.1

Table 11-3.   FEMALES: Has Your Spouse Ever Hit You?
MALES: Have You Ever Hit Your Spouse?

	LIVING TOGETHER	
	F	M
	N = 303	N = 23
Never	52.1	60.9
Once	17.2	4.3
Two or three times	23.1	22.7
Often	7.6	13.0

Table 11-4
How Do You Feel About Husbands Hitting Their Wives?

	Same Religion	Different Religion	Same Ethnic Group	Different Ethnic Group
	N = 269	N = 70	N = 252	N = 89
It's OK	--	1.4	.4	--
It's not good, but sometimes it's necessary	8.2	12.9	7.9	13.5
It's not OK, but may happen when he's angry or drunk	17.1	30.0	21.4	14.6
It should never happen	74.7	55.7	70.2	71.9

Table 11-5
How Do You Feel About Husbands Hitting Their Wives?

	N. CALIF. F	N. CALIF. M	NORTHWEST F	NORTHWEST M	SO. CALIF. F	SO. CALIF. M
	N = 162	N = 29	N = 302	N = 46	N = 573	N = 279
It's OK	--	3.4	--	4.3	.5	2.2
It's not good, but sometimes it's necessary	5.6	17.2	7.3	10.9	5.6	13.6
It's not OK, but may happen when he's angry or drunk	13.6	13.8	15.9	21.7	17.6	14.0
It should never happen	80.9	65.5	76.8	63.0	76.3	70.3

	NM-TX F	NM-TX M	MIDDLE WEST F	MIDDLE WEST M	NORTHEAST F	NORTHEAST M	SOUTHEAST F	SOUTHEAST M
	N = 311	N = 79	N = 516	N = 170	N = 236	N = 76	N = 247	N = 54
It's OK	.3	3.8	.4	4.7	.8	5.3	.4	--
It's not good, but sometimes it's necessary	2.9	10.1	7.8	10.6	7.2	13.2	11.7	24.1
It's not OK, but may happen when he's angry or drunk	15.4	12.7	16.1	9.4	12.7	13.2	18.2	20.4
It should never happen	81.4	73.4	75.8	75.3	79.2	68.4	69.6	55.6

Table 11-6
How Do You Feel About Husbands Hitting Their Wives?

PARENT'S INCOME

| | UNDER $5000 | | $5000-$10000 | | $10000-$20000 | | $20000-$50000 | | OVER $50000 | |
| | F | M | F | M | F | M | F | M | F | M |
	N = 275	N = 56	N = 380	N = 86	N = 578	N = 162	N = 555	N = 216	N = 148	N = 74
It's OK	1.5	1.8	.3	1.2	--	4.3	.2	2.8	.7	8.1
Not good, but sometimes necessary	8.7	16.1	8.2	15.1	6.1	14.8	3.8	9.7	2.0	13.5
Not OK, but may happen when he's angry/drunk	25.8	17.9	19.2	17.4	15.4	17.3	11.7	13.0	9.5	4.1
Should never happen	64.0	64.3	72.4	66.3	78.5	63.6	84.3	74.5	87.8	74.3

Table 11-7
How Do You Feel About Husbands Hitting Their Wives?

ETHNIC GROUPS

| | BLACK | | ANGLO | | ASIAN | | NATIVE AMERICAN | | HISPANIC | |
| | F | M | F | M | F | M | F | M | F | M |
	N = 407	N = 59	N = 1338	N = 399	N = 29	N = 15	N = 113	N = 46	N = 401	N = 144
It's OK	.7	3.4	.2	3.8	3.4	6.7	--	2.2	.7	2.1
Not good, but sometimes necessary	15.7	25.4	4.1	9.8	10.3	20.0	7.1	13.0	4.7	17.4
Not OK, but may happen when he's angry/drunk	20.6	22.0	12.3	11.5	17.2	26.7	27.4	15.2	20.9	15.3
Should never happen	62.9	49.2	83.4	74.9	69.0	46.7	65.5	69.6	73.6	65.3

Table 11-8
How Do You Feel About Husbands Hitting Their Wives?

	NEVER PREGNANT N = 1235	MOTHERS N = 432	FATHERS N = 50
It's OK	.4	.9	8.0
Not good, but sometimes necessary	4.5	9.0	20.0
Not OK, but may appen when he's angry or drunk	13.3	18.8	18.0
Should never happen	81.9	71.3	54.0

Category Definition

"No hitting": Respondent replied "It should never happen" when asked "How do you feel about husbands hitting wives?"

"Tolerates hitting": Respondent replied, "It's OK,", "It's not good, but sometimes it's necessary," or "It's not OK, but it may happen when he's angry or drunk" to the above question.

Table 11-9
How is your relationship with your mother?

	TOLERATES HITTING		NO HITTING	
	F	M	F	M
	N = 532	N = 203	N = 1762	N = 463
Very good	40.2	39.4	42.7	44.9
Good	32.5	34.5	31.1	35.9
Fair	18.6	18.2	18.1	12.5
Poor	4.9	3.9	5.7	4.1
No relationship	3.8	3.9	2.4	2.6

How is your relationship with your father?

	TOLERATES HITTING		NO HITTING	
	F	M	F	M
	N = 526	N = 201	N = 1717	N = 453
Very good	17.9	30.8	27.3	31.3
Good	29.8	31.3	29.5	32.9
Fair	23.8	14.4	22.5	19.2
Poor	12.5	10.9	9.7	8.2
No relationship	16.0	12.4	11.1	8.4

Table 11-10

How Do You Feel About A Young Couple Living With Either His Or Her Parents?

	N = 531	N = 203	N = 1759	N = 460
Good idea	6.4	11.8	3.1	6.7
OK until we save some money	36.2	31.5	31.6	29.6
I would rather not	47.5	40.4	51.8	50.7
I'm totally against it	10.0	16.3	13.5	13.0

Table 11-11

When A Couple Has An Argument, Who Should Usually Have The Final Say?

	TOLERATES HITTING		NO HITTING	
	F	**M**	**F**	**M**
	N = 530	N = 201	N = 1765	N = 460
Male	7.2	33.8	4.9	13.0
Female	10.8	1.5	6.1	1.5
It doesn't matter	82.1	64.7	89.1	85.4

Table 11-12

If You Are Upset With Your Partner, What Do You Do?

	N = 393	N = 170	N = 1260	N = 365
Tell him/her you are upset	51.7	42.4	66.0	56.4
Hit him/her	3.6	11.8	2.2	2.7
Leave and think it through	28.5	25.3	20.9	29.9
Tell a friend or or parent, but not your partner	6.1	4.7	4.9	5.2
I don't do anything	10.2	15.9	6.0	5.8

Table 11-13

In A Good Marriage, Who Should Be Responsible For The Following Tasks?

	TOLERATES HITTING		NO HITTING	
	F	M	F	M
Vacuuming house	N = 531	N = 200	N = 1773	N = 465
Husband	2.1	5.5	.8	1.3
Wife	45.2	52.5	36.4	37.6
Both	32.2	24.0	43.3	40.6
It doesn't matter	20.5	18.0	19.5	20.4
Mopping floors	N = 533	N = 202	N = 1771	N = 463
Husband	2.4	3.0	1.3	1.9
Wife	51.0	60.4	45.4	50.1
Both	29.3	20.3	36.4	30.0
It doesn't matter	17.3	16.3	16.9	17.9
Preparing meals	N = 532	N = 199	N = 1756	N = 462
Husband	.9	3.5	.7	1.1
Wife	47.6	48.2	34.3	38.1
Both	41.2	35.2	52.6	45.7
It doesn't matter	10.3	13.1	12.4	15.2
Washing dishes	N = 532	N = 200	N = 1769	N = 466
Husband	1.9	4.5	1.3	2.4
Wife	32.0	39.0	21.8	22.7
Both	55.6	45.5	66.5	62.0
It doesn't matter	10.5	11.0	10.3	12.9
Washing clothes	N = 535	N = 202	N = 1764	N = 466
Husband	2.1	5.0	1.6	1.5
Wife	59.4	57.9	54.5	49.4
Both	30.3	22.8	34.2	34.8
It doesn't matter	8.2	14.4	9.7	14.4
Washing the car	N = 529	N = 199	N = 1754	N = 464
Husband	38.8	58.8	29.6	44.6
Wife	1.7	9.0	.6	1.5
Both	41.4	18.6	50.7	33.6
It doesn't matter	18.1	13.6	19.1	20.2
Mowing the lawn	N = 533	N = 201	N = 1764	N = 462
Husband	64.2	65.7	54.1	73.2
Wife	1.1	5.0	.7	1.9
Both	22.9	20.4	31.1	14.3
It doesn't matter	11.8	9.0	14.0	10.6

Table 11-14

In A Good Marriage, Who Should Be
Responsible For The Following Tasks?

	TOLERATES HITTING		NO HITTING	
	F	M	F	M
Playing with the children	N = 533	N = 198	N = 1773	N = 459
Husband	1.1	4.0	.8	1.3
Wife	.6	7.6	.6	3.3
Both	94.7	81.3	96.6	87.8
It doesn't matter	3.6	7.1	2.1	7.6
Feeding babies and children	N = 533	N = 199	N = 1763	N = 463
Husband	.6	3.0	.3	.6
Wife	20.3	31.7	13.3	22.7
Both	71.5	55.8	81.4	66.1
It doesn't matter	7.7	9.5	4.9	10.6
Changing baby's diapers	N = 534	N = 197	N = 1762	N = 463
Husband	.9	2.0	.5	.4
Wife	19.3	47.2	11.9	34.6
Both	69.1	39.1	80.2	54.4
It doesn't matter	10.7	11.7	7.4	10.6
Disciplining children	N = 532	N = 196	N = 1763	N = 463
Husband	3.6	14.3	1.6	4.5
Wife	3.2	7.7	1.2	3.9
Both	86.7	72.4	94.7	84.7
It doesn't matter	6.6	5.6	2.4	6.9
Bathing baby	N = 534	N = 199	N = 1765	N = 466
Husband	.7	2.0	.4	.2
Wife	37.3	42.2	26.2	35.2
Both	54.5	39.7	65.2	52.4
It doesn't matter	7.5	16.1	8.2	12.2
Putting baby to bed	N = 531	N = 199	N = 1764	N = 465
Husband	.4	3.5	.6	.2
Wife	16.6	19.6	9.3	16.3
Both	70.6	57.3	81.9	69.9
It doesn't matter	12.4	19.6	8.3	14.6
Putting toddler to bed	N = 529	N = 198	N = 1754	N = 463
Husband	3.2	6.1	1.5	1.5
Wife	14.7	25.8	7.9	15.6
Both	69.6	45.5	79.2	65.7
It doesn't matter	12.5	22.7	11.4	17.3

Table 11-15

Do You Think Marrying A Person From A Different
Ethnic Group Would Usually Cause
Problems Within A Marriage?

	TOLERATES HITTING		NO HITTING	
	F	M	F	M
	N = 532	N = 203	N = 1761	N = 466
Absolutely	6.2	11.8	5.8	5.6
Probably	21.6	23.2	23.8	19.7
I don't know	41.9	37.4	41.5	43.3
Probably not	22.7	23.2	23.9	22.3
Absolutely not	7.5	4.4	5.1	9.0

Table 11-16

When You Get Married, Do You Expect It To
Last The Rest Of Your Life?

	TOLERATES HITTING		NO HITTING	
	F	M	F	M
	N = 532	N = 203	N = 1758	N = 464
Absolutely	55.8	51.2	71.4	59.5
Probably	26.5	25.1	20.8	29.5
I don't know	3.8	9.9	2.0	4.3
Probably not	12.2	8.4	4.9	5.0
Absolutely not	1.7	5.4	.9	1.7

Table 11-17

Do You Think Being Married Would Tie You Down?

	TOLERATES HITTING		NO HITTING	
	F	M	F	M
	N = 532	N = 201	N = 1731	N = 456
Absolutely	10.7	19.4	12.4	15.6
Probably	29.3	40.3	31.3	35.3
I don't know	27.4	19.9	22.5	23.2
Probably not	21.6	11.4	23.7	19.5
Absolutely not	10.9	9.0	10.1	6.4

Table 11-18

Do You Think A Couple Should Have Sexual Intercourse Before They Are Married?

	TOLERATES HITTING		NO HITTING	
	F	M	F	M
	N = 527	N = 202	N = 1719	N = 457
Absolutely	10.4	35.6	9.4	19.7
Probably	15.6	15.3	12.4	14.2
It doesn't matter	46.1	28.2	44.2	38.1
Probably not	13.7	11.4	14.8	14.9
Absolutely not	14.2	9.4	19.2	13.1

Table 11-19

How Do You Feel About A Man And A Woman Living Together
If They Aren't Married?

	TOLERATES HITTING		NO HITTING	
	F	M	F	M
	N = 533	N = 204	N = 1772	N = 465
It's OK	40.9	61.8	39.4	53.5
OK if they plan to marry	32.1	24.0	25.3	25.2
OK but I wouldn't do it	13.9	7.8	16.1	6.0
I think it's wrong	13.1	6.4	19.1	15.3

Table 11-20

Do You Think It Is Important That A Husband And Wife
Agree On How They Spend Money?

	TOLERATES HITTING		NO HITTING	
	F	M	F	M
	N = 533	N = 203	N = 1751	N = 461
Absolutely	78.0	68.0	83.4	73.3
Probably	15.8	19.7	13.9	21.3
I don't know	2.4	5.4	1.9	3.3
Probably not	1.9	2.5	.7	1.3
Absolutely not	1.9	4.4	.1	.9

Table 11-21

Do You Expect Your Wife To Work Outside
Your Home Until You Have Children?

	TOLERATES HITTING	NO HITTING
	N = 194	N = 441
Absolutely	19.1	7.9
Probably	32.0	35.8
It doesn't matter	33.5	42.0
Probably not	7.2	9.1
Absolutely not	8.2	5.9

Table 11-22

Do You Expect Your Wife To Work Outside
Your Home While You Have Children Under Two Years Of Age?

	TOLERATES HITTING	NO HITTING
	N = 192	N = 440
Absolutely	6.3	3.4
Probably	6.3	8.4
It doesn't matter	17.2	22.0
Probably not	38.5	42.5
Absolutely not	31.8	23.6

Table 11-23

Do You Expect Your Wife To Work Outside
Your Home After Your Children Are All In School?

	TOLERATES HITTING	NO HITTING
	N = 191	N = 440
Absolutely	19.4	7.3
Probably	30.9	32.0
It doesn't matter	34.6	43.9
Probably not	8.4	11.1
Absolutely not	6.8	5.7

Table 11-24

Would You Be Jealous If Your Partner:

	TOLERATES HITTING		NO HITTING	
	F	M	F	M
Looked at opposite sex?	N = 515	N = 178	N = 1716	N = 434
Absolutely	23.1	26.1	20.1	17.7
Probably	36.7	31.9	35.0	34.1
I don't know	11.7	13.3	11.3	16.8
Probably not	21.9	22.9	27.0	24.2
Absolutely not	6.6	5.9	6.5	7.1
Talked w/opposite Sex?	N = 518	N = 189	N = 1709	N = 433
Absolutely	16.8	13.2	10.8	7.4
Probably	26.3	29.1	21.9	25.4
I don't know	18.7	15.3	15.0	20.6
Probably not	30.5	33.9	41.1	36.3
Absolutely not	7.7	8.5	11.3	10.4
Worked w/opposite sex?	N = 515	N = 191	N = 1714	N = 433
Absolutely	10.1	11.5	4.8	6.7
Probably	17.7	22.0	11.8	18.5
I don't know	17.9	22.0	15.6	24.5
Probably not	38.8	33.0	44.2	39.0
Absolutely not	15.5	11.5	23.6	11.3
Attended school w/opposite sex?	N = 518	N = 190	N = 1712	N = 432
Absolutely	11.2	12.1	5.8	6.7
Probably	15.8	20.0	11.3	13.4
I don't know	13.3	15.3	11.9	19.4
Probably not	38.0	37.9	41.7	43.3
Absolutely not	21.6	14.7	29.3	17.1
Attended concert w/opposite sex?	N = 516	N = 190	N = 1709	N = 431
Absolutely	62.2	57.4	60.5	44.3
Probably	20.5	22.6	25.2	34.6
I don't know	7.0	6.3	6.0	11.1
Probably not	5.2	9.5	4.3	5.6
Absolutely not	5.0	4.2	4.0	4.4
Had close friend of opposite sex?	N = 515	N = 188	N = 1706	N = 424
Absolutely	31.1	30.9	23.8	26.2
Probably	27.2	30.9	26.6	27.6
I don't know	20.6	16.0	22.9	23.6
Probably not	15.3	14.4	20.4	16.3
Absolutely not	5.8	8.0	6.3	6.4

Questionnaire — Nationwide Survey
TEEN ATTITUDES TOWARD MARRIAGE

1. **How old are you?**
   A. 14 or younger.   B. 15   C. 16   D. 17   E. 18 or older.

2. **What grade are you in at school?**
   A. 8th or lower.   B. 9-10   C. 11   D. 12   E. Not in school.

3. **What kind of school do you attend?**
   A. "Regular" public school.   B. Private school.   C. Continuation school.
   D. Special school for pregnant adolescents and/or school-age parents.   E. Other.

4. **What sex are you?**
   A. Male   B. Female

5. **Where do you live?**
   A. Inner City.   B. Urban area.   C. Suburb.
   D. Town of 10,000 or less.   E. On a farm.

6. **To which ethnic group do you feel you belong?**
   A. White.   B. Black.   C. Latino/Hispanic.   D. Asian.   E. Native American.

7. **Within which religious group do you feel you belong?**
   (If none, leave blank.)
   A. Catholic.   B. Protestant.   C. Born-Again Christian.   D. Jewish.   E. Other.

8. **What is your marital status?**
   A. Single.   B. Engaged.   C. Married.   D. Separated.   E. Divorced or widowed.

9. **About how much money do your parents earn each year?**
   A. Under $5000.   B. $5000-$10,000.   C. $10,000-$20,000.
   D. $20,000-$50,000.   E. Over $50,000.

NOTE: Answer both #10 and #11 only if both apply to you.

10. **With whom do you live?**
    A. Mother only.   B. Father only.   C. Both parents.
    D. Guardian.   E. Foster home.

11. **With whom do you live?**
    A. Husband/Wife.   B. Boy/Girl friend.   C. Other friend(s).
    D. Relative(s).   E. Other.

12. **FOR GIRLS: Are you now or have you ever been pregnant?**
    A. I have never been pregnant.   B. I was pregnant, but I had an abortion.
    C. I have had a child.   D. I'm pregnant now.

    FOR BOYS: Have you ever gotten a girl pregnant?
    A. No.   B. Yes.   C. I don't know.

13. **FOR BOYS AND GIRLS: Do you already have one or more children?**
    A. No.   B. Yes—One child.   C. Yes—Two children.
    D. Yes—Three children.   E. Yes—Four children.

14. FOR BOYS AND GIRLS. If you already have a child, how old is s/he? (If you have more than one child, mark the age of each child.)

A. 0-6 months.   B. 6-12 months.   C. 12-18 months. D. 18-24 months.   E. Two years or older.

15. If you have a child, who is mostly responsible for her/his care?

GIRLS: A. I am.   B. The child's father.   C. My parent(s) E. Baby's father's parent(s).   E. Other.

BOYS: A. I am.   B. The child's mother.   C. My parent(s) E. Baby's mother's parent(s).   E. Other.

16. What do you think is the best age for women to get married?

A. 17 or younger.   B. 18-19.   C. 20-24.   D. 25-29.   E. 30 or older.

17. What do you think is the best age for men to get married?

A. 17 or younger.   B. 18-19.   C. 20-24.   D. 25-29.   E. 30 or older.

18. How is your relationship with your mother?

A. Very good.   B. Good.   C. Fair.   D. Poor.   E. No relationship.

19. How is your relationship with your father?

A. Very good.   B. Good.   C. Fair.   D. Poor.   E. No relationship.

20. How do you feel about a young couple living with either his or her parents?

A. Good idea.   B. OK until we save some money.   C. I would rather not. D. I'm totally against it.

21. How do you feel about a man and a woman living together if they aren't married?

A. It's OK.   B. It's OK *if* they plan to get married later. C. It's OK but I wouldn't do it.   D. I think it's wrong.

22. If you have a problem, to whom do you talk? (More than one answer is OK.)

A. Nobody.   B. Parents   C. Teacher, counselor, or minister. D. Another friend.   E. Boy/Girl friend (or husband/wife).

23. When a couple has an argument, who should usually have the final say?

A. Male.   B. Female.   C. It doesn't matter.

24. If you are upset with your partner, what do you do? (More than one answer is OK.)

A. Tell him/her you are upset.   B. Hit him/her.   C. Leave and think it through. D. Tell a friend or parent, but not your partner.   E. I don't do anything.

25. When you and your boyfriend/girlfriend have an argument, how do you settle it? (More than one answer is OK.)

A. Slug it out.   B. Talk it through together.   C. Yell to get rid of bad feelings. D. Quit talking to each other.   E. Get a referee.

26. How do you feel about husbands hitting their wives?

A. It's OK.   B. It's not good, but sometimes it's necessary. C. It should never happen. D. It's not OK, but it may happen when he's angry or drunk.

27. How do you feel about wives hitting their husbands?
A. It's OK.   B. It's not good, but sometimes it's necessary.
C. It should never happen.
D. It's not OK, but it may happen when she's angry or drunk.

HOW MUCH DO YOU THINK GETTING MARRIED AT AGE 18 OR YOUNGER WOULD CHANGE YOUR LIFE IN THE FOLLOWING AREAS? (If you are already married, how has marriage changed your life?)

28. MONEY:
A. I'd have more money.   B. I'd have less money.   C. No change.

29. FRIENDS:
A. More friends.   B. Fewer friends.   C. Different friends.   D. No change.

30. RECREATION/PARTYING:
A. More.   B. Less.   C. No change.

31. FREE TIME:
A. More.   B. Less.   C. No change.

32. RELATIONSHIP WITH YOUR FAMILY:
A. Closer.   B. Less close.   C. No change.

33. HIGH SCHOOL ATTENDANCE:
A. I'd drop out.   B. I'd continue going to school.   C. I would graduate
D. Marriage wouldn't change my attendance.

34. COLLEGE/TRADE SCHOOL:
A. I'd be more likely to attend.   B. Less likely to attend.   C. No change.

IN A *GOOD* MARRIAGE, WHO SHOULD BE RESPONSIBLE FOR THE FOLLOWING TASKS?

35. EARNING MONEY:
A. Husband.   B. Wife.   C. Both.   D. It doesn't matter.

36. DECIDING HOW MONEY IS SPENT:
A. Husband.   B. Wife.   C. Both.   D. It doesn't matter.

37. PAYING BILLS:
A. Husband.   B. Wife.   C. Both.   D. It doesn't matter.

38. VACUUMING THE HOUSE:
A. Husband.   B. Wife.   C. Both.   D. It doesn't matter.

39. MOPPING FLOORS:
A. Husband.   B. Wife.   C. Both.   D. It doesn't matter.

40. PREPARING MEALS:
A. Husband.   B. Wife.   C. Both.   D. It doesn't matter.

41. CLEANING UP AFTER MEALS:
A. Husband.   B. Wife.   C. Both.   D. It doesn't matter.

42. WASHING THE CAR:
A. Husband.   B. Wife.   C. Both.   D. It doesn't matter.

43. MOWING THE LAWN:
A. Husband.   B. Wife.   C. Both.   D. It doesn't matter.

44. PLAYING WITH THE CHILDREN:
    A. Husband.   B. Wife.   C. Both.   D. It doesn't matter.

45. FEEDING BABIES/CHILDREN:
    A. Husband.   B. Wife.   C. Both.   D. It doesn't matter.

46. CHANGING BABY'S DIAPERS:
    A. Husband.   B. Wife.   C. Both.   D. It doesn't matter.

47. DISCIPLINING CHILDREN:
    A. Husband.   B. Wife.   C. Both.   D. It doesn't matter.

48. BATHING BABY:
    A. Husband.   B. Wife.   C. Both.   D. It doesn't matter.

49. PUTTING BABY TO BED:
    A. Husband.   B. Wife.   C. Both.   D. It doesn't matter.

50. PUTTING TODDLER TO BED:
    A. Husband.   B. Wife.   C. Both.   D. It doesn't matter.

51. DOING FAMILY'S LAUNDRY:
    A. Husband.   B. Wife.   C. Both.   D. It doesn't matter.

52. Do you want to marry a person from your own ethnic group or race?
    A. Absolutely.   B. Probably.   C. It doesn't matter.
    D. Probably not.   E. Absolutely not.

53. Do you think marrying a person from a different ethnic group would usually cause problems within a marriage?
    A. Absolutely.   B. Probably.   C. I don't know.
    D. Probably not.   E. Absolutely not.

54. Do you want to marry a person who has the same religious beliefs as you do?
    A. Absolutely.   B. Probably.   C. It doesn't matter.
    D. Probably not.   E. Absolutely not.

55. Do you think marrying a person with a religious faith different from your own would cause problems in your marriage?
    A. Absolutely.   B. Probably.   C. I don't know.
    D. Probably not.   E. Absolutely not.

56. Do you want your marriage to be much like your parents' marriage?
    A. Absolutely.   B. Probably.   C. It doesn't matter.
    D. Probably not.   E. Absolutely not.

57. When you get married, do you expect it to last the rest of your life?
    A. Absolutely.   B. Probably.   C. It doesn't matter.
    D. Probably not.   E. Absolutely not.

58. Is sex an important part of marriage?
    A. Absolutely.   B. Probably.   C. I don't know.
    D. Probably not.   E. Absolutely not.

59. Do you think a couple should have sexual intercourse before they are married?
    A. Absolutely.   B. Probably.   C. It doesn't matter.
    D. Probably not.   E. Absolutely not.

60. When a high school-age girl gets pregnant, should she and her boy friend get married?
A. Absolutely. B. Probably. C. It doesn't matter.
D. Probably not. E. Absolutely not.

61. Do you think it is important for a child to live with both of his/her parents?
A. Absolutely. B. Probably. C. It doesn't matter.
D. Probably not. E. Absolutely not.

62. For how long have you lived with both of your parents?
A. All my life. B. 10-15 years. C. 5-10 years. D. 0-5 years. E. Never.

63. Do you think having "enough" money is an important part of a good marriage?
A. Absolutely. B. Probably. C. I don't know.
D. Probably not. E. Absolutely not.

64. Do you think it is important that a husband and wife agree on how they spend money?
A. Absolutely. B. Probably. C. I don't know.
D. Probably not. E. Absolutely not.

65. Do you think it is important for a husband and a wife to agree on how to discipline their children?
A. Absolutely. B. Probably. C. I don't know.
D. Probably not. E. Absolutely not.

66. If you were married, would you want your spouse to continue his/her education?
A. Absolutely. B. Probably. C. It doesn't matter.
D. Probably not. E. Absolutely not.

67. Would you like your spouse to be more intelligent than you are?
A. Absolutely. B. Probably. C. It doesn't matter.
D. Probably not. E. Absolutely not.

68. Do you think being married would tie you down?
A. Absolutely. B. Probably. C. I don't know.
D. Probably not. E. Absolutely not.

69. In a good marriage, should the husband earn most of the money?
A. Absolutely. B. Probably. C. It doesn't matter.
D. Probably not. E. Absolutely not.

71. In a good marriage, should the wife be a good housekeeper?
A. Absolutely. B. Probably. C. It doesn't matter.
D. Probably not. E. Absolutely not.

72. In a good marriage, should the husband take care of the car and lawn?
A. Absolutely. B. Probably. C. It doesn't matter.
D. Probably not. E. Absolutely not.

72. In a good marriage, should the wife do most of the cooking?
A. Absolutely. B. Probably. C. It doesn't matter.
D. Probably not. E. Absolutely not.

FOR BOYS ONLY: (Girls—Please skip #73 - #78.)

73. Do you expect your wife to work outside your home until you have children?
    A. Absolutely. B. Probably. C. It doesn't matter.
    D. Probably not. E. Absolutely not.

74. Do you expect your wife to work outside your home while you have children under two years of age?
    A. Absolutely. B. Probably. C. It doesn't matter.
    D. Probably not. E. Absolutely not.

75. Do you expect your wife to work outside your home after your children are all in school?
    A. Absolutely. B. Probably. C. It doesn't matter.
    D. Probably not. E. Absolutely not.

76. Would it be all right with you if your wife wanted to get a job?
    A. Absolutely. B. Probably. C. I don't know.
    D. Probably not. E. Absolutely not.

77. Would it be all right with you if your wife made more money than you did?
    A. Absolutely. B. Probably. C. I don't know.
    D. Probably not. E. Absolutely not.

78. Would it be all right with you if your wife chose to stay home instead of getting a job?
    A. Absolutely. B. Probably. C. I don't know.
    D. Probably not. E. Absolutely not.

FOR GIRLS ONLY: (Boys—Please skip #79 - #84.)

79. Do you expect to work outside your home until you have children?
    A. Absolutely. B. Probably. C. It doesn't matter.
    D. Probably not. E. Absolutely not.

80. Do you expect to work outside your home while you have children under two years of age?
    A. Absolutely. B. Probably. C. It doesn't matter.
    D. Probably not. E. Absolutely not.

81. Do you expect to work outside your home after your children are all in school?
    A. Absolutely. B. Probably. C. It doesn't matter.
    D. Probably not. E. Absolutely not.

82. Would it be all right with you if your husband said you should *not* get a job?
    A. Absolutely. B. Probably. C. I don't know.
    D. Probably not. E. Absolutely not.

83. Would it be all right with you if your husband said you *must* get a job?
    A. Absolutely. B. Probably. C. I don't know.
    D. Probably not. E. Absolutely not.

84. Would it be all right with you if your *husband* wanted to stay home while you got a job to support your family?
A. Absolutely. B. Probably. C. I don't know.
D. Probably not. E. Absolutely not.

FOR BOYS ONLY: (Girls—Please skip #85 - #90.)

WOULD YOU BE JEALOUS IF YOUR GIRL FRIEND OR YOUR WIFE

85. Looked at other boys?
A. Absolutely. B. Probably. C. I don't know.
D. Probably not. E. Absolutely not.
86. Talked with other boys?
A. Absolutely. B. Probably. C. I don't know.
D. Probably not. E. Absolutely not.
87. Worked with boys?
A. Absolutely. B. Probably. C. I don't know.
D. Probably not. E. Absolutely not.
88. Went to school with boys?
A. Absolutely. B. Probably. C. I don't know.
D. Probably not. E. Absolutely not.
89. Went to a concert with another boy?
A. Absolutely. B. Probably. C. I don't know.
D. Probably not. E. Absolutely not.
90. Had a close male friend?
A. Absolutely. B. Probably. C. I don't know.
D. Probably not. E. Absolutely not.

FOR GIRLS ONLY: (Boys, please skip #91 — #96.)

WOULD YOU BE JEALOUS IF YOUR BOY FRIEND OR YOUR HUSBAND:

91. Looked at other girls?
A. Absolutely. B. Probably. C. I don't know.
D. Probably not. E. Absolutely not.
92. Talked with other girls?
A. Absolutely. B. Probably. C. I don't know.
D. Probably not. E. Absolutely not.
93. Worked with girls?
A. Absolutely. B. Probably. C. I don't know.
D. Probably not. E. Absolutely not.
94. Went to school with girls?
A. Absolutely. B. Probably. C. I don't know.
D. Probably not. E. Absolutely not.
95. Went to a concert with another girl?
A. Absolutely. B. Probably. C. I don't know.
D. Probably not. E. Absolutely not.

96. Had a close female friend?
    A. Absolutely. B. Probably. C. I don't know.
    D. Probably not. E. Absolutely not.

FOR BOYS AND GIRLS: HOW IMPORTANT DO YOU THINK
IT IS FOR A *HUSBAND* TO HAVE THE FOLLOWING
QUALITIES?

97. Good money manager.
    A. Very important. B. Somewhat important.
    C. Not important. D. It doesn't matter at all.
98. Loves and cares about children.
    A. Very important. B. Somewhat important.
    C. Not important. D. It doesn't matter at all.
99. Good cook.
    A. Very important. B. Somewhat important.
    C. Not important. D. It doesn't matter at all.
100. Good housekeeper.
    A. Very important. B. Somewhat important.
    C. Not important. D. It doesn't matter at all.
101. Knows how to repair the plumbing.
    A. Very important. B. Somewhat important.
    C. Not important. D. It doesn't matter at all.
102. Doesn't get upset easily.
    A. Very important. B. Somewhat important.
    C. Not important. D. It doesn't matter at all.
103. Takes care of the yard.
    A. Very important. B. Somewhat important.
    C. Not important. D. It doesn't matter at all.
104. Takes charge of home and family.
    A. Very important. B. Somewhat important.
    C. Not important. D. It doesn't matter at all.
105. Good sex partner.
    A. Very important. B. Somewhat important.
    C. Not important. D. It doesn't matter at all.
106. Shares common interests with spouse.
    A. Very important. B. Somewhat important.
    C. Not important. D. It doesn't matter at all.
107. Spends most of his spare time with his spouse.
    A. Very important. B. Somewhat important.
    C. Not important. D. It doesn't matter at all.

FOR BOYS AND GIRLS: HOW IMPORTANT DO YOU THINK
IT IS FOR A *WIFE* TO HAVE THE FOLLOWING QUALITIES?

108. Good money manager.
    A. Very important. B. Somewhat important.
    C. Not important. D. It doesn't matter at all.

109. **Loves and cares about children.**
   A. Very important.   B. Somewhat important.
   C. Not important.   D. It doesn't matter at all.

110. **Good cook.**
   A. Very important.   B. Somewhat important.
   C. Not important.   D. It doesn't matter at all.

111. **Good housekeeper.**
   A. Very important.   B. Somewhat important.
   C. Not important.   D. It doesn't matter at all.

112. **Knows how to repair the plumbing.**
   A. Very important.   B. Somewhat important.
   C. Not important.   D. It doesn't matter at all.

113. **Doesn't get upset easily.**
   A. Very important.   B. Somewhat important.
   C. Not important.   D. It doesn't matter at all.

114. **Takes care of the yard.**
   A. Very important.   B. Somewhat important.
   C. Not important.   D. It doesn't matter at all.

115. **Takes charge of home and family.**
   A. Very important.   B. Somewhat important.
   C. Not important.   D. It doesn't matter at all.

116. **Good sex partner.**
   A. Very important.   B. Somewhat important.
   C. Not important.   D. It doesn't matter at all.

117. **Shares common interests with spouse.**
   A. Very important.   B. Somewhat important.
   C. Not important.   D. It doesn't matter at all.

118. **Spends most of her spare time with her spouse.**
   A. Very important.   B. Somewhat important.
   C. Not important.   D. It doesn't matter at all.

Questionnaire — Married/Living-Together

IF YOU ARE MARRIED OR LIVING WITH YOUR PARTNER, PLEASE ANSWER THE FOLLOWING QUESTIONS:

119. **Are you (or were you)**
   A. Married and living together.   B. Married, but *not* living together.
   C. Married, but now separated or divorced.   D. Living together, but not married.
   E. Lived together for awhile, but are no longer together.

120. **How long have you been living together? (If you aren't now together, how long did you live together?)**
   A. 0-3 months.   B. 3-6 months.   C. 6-12 months.   D. 1-2 years.   E. More than 2 years.

121. **How long have you been married? (If you are separated or divorced, how long were you married?) If you are not married, leave blank.**
   A. 0-3 months   B. 3-6 months.   C. 6-12 months.   D. 1-2 years.   E. More than 2 years.

122. FOR GIRLS: Were you pregnant or a parent when you got married and/or started living together? (If more than one answer applies, check both.)
A. No.   B. I was pregnant.
C. My partner and I already had a child.   D. I already had a child by a different man.

FOR BOYS: Was your partner pregnant and/or a parent when you got married and/or started living together? (If more than one answer applies, check both.)
A. No.   B. She was pregnant.
C. We already had a child.   D. She already had a child by a different man.

123. Do you and your partner belong to the same ethnic group?
A. Yes.   B. No.

124. If you do not belong to the same ethnic group, how has this affected your relationship? (Leave blank if you belong to the same ethnic group.)
A. No problem at all.   B. It's a problem only to our parents.
C. This occasionally causes problems for us.   D. It's a big problem for us.

125. Do you and your partner have similar religious beliefs?
A. Yes.   B. No.

126. Does either of you belong to a church?
A. Yes.   B. No.

127. Do you and your partner belong to the same church?
A. Yes.   B. No.

128. If you do not belong to the same church or practice the same faith, how has this affected your relationship? (Leave blank if this does not apply to your situation.)
A. No problem at all.   B. It's a problem only to our parents.
C. This occasionally causes a problem for us.   D. It's a big problem for us.

129. How important is religion in your relationship?
A. Very important.   B. Mildly important.   C. Not important.

130. While living together, have you and your partner always lived by yourselves?
A. Yes.   B. No.

131. If you have not always lived by yourselves, with whom have you lived? (Leave blank — or check one or more as necessary.)
A. His parents.   B. Her parents.   C. Other relatives.   D. Friends.   F. Other.

132. If you have a child, what effect has this had on your relationship?
A. No effect.   B. Very good effect.   C. Somewhat good.
D. Somewhat bad.   E. Very bad.

133. Has money — or lack of it — been a problem in your relationship?
A. Always.   B. Most of the time.   C. Sometimes.   D. Not often.   E. Never.

134. Has money — or the lack of it — been a greater problem than you had expected?
A. Yes, much greater.   B. Yes, somewhat greater.   C. No.

135. Do you and your partner have similar interests?
A. Yes.   B. No.   C. Sometimes.

136. Is a lack of similar interests ever a problem?
A. Yes.   B. No.   C. Sometimes.

137. Do you and your partner find it easy to communicate (talk, share feelings) with each other?
A. Yes.   B. No.   C. Sometimes.

138. Do you think communication with your partner — or lack of communication — is a problem in your relationship?
A. Yes.   B. No.   C. Sometimes.

139. Has your partner changed much since you were married or started living together?
A. No change.   B. Some positive change.   C. Much positive change.
D. Some negative change.   E. Much negative change.

140. Has your spouse ever hit you?
A. Never.   B. Once.   C. Two or three times.   D. Often.

141. Have you ever hit your spouse?
A. Never.   B. Once.   C. Two or three times.   D. Often.

142. Compared to what you expected before you started living together, is living together:
A. Easier?   B. Harder?   C. About what you expected?

143. Are you happy with your partnership?
A. Yes.   B. Most of the time, yes.   C. Most of the time, no.   D. No.

OPEN-ENDED QUESTIONS — Please answer on a separate sheet of paper, then attach the paper to your answer sheet.

144. What do you feel you have given up because of your partnership?

145. What is the subject of most of your arguments? (Money? Household chores? In-laws? Recreation? Children? Or???)

146. When, where, and why do most of your arguments occur?

147. What effect has education — or lack of it — had on your relationship?

148. What are the biggest problems in your partnership?

149. What is good about your partnership?

150. Do you think your partnership will last "forever"? Please comment.

Questionnaire — Teen Mother Program Alumnae

If you are or have been married or if you've ever lived with a partner, please answer the following questions. Your answers will be completely confidential. Please circle or check the answer closest to what you think or what you have experienced. If you want to comment on any of the questions, please do so.

NOTE: If you have been married more than once — or if you have lived with more than one partner, please answer the questions based on your *first* experience of marriage and/or living with your partner.

1. How old were you when you and your partner started living together?_____

2. Are you still living with your "first" partner? Yes_____ No_____

3. How long have you been living together — or if not now together, how long did you live together? _____

4. As a couple, did you ever live with his or your parents or other relatives? Yes_____ No_____. If yes, how did you feel about this? _____

5. Are your parents married to each other now? Yes_____ No_____. If not, how old were you when they separated? _____

6. Do you want your marriage to be much like your parents' marriage? Yes_____ No_____. Why or why not? _____

7. Does/Did being married/living together tie you down? Yes_____ Sometimes_____ No_____

8. Is sex an important part of your marriage? Very important_____ Somewhat important_____ Not important_____

9. Do/Did you and your partner agree on how you spend money?
   Almost always____ Sometimes____ No, almost never____

10. In your partnership, does/did your partner earn most of the money? Yes____ No____

11. Does/Did your partner want you to work away from home?
    Yes____ No____ He didn't care____

12. Do/Did you and your partner agree on how to discipline your child(ren)?
    Yes, almost always____ Sometimes____ No, almost never____

13. Is jealousy a problem in your partnership?
    Yes____ No ____ Please comment. _____
    _____

14. In your *first* marriage or living-together partnership, who was/is responsible for the following tasks:

	I am	He is	Mostly me	Mostly him	Both
Deciding how money is spent	____	____	____	____	____
Paying bills	____	____	____	____	____
Vacuuming the house	____	____	____	____	____
Mopping floors	____	____	____	____	____
Washing dishes	____	____	____	____	____
Washing the car	____	____	____	____	____
Mowing the lawn	____	____	____	____	____
Doing family's laundry	____	____	____	____	____
Grocery shopping	____	____	____	____	____
Playing with children	____	____	____	____	____
Feeding babies/children	____	____	____	____	____
Changing baby's diapers	____	____	____	____	____
Disciplining children	____	____	____	____	____
Bathing baby	____	____	____	____	____

MAIL ORDER FORM

Teens Look at Marriage: Rainbows, Roles, and Reality
Trade: $9.95; Cloth: $15.95

Teenage Marriage: Coping with Reality
Trade: $8.95; Cloth: $14.95
Teacher's Guide, $2.95; 48-pp. Consumable Study Guide, $2.50

Other Books by Jeanne Lindsay

Teens Parenting: The Challenge of Babies and Toddlers
A parenting book written especially for very young parents. Includes many comments
and suggestions from young mothers. Excellent for Child Development/Parenting classes.
Trade: $9.95; Cloth: $14.95
Teacher's Guide: $5.95; Student Guide: $2.50

Pregnant Too Soon: Adoption Is an Option
Latest information on adoption together with personal stories of
young birth mothers who released their babies for adoption.
Trade: $6.95; Cloth: $13.95
Consumable Student Study Guide, 16 pages: $1.00; 10/$5.00

Do I Have a Daddy? A Story About a Single-Parent Child
Picture story for children whose parents never married.
Includes 10-page section of suggestions for single parents.
Cloth: $7.95

MORNING GLORY PRESS
6595-B San Haroldo Way / Buena Park, CA 90620

Quantity		Price	Total
	Teens Look at Marriage: Rainbows, Roles and Reality		
_____	Trade, ISBN 0-930934-15-6.........................$ 9.95		_____
_____	Cloth, ISBN 0-930934-16-4.........................$15.95		_____
	Teenage Marriage: Coping with Reality		
_____	Trade, ISBN 0-930934-11-3.........................$ 8.95		_____
_____	Cloth, ISBN 0-930934-12-1.........................$14.95		_____
_____	Consumable Study Guide..................$ 2.50, 10/$20.00		_____
_____	Teacher's Guide....................................$2.95		_____
	Teens Parenting: The Challenge of Babies and Toddlers		
_____	Trade, ISBN 0-930934-06-7.........................$ 9.95		_____
_____	Cloth, ISBN 0-930934-07-5.........................$14.95		_____
_____	Teacher's Guide, ISBN 0-930934-09-1.................$ 5.95		_____
_____	Student Study Guide, ISBN 0-930934-08-3.....$2.50, 10/$20.00		_____
	Pregnant Too Soon: Adoption Is an Option		
_____	Trade, ISBN 0-88436-778-9.........................$ 6.95		_____
_____	Cloth, ISBN 0-930934-05-9.........................$13.95		_____
	Do I Have a Daddy?		
_____	Cloth, ISBN 0-930934-10-5.........................$ 7.95		_____

Quantity Discounts Available

TOTAL _____

Please add 10% postage/handling (min. $1.50, max. $10.00) _____

California residents add 6% sales tax _____

TOTAL ENCLOSED _____

NAME _____

ADDRESS _____

_____

Index